D0163321

A SHORT SYNTAX

OF

NEW TESTAMENT GREEK

By the same author

THE ELEMENTS OF NEW TESTAMENT GREEK.
A Method of studying the Greek New Testament with exercises.

Crown 8vo.

KEY TO THE ELEMENTS OF NEW TESTAMENT GREEK

Crown 8vo.

AN INTRODUCTION TO ECCLESIASTICAL LATIN

Crown 8vo.

CAMBRIDGE UNIVERSITY PRESS

A SHORT SYNTAX
OF
NEW TESTAMENT GREEK

Charl R Wescombe

by

The Rev. H. P. V. NUNN, M.A.

St John's College, Cambridge, sometime lecturer at
St Aidan's College, Birkenhead

Cambridge
at the University Press
1949

PUBLISHED BY
THE SYNDICS OF THE CAMBRIDGE UNIVERSITY PRESS

London Office: Bentley House, N.W.1
American Branch: New York

Agents for Canada, India, and Pakistan: Macmillan

First Edition,	1912
Second Edition,	1913
Third Edition,	1920
Fourth Edition,	1924
Reprinted,	1931
Fifth Edition,	1938
Reprinted,	1943
"	1945
"	1949

Printed in Great Britain at the University Press, Cambridge
(Brooke Crutchley, University Printer)

PREFACE TO THE FIFTH EDITION

THIS book is not intended to be a complete syntax of New Testament Greek; its aim is to present the main features of that subject for the benefit of students in Theological Colleges and of those who take up the study of Greek towards the end of their school life, or after they have left school, chiefly with a view to reading the New Testament.

It is founded wholly on the Greek of the New Testament, but it is hoped that it may be useful to those who expect to read a little Classical Greek as well. It seems to the writer that those who do not begin to learn Greek early, and who do not expect to make a thorough study of the Classical authors, may best begin the study of the language with the New Testament. The style of the writers of the Gospels and the Acts is very simple, and may generally be translated straight into English, while the style even of such a simple Classical author as Xenophon needs considerable adaptation. Moreover the vocabulary of such books as the Gospel and Epistles of St John is so limited that the student is not burdened at the beginning of his course with a long, and daily increasing, list of new words. Most of the words which he meets with are easily learnt from their frequent repetition.

Care has been taken to indicate all deviations from Classical usage, and occasional notes have been added on usages which are confined to, but common in Classical Greek.

Some of the rules are illustrated by Latin[1] as well as by Greek examples. The student probably has some knowledge of Latin, and it is believed that these examples will help him to remember the Greek rules either as parallels or contrasts.

The section on English Grammar covers, as far as possible, the ground which is common to English, Latin, and Greek Grammar.

Everything in it should be known by those who take up the study of any language, other than their own, before they begin that study.

[1] The Latin quotations are generally taken from the Vulgate: but in a few instances the version of Beza published by the Bible Society has been used instead.

It is hoped that this preliminary section, if it does not convey any fresh information to the student, may at least serve to remind him of what he knows already, and to indicate those points of English Grammar which must be thoroughly understood by anyone who wishes to study Greek or Latin to any profit.

The chapter on Prepositions is placed at the beginning of the second part of the book because Prepositions are of such frequent occurrence, and an exact acquaintance with their meaning is of such importance to correct translation, that it is well to master them thoroughly as soon as possible.

In writing the first edition of this book the author received much valuable help from his friend the Rev. W. L. Walter, at that time Vice-Principal of St Aidan's College, Birkenhead, and some kind assistance in the final revision from the late Professor Moulton, whose untimely death was such a loss to New Testament scholarship.

In the compiling of subsequent editions many useful suggestions made by the Rev. G. H. Casson of the Theological Hall, Mengo, Uganda, and other friends were adopted.

In the last edition a brief summary of the explanation given by Dr Burney in his *Aramaic Origin of the Fourth Gospel* of the peculiar uses of ἵνα to be found in the Gospels has been added. Dr Torrey of Yale University in his new translation of the Gospels and in his book *Our Translated Gospels* has added many arguments to those of Dr Burney to prove that the peculiar Greek to be found in the Gospels (and nowhere else) is "translation Greek."

The satisfactory explanation that he gives of many obscure verses in the Greek of the Gospels makes his theory both interesting and valuable.

Before beginning to use this book the student is expected to be familiar with the declensions of the nouns, pronouns and adjectives commonly given in elementary Greek grammars and with the conjugation of the verbs. The author's *Elements of New Testament Greek* published by the Cambridge University Press gives what is required with exercises and simple pieces for reading.

The principal books which were consulted in the preparation of this work were Professor Goodwin's *Greek Grammar*, Dr Blass' *Grammar of New Testament Greek*, Professor J. H. Moulton's *Prolegomena*, Professor

Burton's *Moods and Tenses of New Testament Greek*, the Rev. E. A. Abbott's *How to Parse* and *Parts of Speech* and the *Parallel Grammar Series*.

To the authors of all these books the writer wishes to express himself deeply indebted.

In the later editions some use has been made of the report of the Committee on Grammatical Terminology.

The selections from the Fathers of the second century and from other writers placed at the end of the book are especially commended to the attention of those who wish to attain some mastery of New Testament Greek. It is fatally easy to think that one knows Greek, because one can translate the New Testament; but the fact that the English version is, or should be, familiar to a theological student, before he begins to translate it, makes this knowledge more apparent than real.

Those who wish to pursue the study further will find some easy Patristic Greek in the admirable volumes of the Loeb Library.

The author will at all times welcome corrections and suggestions.

H. P. V. N.

3 DAVENPORT PARK ROAD,
STOCKPORT.

CONTENTS OF PART I

PAGE

1. Parts of Speech 1

2. Parsing 2

3. Nouns 5

4. Adjectives 6

5. Verbs 6
   - (a) Transitive and Intransitive 6
   - (b) Active and Passive Voice 6
   - (c) Deponent Verbs 7
   - (d) Formation of the Passive Voice 7
   - (e) Auxiliary Verbs, Impersonal Verbs, the Copulative Verb, Verbs of Incomplete Predication . . . 8
   - (f) Person and Number 9
   - (g) Tense 10
   - (h) Mood 11
   - (i) Participles 12
   - (j) Verbal Nouns : Infinitive Mood, Gerund . . . 13

6. Sentences 14

7. Equivalents 17

8. Simple and Complex Sentences 18

9. Substantival or Noun Clauses 19

10. Adjectival Clauses 21

11. Adverbial Clauses 22

12. Preparatory *it* and *there* 24

CONTENTS OF PART II

	PAGE
The Greek of the New Testament	25
Prepositions	28
Subject and Predicate	37
Cases and their meanings	37
Notes on the use of the Oblique cases	39
Adjectives	49
Pronouns	50
The Definite Article	55
The Verb—Mood, Voice, Tense	61
Sentences	80
The use of the Subjunctive in independent sentences, etc.	82
The Imperative	83
Prohibitions	84
The Infinitive and its equivalents in Noun Clauses and certain Adverbial Clauses	87
Adverbial Clauses	110
Adjectival Clauses	120
Participles	121
Use of οὐ and μή	126
Questions	127
The Particle ἄν	128
List of Irregular Verbs	129
Appendix	135
Indices	171

GLOSSARY OF GRAMMATICAL TERMS

ANACOLUTHON (ἀ, negative, and ἀκολουθέω, I follow). A break in the construction of a sentence where a clause is left unfinished and one of a new construction begun. Very common in the Epistles of St Paul. See 2 Tim. iii. 10—11.

ANALYSIS (ἀνά, back, and λύω, I loose). A loosing or division of a sentence into its parts :—Subject, Predicate, etc. A language like English which makes its verb-forms with auxiliary verbs instead of with endings is said to be analytical.

ANOMALY (ἀ, negative, and ὁμαλός, level). A construction which does not conform to rule.

ANTITHESIS (ἀντί, against: τίθημι, I place). Placing a word or clause over against another by way of contrast.

APPOSITION (ad, to: pono, I place). When two nouns or a noun and a pronoun are placed together so that the second explains the meaning of the first more fully they are said to be in apposition. They must always be in the same case.

Examples: I, your mother, call you.

William the Conqueror died in 1087.

ARCHAISM (ἀρχαῖος, ancient). An expression belonging to an ancient form of any language.

CARDINAL (cardo, a hinge). That on which anything hinges, that which is important. The name given to the more important forms of numeral adjectives, One, Two, Three, etc. from which the Ordinal numbers are formed, First, Second, etc.

CASE (casus, falling). The name given to the various forms which nouns etc. assume in Latin and Greek. The Ancients regarded the Substantive form of the noun (the Nominative Case) as standing upright and the other forms as falling away from it. Hence the name Oblique Cases applied to the cases other than the nominative, and the term declension or falling away given to the list of these cases.

COGNATE (*con*, together : *natus*, born). Words derived from the same root, or even of the same meaning, are said to be cognate. Intransitive verbs may take a noun of cognate meaning after them which must not be confused with the object.
Examples : He went his way. I have lived a long life.

COMPLEMENT (*compleo*, I fill up). A word or phrase that fills up the meaning of a verb of incomplete predication such as the verb *to be*.
Example : He is a man to be thoroughly trusted.

CONJUGATION (*con*, together : *jugo*, I yoke). The name given to a number of verbs of generally similar inflections joined in one class.

CONSONANT (*con*, together : *sono*, I sound). Letters that can only be sounded together with a vowel.
Examples : B, C, D.

CORRELATIVES. Words that mutually answer to one another.
Examples : Where, there, When, then.

DECLENSION : see Case.

DIPHTHONG (δι, twice : φθόγγος, sound). Two vowel-sounds produced as one.
Example : Caesar.

ELLIPSIS. The omission of words in a sentence which can be understood from the context.

ETYMOLOGY (ἔτυμος, true : λόγος, meaning). The science of the true or original meaning of words.
All the Greek and Latin words placed in brackets in this glossary show the etymological meaning of the English words.

EUPHONY (εὖ, well : φωνή, sound). That which sounds well. Many of the varying forms of words are due to the fact that certain combinations of letters were not easy to pronounce and so were modified for the sake of euphony.

GERUND (*gero*, I carry on). A verbal noun which denotes *the carrying on* of the action of the verb.
Examples : loving, fearing.

IDIOM (ἴδιος, private, peculiar). A mode of expression peculiar to a language.

INFLECTION (*inflecto*, I bend). The bending or changing of a word from its simple form ; see Case.

METAPHOR (μετά, from one to another: φέρω, I carry). The transference of a word properly referring to one set of objects to another set of objects. For example, when a ship is said *to plough a furrow in the sea* we are transferring language, which properly applies only to the land, to the sea, by metaphor. This use is exceedingly common. In dictionaries the abbreviations **Metaph. Figurat. Transf.** (i.e. by transference) and **Trop.** (Tropologice) are used to denote the metaphorical or extended meanings of the words. These are often the most important.

MONOSYLLABLE (μόνος, alone: συλλαβή, a syllable). A word of one syllable.

MOOD: see page 11.

OBLIQUE: see Case.

ORDINAL (*ordo*, order). A numeral adjective which answers the question, *In which order?*—Second, Third, etc.

PARENTHESIS (παρά, beside: ἔνθεσις, insertion). A word, phrase, or sentence inserted in another sentence yet not grammatically connected with any word in it.
Example: Ye were the servants of sin; but now—God be thanked —ye are so no more.

PARTICIPLE (*participo*, I partake). A form of the verb which partakes of the nature both of a verb and of an adjective.

PERIOD (περί, around: ὁδός, a way). (1) The full rounded path of a complex sentence. (2) A full stop.

POLYSYLLABLE (πολύς, many: συλλαβή, syllable). A word of many syllables, generally three or more.

PRIMARY TENSES. The Present, Future, Future Perfect and Present Perfect tenses.

SECONDARY TENSES. The Past, Imperfect and Pluperfect tenses.

SIMILE (*similis*, like). A sentence or clause expressing the likeness of one action to another.
Example: Then like an arrow swift he flew
            Shot by an archer strong.

SYLLABLE (σύν, together: λαβ-, take). A group of letters taken together to form one sound.

SYNTAX (σύν, together: τάξις, arrangement). The science of arranging words to form sentences.

VOWEL (*Vocalis*, having a voice). The letters which can be sounded by themselves: A, E, I, O, U.

PART I

1. PARTS OF SPEECH

BY **parts of speech** we mean the various classes under which all words used in speaking and writing may be arranged.

The names of the parts of speech are as follows:

Noun. Pronoun. Adjective.

Verb. Adverb.

Preposition. Conjunction. Interjection.

The Article, definite and indefinite, is also sometimes classed as a separate part of speech.

A NOUN is the name of anything. (Latin *nomen*, name.)

Examples: John, boy, sweetness.

A PRONOUN is a word used instead of a noun to indicate, or enumerate persons or things without naming them. (Latin *pro*, for: *nomen*, name.)

Examples: I, you, they, who, that.

An ADJECTIVE is a word used with a noun to describe, indicate, or enumerate what is denoted by the noun. (Latin *adjectum*, a thing thrown to.)

Examples: Good, many.

A VERB is a word by means of which we can make a statement, ask a question, or give a command about some person or thing. (Latin *verbum*, a word, so called as being the principal word in the sentence.)

Examples: I run, we see.

An ADVERB is a word used with a verb or an adjective or another adverb to describe, indicate, or enumerate what is denoted by the verb, adjective, or other adverb.

Examples: Slowly, very, there.

A PREPOSITION is a word joined with, and generally placed before, a noun or its equivalent[1], so that the preposition together with the noun forms a phrase equivalent to an adverb or adjective. (Latin *praepono*, I place before.)

Examples: At, with, by.

A CONJUNCTION is a word that joins together sentences, clauses or words. (Latin *conjungo*, I join.)

Examples: And, but, for.

[1] See page 17.

AN INTERJECTION is a word thrown into a sentence to express a feeling
of the mind. (Latin *interjicio*, I throw in.)
Examples: Hallo, ha.
The DEFINITE ARTICLE *The* and the INDEFINITE ARTICLE *A* are always
joined with nouns like adjectives.

2. PARSING

As this book is intended for older students it has not been thought
necessary to adopt the method of deriving the reason for the names of
the different parts of speech from examples.

This is excellently done in a little book called *How to tell the Parts
of Speech*, by the Rev. E. A. Abbott, published by Seeley, which the
student who is altogether unacquainted with this subject is advised
to get.

A few rules and examples are however given which may be of
assistance in determining the parts of speech.

The first principle to be remembered is that no word should ever
be parsed without careful reference to the function which it performs
in the sentence where it occurs.

In English many words having exactly the same form must be
regarded as entirely different parts of speech, according to the place
which they occupy in the sentence, and must be translated by wholly
different words in Latin and Greek, according as their meaning varies.

For example the word *that* may be (1) A demonstrative Pronoun.
(2) A demonstrative Adjective. (3) A relative Pronoun. (4) A Conjunction[1].

(1) That is the man. (2) Give me that book. (3) This is the book
that I want. (4) He said that this was the book. (4) He came that
he might find the book.

Again, the word *considering* may be (1) A verbal noun. (2) A
participle.

(1) Considering is slow work. (2) He went away considering the
matter.

Many words may be nouns or verbs, according to the place which
they occupy in the sentence

[1] Consider the meaning of the word *that* in the following sentence, *He
said that that that that man said was false.*

Some such words are : Bite, fly, rose, scale and sign.

Other words may be adjectives or nouns, such as : Base, last, stout, spring, kind.

Other words may be adjectives or verbs, such as: Lean, clean, blunt, idle, free.

Remembering then always to consider the word in connection with its sentence, the student should ask himself the following questions before parsing a word. They will help him to find out what part of speech it is.

(1)   Is it the name of anything?

Then it is a **noun**.

(2)   Can a noun which is mentioned or thought of before be substituted for the word without altering the meaning of the sentence?

Then it is a **pronoun**.

(3)   Does it answer any of the questions : *What kind? How many? How much? Which? Whose? In what order?* with regard to some noun?

Then it is an **adjective**.

(4)   Does it make a statement, ask a question, or give a command?

Then it is a **verb**.

(5)   Does it answer the questions *How? When? Where?*

Then it is an **adverb**.

Note.   The words *How? When?* and *Where?* are themselves adverbs.

(6)   Does it stand before a noun or its equivalent making with it a phrase which is equivalent to an adverb or adjective?

Then it is a **preposition**.

(Another test of a preposition is that it is a word which is not a verb but which can stand before *him* and *them*, but not before *he* or *they*.)

(7)   Does it join sentences, clauses or words?

Then it is a **conjunction**.

The words in the following sentence are parsed as an example. *The man went quickly down the street and did not turn to his right hand or to his left.*

THE	Limits the application of the word *man*. Tells us which man it was, i.e. some man already known.	Therefore it is that kind of adjective to which the name Definite Article is given.
MAN	Is the name of something.	Therefore it is a noun.
WENT	Makes a statement about the man.	Therefore it is a verb.
QUICKLY	Qualifies the verb *went*, tells us how he went.	Therefore it is an adverb.
DOWN	Stands before the noun *street*, making with it a phrase equivalent to an adverb because it qualifies the verb *went*, telling us where he went.	Therefore it is a preposition.
THE	See above.	
STREET	Is the name of something.	Therefore it is a noun.
AND	Joins together two clauses.	Therefore it is a conjunction.
DID TURN	Makes a statement about the man.	Therefore it is a verb.
NOT	Qualifies the verb *did turn* because it tells us how he did turn, i.e. not at all.	Therefore it is an adverb.
TO	See *down* above.	
HIS	The noun *man's* can be substituted for this.	Therefore it is a pronoun.
	But it also qualifies the noun *hand*, telling whose hand it is.	Therefore it is an adjective as well. Such words are called Pronominal adjectives.
RIGHT	Qualifies the noun *hand*, telling us which hand it is.	Therefore it is an adjective.
HAND	Is the name of something.	Therefore it is a noun.
OR	Joins together the two clauses *did not turn to his right hand* and (*did not turn*) *to his left*.	Therefore it is a conjunction.
TO	See above.	
HIS	See above.	
LEFT	See above.	

3. NOUNS

There are four kinds of nouns :

(1) **Proper Nouns.** A Proper noun is the name appropriated to any particular person, place or thing (Latin *proprius,* belonging to a person).

Examples : John, Mary, London, England.

(2) **Common Nouns.** A Common noun is the name which all things of the same kind have in common (Latin *communis,* belonging to all).

Examples : Boy, girl, town, country.

(3) **Collective Nouns.** A Collective noun is the name of a number of persons or things forming one body.

Examples : Committee, jury, army.

(4) **Abstract Nouns.** An Abstract noun is the name of some quality, state, or action considered apart from the person or thing in which it is embodied (Latin *abstractus,* withdrawn).

Examples : Goodness, whiteness, purity, servitude, running, walking.

Number, Gender, Case

Number. Nouns are inflected or changed in form to show whether they are singular or plural in number.

A noun in the **Singular number** is the name of a single person or thing, unless it is a Collective noun (see above).

A noun in the **Plural number** is the name of more than one person or thing.

Examples :	Singular	Plural
	Horse	horses
	Man	men
	Ox	oxen.

Gender. In English all names of men or male animals are in the **Masculine gender,** all names of women or female animals are in the **Feminine gender,** all names of things without life are in the **Neuter gender.** Nouns used to denote persons of either sex such as *parent, sovereign,* are said to be of **Common gender.**

In Latin and Greek, although all names of men and male animals are Masculine, and all names of women or female animals are Feminine, names of things without life may be Masculine or Feminine in gender as well as Neuter.   The gender of a noun is generally determined by the ending of the Nominative Singular.

Case.   Nearly all traces of case-endings have disappeared from English nouns.   The only surviving ending is that of the Possessive or Genitive case which is formed by adding 's to the end of a noun in the singular and s' to the end of the noun in the Plural.

Example	Nominative	Possessive Singular	Possessive Plural
	horse	horse's	horses'

4.   ADJECTIVES

In English, adjectives are never inflected, but have the same ending whether they qualify singular or plural, masculine or feminine nouns.

In Latin and Greek they are inflected to show gender, number, and case.

5.   VERBS

Verbs are of two kinds—Transitive and Intransitive.

(a)   **Transitive Verbs.**   Transitive verbs are so called because they denote an action which necessarily affects or passes over to some person or thing other than the subject of the verb (Latin *transire,* to pass over).

Examples: I *throw,* I *take.*   These statements are not complete; we ask immediately, What do you *throw* or *take?* The name of the person or thing affected by the action of the verb must be supplied in order to make a complete sentence—*I throw a ball, I take an apple.*   The name of the person or thing which is affected by the action of the verb is called the **direct object.**

A transitive verb is one which must have a direct object expressed in order to make a complete sentence.

Intransitive Verbs.   Intransitive verbs are so called because they denote an action which does not affect or pass over to any person or thing besides the subject of the verb.

Examples: I *stand,* The sun *shines.*   These sentences are complete statements in themselves.

Many transitive verbs may also be used intransitively.

Examples: The dog bit the man.   The dog bites.

(b)   **Active Voice.**   A verb is said to be in the Active voice when its subject is spoken of as acting or doing something (Latin *ago,* I act).

Passive Voice. A verb is said to be in the Passive voice when its subject is spoken of as suffering or being acted upon (Latin *patior*, I suffer).

Examples: Active, I love, I was hearing.

              Passive, I am loved, I was being heard.

N.B. Only Transitive verbs can have a Passive voice.

There are certain verbs such as *I fall, I slip*, etc. which do not speak of the subject as acting ; these are however regarded as Active verbs because they are Intransitive.

(c) **Deponent Verbs.** In Latin and Greek there are many verbs which are called Deponent verbs. These are verbs which have the form of Passive verbs, but which are Active in meaning.

They are called *Deponent* because they have *laid aside* (Latin *depono*) a passive sense and assumed an active.

Examples : *patior,* I suffer. ἀποκρίνομαι, I answer.

(d) **The English Passive voice** of any verb is formed by using the proper tenses of the verb *to be* with the PASSIVE PARTICIPLE (which usually ends in *ed*) of the verb of which we desire to form the Passive voice.

Present simple Active	I love.
Present simple Passive	I am loved.
Past simple Active	I loved.
Past simple Passive	I was loved.
Future simple Active	I shall love.
Future simple Passive	I shall be loved.

This formation must be carefully distinguished from the use of the same Auxiliary verb *to be* with the ACTIVE PARTICIPLE which forms the Continuous Active tenses of the verb.

Present continuous Active	I am loving.
Past continuous Active	I was loving.
Future continuous Active	I shall be loving.

The student should be able to tell readily what voice, tense, and person any English verb is in ; unless he can do this he cannot possibly translate from another language with accuracy.

It is good practice to go through the tenses of an English verb, first in the Active, and then in the Passive.

(e) **Auxiliary Verbs.** Auxiliary verbs are verbs which are used as aids (Latin *auxilia*) to enable other verbs to form moods and tenses, which cannot be expressed within the compass of one word.

Examples : I SHALL go. I WOULD HAVE gone. I SHALL HAVE BEEN sent.

In English the use of these verbs is very common, no tense in the Active Voice except the Past can be formed without them, and they are used in every tense of the Passive voice.

In Latin and Greek they are rarely used. The only verb used in these languages as an auxiliary verb is the verb *to be*.

Impersonal Verbs. Impersonal verbs are verbs which are not used in the first and second persons, but only in the third.

Examples : It rains, it snows.

The Copulative Verb, Verbs of Incomplete Predication.

The verb *to be* has two meanings :

(1) It is used in the sense of *to exist* as in the sentence *God is.*

(2) It is used to join together two nouns or noun equivalents which denote the same person or thing when the person or thing denoted by the one is said to be identical with the person or thing denoted by the other.

Examples : William, was Duke of Normandy. I am the governor. This is he.

As the nouns or noun equivalents joined together by the verb *to be* denote the same person or thing, they must always be in the same case. It is grammatically incorrect to say *I am him, It is me*, because *him* and *me* are in the Accusative case, and *I* and *it* are in the Nominative case.

It is necessary to observe this rule very carefully in Latin and Greek where the Nominative and Accusative cases generally have different forms.

This rule is sometimes stated as follows :

" The verb ' to be ' takes the same case after it as before it."

The verb *to be* may also join together a noun or a noun equivalent and an adjective, making a sentence which asserts that the quality denoted by the adjective is an attribute of the person or thing denoted by the noun or noun equivalent. This adjective always agrees with the noun in number, gender and case, in such languages as Latin and Greek.

Examples : The king is proud.   He is good.   To err is human.

From its power of joining nouns to other nouns or adjectives the verb *to be* is called the **Copulative Verb**.   (Latin *copulo*, I link.)

It is also called a verb of **Incomplete Predication** because it does not make sense when it stands by itself (except when used in the sense of *to exist*), but requires to be followed by a noun or an adjective which is called the **Complement**, because it fills up the sense (Latin *compleo*, *I fill up*).

There are other verbs of Incomplete Predication besides the verb *to be*, some Intransitive and some Transitive.

Such verbs are : Intransitive—become, seem, appear, etc.
Transitive—make, declare, choose, think, consider, etc.

When a verb of Incomplete Predication is Intransitive, or Transitive and in the Passive voice, the Complement refers to the same person or thing as the subject of the sentence, and must therefore be in the Nominative case.

Examples :   Peter became an Apostle.
This place seems healthy.
He is called our king.

But when a verb of Incomplete Predication is Transitive and in the Active voice, the Complement refers to the same person or thing as the object of the sentence, and is therefore in the Accusative case.

Examples :   They made him captain.
We choose you king.
You consider me happy.

This principle is obviously of great importance in Greek and Latin.

(*f*) Person and Number.

The **First Person** of the verb is used when the speaker is speaking of himself.

The **Second Person** is used when the speaker is speaking to another person or thing.

The **Third Person** is used when the speaker is speaking of another person or thing.

Examples : 1st person, I love.　2nd person, You love.　3rd person, He loves.

The use of the **Singular Number** denotes that only one person or thing is being spoken about.

The use of the **Plural Number** denotes that more than one person or thing is being spoken about.

Rule.　**The verb agrees with its subject in Number and Person**.

Note.　The Plural of the second person *You* is almost always used in modern English instead of the second person Singular, even where only one person is being spoken to.

But in Latin and Greek the Singular is always used when one person is being spoken to.

(*g*) **Tense.**　Tenses are forms which verbs assume to show at what time the action of the verb is represented as taking place.

The times when the action may take place are (i) Past, (ii) Present, (iii) Future.

The tenses in English have further subdivisions to show whether the action is represented as being (1) continuous or in progress, (2) indefinite or simple, (3) perfect or completed.

Below is a table of the Tenses of an English verb in the Indicative Mood with the corresponding tenses of a Greek and Latin verb, given, where possible, with the names by which the tenses are generally called in Latin and Greek Grammars.

It will be seen that there are more tense-forms in English than in Latin and Greek.

The Latin and Greek Present stands both for the English Present Continuous and Present Simple, and the Latin and Greek Future for the English Future Continuous and Future Simple.

The Latin Perfect has two meanings, one of which corresponds to the English Past Simple, and the other to the English Present Perfect or Perfect, as it is generally called.

TIME

STATE	Past	Present	Future
Simple	I loved	I love	I shall love
	Amavi (Perfect)	Amo (Present)	Amabo (Future)
	ἐφίλησα (Aorist)	φιλῶ	φιλήσω
Continuous	I was loving	I am loving	I shall be loving
	Amabam (Imperfect)	Amo (Present)	Amabo (Future)
	ἐφίλουν	φιλῶ	φιλήσω
Perfect	I had loved	I have loved	I shall have loved
	Amaveram (Pluperfect)	Amavi (Perfect)	Amavero (Future perfect)
	ἐπεφιλήκειν	πεφίληκα	πεφιλήσομαι

(*h*) **Moods**. Moods are forms which verbs assume to show the way in which the action or state denoted by the verb is to be regarded, i.e. if it is a statement or fact, a command, a wish, or a thought.

The **Indicative Mood** generally makes a statement, or asks a question.

Examples: He goes. We shall run. Were you listening?

The **Imperative Mood** gives a command.

Examples: Go. Come. Make haste.

The **Subjunctive Mood** expresses a thought or wish rather than an actual fact.

The uses of the Subjunctive Mood are so various, and its use in English is so different from its use in Latin and Greek, that it is impossible to bring it under any more exact definition.

The student is warned against connecting any particular English meaning with the Latin and Greek Subjunctive, or with the Greek Optative such as *that I might love, I should, or would, love.*

Practice, and the observance of seemingly arbitrary rules, will alone enable him to use these moods correctly.

The use of tenses formed with *may, might, should, would,* etc. in English is a most unreliable guide to the use of the Subjunctive and Optative in Latin and Greek.

(*i*) **Participles.** Participles are verbal adjectives resembling verbs in that they can have subjects and objects, tenses and voices, and resembling adjectives in that they can qualify nouns.

There are two Participles in English—the Active Participle ending in *ing*, and the Passive Participle ending generally in *ed* or *d*.

Examples: *Loving, Loved.*

There is also a Past Active Participle formed with the auxiliary *having* and the Passive Participle.

Example: *Having loved.*

The Past Passive Participle is formed with the auxiliary verbs *having been* and the Passive Participle.

Example: *Having been loved.*

The Present Participle Passive is *being loved.*

There is no Past Participle Active in Latin except in the case of Deponent verbs, nor is there any Present Participle Passive. Both however are found in Greek.

As the verbal noun or Gerund in English ends in *ing* as well as the Active Participle care must be taken to distinguish them.

If the word is a Participle, it can always be replaced by such a clause beginning with a Conjunction or a Relative.

When it is a verb-noun it cannot be replaced by a clause.

Examples: (1) Skating is a fine exercise.

Here *skating* is a verb-noun and the subject of the sentence.

(2) I like to see the boys skating.

Here *skating* can be replaced by the clause *when they are skating*, and is therefore a Participle.

(3) There is a dancing bear.

Here *dancing* can be replaced by the Relative clause *that is dancing*. Therefore it is a Participle.

Participles are also used with auxiliary verbs to form certain tenses of the verb as shown above.

(*j*) **Verbal Nouns, Infinitive, Gerund.** The so-called Infinitive Mood *to go, to see, to hear* is really a verbal noun.

The other verbal noun in English is called the Gerund, and ends in *ing—going, seeing, hearing.*

Verbal nouns resemble verbs in that they can have a subject and an object, tenses and voices: they resemble a noun in that they themselves can be the subject or object of another verb.

Examples of the use of the Infinitive.

(1) As Subject—*To err is human.* Here *to err* is the subject of the sentence.

As is explained more fully in section 12, sentences in which the Infinitive stands as a Subject are more usually expressed in the following form with an anticipatory *it* standing as the grammatical subject before the verb:

It is human to err.

It is a pleasure to see you.

It is advisable to make haste.

The object of an Infinitive standing as the subject of a sentence may be expressed as in the following example : *To forgive such crimes is difficult,* or *It is difficult to forgive such crimes.*

Here *such crimes* is the object of *to forgive.*

The only way in which the subject of an Infinitive standing as the subject of a sentence can be expressed in English is by inserting *for* in front of it and making it depend on the predicate of the principal clause : *It is difficult* for a king *to forgive such crimes.*

(2) As Object—*They desire to live.* Here *to live* is the Object of the verb *desire.*

I desire him to live. Here *him* is the subject of the Infinitive *to live* and the clause *him to live* is the Object of the verb *desire.*

(3) The Infinitive is also used after certain nouns and adjectives in an explanatory or epexegetic sense.

Examples : I have not the heart to do it.

We are not worthy to gather up the crumbs under Thy table.

It is time to depart.

He was not able to answer a word.

(4) The use of the Gerund is seen in the following examples :

As Subject—Playing the violin is delightful.

As Object—He loves playing the violin.

If the student keeps in mind that the Infinitive and the Gerund are essentially *nouns* their uses in the various constructions in which they occur will explain themselves.

Note on the form of the English Infinitive. The English Infinitive is nearly always found with the preposition *to* in front of it.

This preposition is no part of the Infinitive, but is a relic of the Dative case of the verbal noun in Old English. The force of the preposition has become so weakened that its presence in the sentence is generally quite neglected, and another preposition may even be put in front of it, as for example— *What went ye out for to see ?*

This Dative case of the verbal noun originally expressed purpose, and this use still survives in such sentences as *I came to see you, He went to hear the band.*

The proposition *to* may be omitted after certain verbs such as *may, can, shall, bid, let, make,* etc.

Examples : *I can do this, Let him go, Make him stay.*

Contrast with these the following examples, *I am able to do this, Allow him to go, Force him to stay.*

6. SENTENCES

A sentence is a group of words expressing a Statement, a Question or a Desire (a command, request, entreaty or wish) or an Exclamation. (C.G.T.)

(1) **The Subject** of a sentence is the word or group of words which denotes the person or thing about which a statement is made, a question asked or a desire is expressed.

(2) **The Predicate** of a sentence is the word or group of words which expresses the statement that is made, the question that is asked or the desire which is expressed about the person or thing denoted by the Subject.

The Predicate of a sentence must not be confused with the Verb, for it includes the Object of the Verb (if any) and also all other words or clauses explanatory of the Verb.

If the Verb in a sentence is Transitive and in the Active voice it must have an Object.

The Object of a sentence is the word or group of words which denotes the person or thing which is affected by the action of the Verb or towards which it is directed.

But "the Sentence and not the Verb is the real unit of speech. A speaker thinks in sentences. Most words carry no meaning if spoken as isolated units or, at least, no specific meaning. The precise meaning of a word is determined by the context." Atkinson, *The Greek Language*, p. 133.

The student must therefore make a habit of looking at a sentence as a whole first and then picking out the main verb.

He can then find the Subject of this verb by asking the question *who?* or *what?* before it.

The Object (if any) can then be found by asking the question *whom?* or *what?* after the verb.

Example: Caesar conquered the Gauls.

Verb: *conquered.*

Who conquered?   Caesar.   Therefore *Caesar* is the Subject of the sentence.

Whom did Caesar conquer?   The Gauls.   Therefore *the Gauls* is the Object of the sentence.

Either the Subject or the Predicate can be omitted when it can easily be supplied from the context. It is therefore possible for a sentence to consist of only one word.

Examples: Go.   Come.   Thank you.   (Subject omitted.)

Who did this? I.   (Predicate omitted.)

The omission of the Subject often occurs in Latin and Greek because the forms of the verbs in these languages leave no doubt as to the number and person of the subject. It only occurs in English in the Imperative mood. When any part of the sentence is omitted it is sometimes said to be *understood.*

Every sentence must fall into one of five forms :

(1) Subject and Intransitive Verb.

Example :	SUBJECT	PREDICATE
	The sun	*shines.*

(2) Subject, Transitive Verb, Object.

Example :	SUBJECT	PREDICATE	
		Verb	Object
	Caesar	*conquered*	*the Gauls.*

(3) **Subject, Transitive Verb, two Objects.**

Example :	SUBJECT		PREDICATE	
		Verb	Indirect Object	Direct Object
	Socrates	*taught*	*Plato*	*philosophy.*

(4) **Subject, Copulative Verb or Intransitive Verb of Incomplete Predication, Predicate Noun or Adjective.**

Example :	SUBJECT		PREDICATE
		Verb	Predicate Noun
	William	*was*	*a king.*
		Verb	Predicate Adjective
	He	*is*	*happy.*
	Alexander	*was called*	*great.*

(5) **Subject, Transitive Verb of Incomplete Predication, Object, Predicate Noun or Adjective.**

Example:	SUBJECT		PREDICATE	
		Verb	Object	Predicate Noun
	Tyranny	*makes*	*men*	*slaves.*
		Verb	Object	Predicate Adjective
	They	*call*	*him*	*happy.*

Note. As was mentioned above the Predicate of a sentence is not necessarily identical with the verb. It includes the verb and the object or complement with all the words which qualify them.

Any part of a sentence may be amplified or extended by the addition of qualifying words. The learner must get into the habit of picking out the Verb and Subject first, and then finding out to which of the above forms the sentence, which he is going to translate, belongs.

Take for example the following sentence :

CAESAR, the great Roman general, completely CONQUERED the Gauls, the inhabitants of modern France, at the siege of Alesia.

This is a sentence of form 2 with amplifications.

A noun or pronoun may be amplified or extended in meaning by an adjective or an adjective equivalent.

A verb, an adjective, or an adverb may be amplified or extended in meaning by an adverb or an adverb equivalent.

7. EQUIVALENTS

The Noun, the Adjective, and the Adverb may be replaced by other parts of speech which can do the same work in the sentence.

A word doing the work of a different part of speech, or a group of words doing the work of a single part of speech, is called an **equivalent**.

A group of words forming an equivalent, and not having a subject or predicate of its own is called a **phrase**.

In the example in the last section the words *the great Roman general*, *inhabitants of modern France* and *at the siege of Alesia* are all Phrases.

A group of words forming an equivalent and having a subject and predicate of its own is called a **clause**.

Example: Caesar, *who was a great Roman general*, completely conquered the Gauls, *who inhabited modern France*, *when he took Alesia*. Here all the groups of words in italics are Clauses.

Noun Equivalents. A noun equivalent may be

(1) A **pronoun**. *You* are happy. *I* am miserable.

(2) A **verb-noun**, an Infinitive or Gerund. I like *to run*. *Sleeping* is pleasant.

(3) An **adjective**.
Both *wise* and *foolish* know this.

(4) A **clause**, generally called a noun or substantival clause.
That you have wronged me doth appear in this.
I see *that you know him*.

Adjective Equivalents. An adjective equivalent may be

(1) A **verbal adjective** or participle, or a participial phrase.
A *loving* mother. A *loved* spot. We saw a man *carrying wood*.

(2) A **noun** in apposition.
Queen Victoria. Edward *the peacemaker*.

(3) A **noun** preceded by a preposition, or in the possessive case.
The Houses *of Parliament*.
Maids' Causeway.
The King *of Britain*. (Compare His Britannic Majesty.)
Dogs *for hunting*.

(4)   An Adjectival **Clause.**

The horse *which I saw* is there.

<u>Adverb Equivalents.</u>   An adverb equivalent may be

(1)   **A noun** preceded by a preposition.

He lives *in the woods.*

He walked *for six hours.*

(2)   **A noun** sometimes qualified by an adjective, but without a preposition.

He died *last night.*

They went *home.*

We hope to live *many years.*

(3)   An Adverbial **clause.**

I will see you *when you come.*

I have come *in order to see him.*

I will see you *if you come.*

(4)   A participle or a participial phrase.

We stood *amazed.*

Hearing this I went home.

The sun having set we went to rest.

(5)   An Infinitive.

We came *to see the spectacle.*

He is too foolish *to be trusted.*

8.   SENTENCES SIMPLE AND COMPLEX

A simple sentence is a sentence which contains a single subject and a single predicate.

Two or more clauses which are not dependent on one another, but which make equally important and independent statements, are said to be combined by **coordination,** and to form a **double or multiple sentence.** Such clauses are generally joined together by the coordinating conjunctions *and, but, or, for,* etc.

Example: You do this, and I do that.

A complex sentence is a sentence which contains a principal clause and one or more subordinate clauses depending on it, or on one another, as noun, adjective or adverb equivalents.

It will be found convenient to keep the name **sentence** for complete statements occurring between two full stops.

Groups of words forming part of a compound or complex sentence, and having a subject and predicate of their own, should be called **clauses.**

Groups of words forming an equivalent to some part of speech, and not having a subject and predicate of their own, should be called **phrases.**

EXAMPLE OF A COMPLEX SENTENCE.

When the captain drew near to the coast, he sent some of his men to land in order that he might get help, if the other ships, which had not yet arrived, should need it.

(1) Main Clause : *he sent some of his men to land.*

Subject : He.   Predicate : Sent some of his men to land.

(2) *when the captain drew near to the coast*
     is an Adverbial Clause qualifying *sent.*
     It tells us when he sent the men.

(3) *in order that he might get help*
     is an Adverbial Clause qualifying *sent.*
     It tells us why he sent the men.

(4) *if the other ships should need it*
     is an Adverbial Clause qualifying *get help.*
     It tells us under what conditions he would need the help.

(5) *which had not yet arrived,*
     is an Adjectival Clause qualifying *ships.*
     It tells us more about the ships.

9. SUBSTANTIVAL OR NOUN CLAUSES

A Substantival or Noun Clause is a clause which stands in the relationship of a noun to the principal clause or to some other clause in a complex sentence.

(1) **As Subject.** *That he is coming* is certain.

(2) **As Object.** He said *that he was king.* (Statement.)

He commanded *that bread should be set before them.* (Command.)

He besought him *that he might be with him.* **(Petition.)**

Do you know *who he is?*
He asked *how it happened.* 〕 (Questions.)
Tell me *where he lives.*

You see *how unjust he is.* (Exclamation.)

(3) **As Complement, or Predicative Noun.**
My hope is *that you may succeed.*

When a Noun Clause which is the object of a verb states a fact, it is generally called a **Dependent Statement.**

When a Noun Clause gives the words of a command or petition, it is generally called a **Dependent Command or Petition.**

When a Noun Clause begins with an interrogative or exclamatory word such as *who, what, where, whether, if, how,* it is generally called a **Dependent Question or Exclamation.**

All the Noun Clauses given above with the exception of the Dependent Questions and Exclamations are introduced by the conjunction *that* and contain a finite verb.

In certain cases however an infinitive or a gerund may be used in Noun Clauses instead of a clause introduced by *that* and containing a finite verb. This is natural because the infinitive and gerund are verbal nouns.

The infinitive is used frequently in Noun Clauses in Greek and Latin, it is therefore important to see how far the same construction prevails in English.

It is used in English as follows :

(1) As Subject. *To err* is human.
It is a pleasure *to see you.* (See section 12.)

(2) As Object. I declare him *to be guilty.* 〕 (Statements.)
We believe him *to be innocent.*
He commanded them *to go away.* (Command.)

(3) As Complement or Predicative Noun.
My hope is *to succeed.*

The use of the infinitive in a dependent statement is only found after a few verbs in English, such as *I declare, I assert, I proclaim, I believe,* etc. A clause introduced by *that* is by far the most common way of expressing a dependent statement in English, and can be used after any verb.

The infinitive is frequently used in dependent commands or petitions in English, and indeed is the most usual way of expressing them.

There are certain verbs such as *I wish, I hope, I am able, I can*, etc. which always take an Infinitive as their object.

These are sometimes called **Modal Verbs** because they are considered to add to the verb new ways of expressing its meaning.

Examples : I wish *to see the king.*
We hope *to live many years.*
They can *do nothing without you.* (See 5*j*.)

The use of the Gerund is seen in such sentences as :

Subject : *Healing the sick* is a noble work.
Object : I deny *using the expression.*

10. ADJECTIVAL CLAUSES

Adjectival clauses are introduced by the relative pronouns *Who, Which, That,* and their equivalents *when, where, such as,* etc. and qualify some noun in another clause just like an adjective.

This is the man *who sent me.*
This is the man *whom I saw.*
We will do this in the evening *when we meet.*
This is the place *where I was born.*
I can sell you a house *such as you require.*

The word to which the relative pronoun refers, and which the clause which it introduces qualifies, is called the **antecedent**.

In the first two sentences the word *the man* is the antecedent, in the others *evening, place,* and *house.*

A Participle qualifying the Antecedent may take the place of an Adjectival Clause.

We may write :

I saw a man clinging to a mast, or
I saw a man who was clinging to a mast.

11. ADVERBIAL CLAUSES

Adverbial Clauses are clauses which stand in the relationship of an adverb to the verb in another clause.

Example : I will do this *on condition that you do that.*

Here the clause *on condition that you do that* qualifies the verb *I will do* just like an adverb.

The sentence might have been written : I will do this *conditionally.*

Example : I will do this *when to-morrow comes.*

Here *when to-morrow comes* is an adverbial clause qualifying *I will do.* The sentence might have been written : I will do this *to-morrow.*

Adverbial Clauses may be divided into eight classes.

(1)   Clauses of **Time** denoting **time when.** (Also called **Temporal** clauses.)

     He ran *when he got on the road.*

(2)   Clauses of **Place** denoting **place where.** (Also called **Local** clauses.)

     He ran *where the road was level.*

(3)   Clauses of **Cause** denoting **cause.** (Also called **Causal** clauses.)

     He ran *because he was late.*

(4)   Clauses of **Purpose** denoting **purpose.** (Also called **Final** clauses.)

     He ran *that he might get home soon.*

(5)   Clauses of **Result** denoting **result.** (Also called **Consecutive** clauses.)

     He ran *so that he got home soon.*

(6)   Clauses of **Condition** denoting **supposition.** (Also called **Conditional** clauses.)

     He ran *if he was late.*

(7)   Clauses of **Concession** denoting **contrast.** (Also called **Concessive** or **Adversative** clauses.)

     He ran *although he was early.*

(8)   Clauses of **Comparison** denoting **comparison.** (Also called **Comparative** clauses.)

     He ran *as he was accustomed to do.*

The names given to these clauses in the brackets are still often given to them in grammars. They are given here for this reason and not because they have anything else to recommend them, for they are sometimes pedantic and obscure.

The names given to these clauses above are those suggested by the Committee of Grammatical Terminology and have the merit of describing the nature of the clause to which they are applied without ambiguity.

THE USE OF PARTICIPLES TO EXPRESS ADVERBIAL CLAUSES.

A Participle may be used to express some kinds of Adverbial Clauses. Care is often needed to distinguish such participles from those which take the place of Adjectival Clauses (see 10 above).

If the participle can be resolved into a clause consisting of a conjunction and a finite verb it is used in place of an Adverbial Clause, but if it can be resolved into a clause introduced by a relative pronoun it is used in place of an Adjectival Clause.

Example (1) : Knowing this, I returned home.

Here *knowing this* obviously means *since I knew this* and is therefore an **adverbial clause** denoting cause.

Example (2): I saw a man clinging to a spar half a mile from shore.

Here *clinging to a spar* might be replaced by *who was clinging to a spar*. This is a clause introduced by a relative pronoun and *clinging to a spar* must therefore be described as an **adjectival clause**.

Example (3): Seeing the man running away, I went after him.
This might be equally well expressed as follows :
Since I saw the man who was running away, I went after him.
When the sentence is put in this form there is no difficulty in analysing it.

Even Relative Clauses are sometimes adverbial if they express cause or purpose.

Example (1). We disliked our master *who seemed to take a pleasure in punishing us.* Here *who seemed* is equivalent to *because he seemed,* and is an **adverbial clause** of cause.

Example (2). They sent men *who should spy out the land.*

Here *who should spy out the land* is equivalent to *in order to spy out the land,* and is an **adverbial clause** of purpose.

In analysing complex sentences pay very little heed to the FORM, but be sure to find out what the MEANING of the clauses is by putting them into other words if necessary.

12. PREPARATORY *IT* AND *THERE*

This construction is so common in English that it seems to require special mention.

The subject is nearly always put before the verb in English ; indeed, as English nouns have no case endings to distinguish the subject from the object, the order of words in a sentence is the only way in which the subject can be distinguished from the object.

But in certain cases, especially where the subject of the sentence is in the infinitive mood, the subject is placed after the verb.

Then the pronoun *it* is placed before the verb to act as a preparatory subject and to show that the real subject is coming.

Example : It is good to walk in the way of righteousness.

Here the real subject is *to walk in the way of righteousness*, and *is good* is the predicate.

It is the preparatory subject, or the grammatical subject as it is sometimes called.

The adverb *there* is used in the same way especially when the verb in the sentence is part of the verb *to be*.

Example : There was once a boy who lived on an island.

In this sentence the subject is *a boy*. *There* should be parsed as a preparatory adverb.

Neither of these constructions exist in Latin or Greek.

The Latin or Greek for the examples given above are as follows :

Bonum est ambulare in via justitiae.

καλόν ἐστι περιπατεῖν ἐν τῇ ὁδῷ τῆς δικαιοσύνης.

Olim fuit puer qui insulam habitabat.

ἦν ποτε παῖς ὃς κατῴκει νῆσον.

PART II

THE GREEK OF THE NEW TESTAMENT

THE Greek language had its origin in the speech of that branch of the Aryan race which settled in the country which we call Greece. These people called themselves Hellenes, and their country Hellas. It consists of a number of small plains divided from one another by steep mountain ridges or by arms of the sea. From the formation of the country it resulted that each of the tribes which inhabited these plains formed a separate state, and spoke a different dialect. The most important of these dialects was the Attic dialect. This was spoken by the inhabitants of Attica, the little strip of country in which the famous city of Athens was situated.

The importance of this dialect was not due to the size of Attica, or to the extent of the Athenian empire ; but to the celebrity of the Athenian men of letters, whose writings were the accepted models for all Greece.

All Grammars of Classical Greek, unless they are specially written to illustrate some dialect, are founded on Attic Greek, and deviations from it are treated as exceptions to rule.

After the conquests of Alexander in the 4th cent. B.C., Greek gradually became the common language of all the various nations inhabiting the countries surrounding the Eastern end of the Mediterranean Sea.

The victorious army of Alexander carried the Greek language to the inland parts of Asia Minor, to Syria, Palestine and Egypt.

The colonies which the Greek states had planted at an earlier stage of their history had carried the language to the coast of Asia Minor, to the islands of the Aegean Sea, to Sicily and to the South of Italy.

After the Roman conquest of Greece the admiration which the Romans felt for the language and literature of that country, and the convenience of the language for trading purposes, caused it to be very commonly spoken in Rome itself.

But the Macedonian conquests had not only opened up the East to Greek influence ; they also broke down the barriers which separated one Greek state from another. Men of all the Greek tribes met in Alexander's army or followed in its train. They soon felt the need of a new manner of speech by means of which they could communicate readily with one another, and so a new dialect was formed from those elements which the old dialects had in common. The literary celebrity of Attic Greek gave its forms a preponderance in the new common dialect ; but the latter contained many expressions, which would not have been tolerated in Attic, and dropped many peculiarities of diction and niceties of phrase, which had been found necessary by the highly cultivated Athenian writers, but which were not required for purposes of ordinary intercourse.

This Common Dialect, or the κοινή, as it is generally called, became the regular means of communication among the nations comprising the Eastern part of the Roman Empire, and between them and Rome. We find the Apostle Paul writing to the Roman Church in Greek, and Clement, Bishop of Rome in the first century, writes to the Corinthians in Greek. The *Shepherd* of Hermas and many of the inscriptions in the Catacombs are written in the same language.

In Egypt the language was thoroughly domesticated.

The papyri, which are being discovered in Egypt, and which have thrown such a valuable light on the Greek of the New Testament, represent the letters and business documents of people of all classes.

The Septuagint, or Greek Version of the Old Testament, was produced at the court of the Ptolemies for the benefit of the Greek-speaking Jews of Egypt, and was soon used even in Palestine and Rome, as we can see from the quotations in the New Testament and in the letter of Clement of Rome.

The Greek of the New Testament is the Greek of this common dialect.

Until a few years ago it was universally held that the peculiarities of New Testament Greek were due to the fact that the writers were accustomed to speak in Aramaic, and to read Hebrew.

But recent discoveries of inscriptions from all parts of the Greek-speaking world and of papyri from Egypt have made it plain that most of these peculiarities existed in countries where there could be no suspicion of Aramaic influence. It is now generally allowed that the New Testament was written in the ordinary Greek in common use in Palestine in the time of Christ, which would be perfectly intelligible to any person of average education in the countries to which the Gospel first penetrated. Its diction is however much influenced by the Septuagint, as might be expected from the nature of the subjects treated, and from the familiarity of its writers with that version of the Old Testament Scriptures.

The chief points in which New Testament Greek differs from Attic Greek are as follows :

(1) The complete disappearance of the Dual.

(2) The almost entire disappearance of the Optative.

(3) The great extension of the use and meaning of clauses introduced by ἵνα.

(4) The extension of the use of μή.

(5) The substitution of the regular endings of the verbs in -ω for those of the verbs in -μι in certain cases.

(6) The general simplification of sentence-construction, and the frequent use of a simple καί or δέ to join sentences or clauses.

PREPOSITIONS

1. Prepositions were originally **Adverbs**, and are so still when they are compounded with verbs. Most of the local and other relations which are now expressed by a Preposition followed by the Accusative, Genitive, or Dative case of a noun or pronoun were originally expressed by the use of a suitable case of the noun or pronoun alone.

In the language from which Greek was derived there were cases which, when standing by themselves, sufficed to denote local, temporal and other derived relations.

The **Accusative** case denoted extension, or motion towards.

The **Ablative** case denoted separation, or motion from.

The **Locative** case denoted the place where, or rest at.

The **Instrumental** case denoted the means by which an action was accomplished, and it had also an idea of association.

In that form of the Greek language with which we are acquainted we find the form which we call the Genitive case used to express the meaning of the Ablative case as well as its own proper meaning.

The form that we call the Dative case expresses the meanings of the Locative and Instrumental cases as well as its own.

We are therefore justified in saying, as a practical rule, that the Genitive in Greek denotes **motion from**, and that the Dative denotes **rest at**, and also can be used to express the **Instrument** of an action, although these are not the proper original meanings of these cases.

As we have already stated, the Accusative denotes **motion towards.**

These cases called in the help of Adverbs to make their meaning more precise, and, when these adverbs had become fixed in this use by custom, they were treated as a separate part of speech, and called Prepositions.

Prepositions do not, properly speaking, "govern" the cases which they precede. The case is really the governing element in the expression : the Preposition only serves to make clear the exact sense in which it is used. But as language developed, the Prepositions mastered the cases. As the horse in the fable called in the man to help him against the stag, and allowed him to get on his back, and then found that he himself had lost his liberty, so the cases called in the help of the Prepositions, and then found themselves weakened, and finally destroyed. In Modern Greek, Italian, French, and English the cases have disappeared, wholly, or in part, and the Prepositions do the work which they once did.

For example we say *of a man* where the Greeks said ἀνθρώπου and *to a man* where the Greeks said ἀνθρώπῳ.

In the Greek of the New Testament we can see this process going on. Prepositions are used with the case of a noun, where the case alone sufficed in Classical Greek.

For example the simple Dative was used in Classical Greek to express the Instrument; but in later Greek ἐν with the Dative was so used.

Example: Lord, shall we strike with the sword?

κύριε, εἰ πατάξομεν ἐν μαχαίρῃ;   Lk. xxii. 49.

In estimating the meaning of a Prepositional phrase (i.e. a Preposition followed by a noun) the proper course to adopt is first to consider the force of the case of the noun and then to add to this the root meaning of the Preposition. The combination of the two ideas will generally explain the meaning of the phrase.

If the proper force of the case is always kept in view, it will explain how the same preposition can have such wholly different meanings with different cases.

We may see the joint influence of the case of the noun and the root meaning of the Preposition best by considering some Preposition that is used with all three cases.

For example παρά means *beside*.

When it is used with the **Accusative** it denotes MOTION TO beside and motion alongside of, hence it gets the derived meanings of *contrary to, beyond*.

Examples : And having departed from thence, Jesus went to the side of the Sea of Galilee.

καὶ μεταβὰς ἐκεῖθεν ὁ Ἰησοῦς ἦλθεν παρὰ τὴν θάλασσαν τῆς Γαλιλαίας.

Mt. xv. 29.

And as he sowed some fell by the way side.

καὶ ἐν τῷ σπείρειν αὐτὸν ἃ μὲν ἔπεσεν παρὰ τὴν ὁδόν.

Mt. xiii. 4.

When it is used with the **Genitive** it denotes MOTION FROM beside.

Example : And they knew truly that I came forth from thee.

καὶ ἔγνωσαν ἀληθῶς ὅτι παρὰ σοῦ ἐξῆλθον.   Jn. xvii. 8.

When it is used with the **Dative** it denotes REST beside and is translated *near*.

Example : Jesus...taking a child, set him near himself.

Ἰησοῦς...ἐπιλαβόμενος παιδίον ἔστησεν αὐτὸ παρ᾽ ἑαυτῷ.   Lk. ix. 47

By analysing the following examples in the way suggested in the English rendering below the force both of the Preposition and the case may be clearly seen.

εἰς τὴν πόλιν.	to the city inwards.
ἀπ᾽ αὐτοῦ.	from him away.
ἐν τῷ τόπῳ.	at the place within.
σὺν αὐτῷ.	in association with him.

2. The uses of the Prepositions given in the following table are those which occur most frequently in New Testament Greek.

The use of Classical Greek is somewhat different.

The meaning printed in capitals after each Preposition may be regarded as indicating the root meaning of the Preposition ; it also generally indicates the meaning of the Preposition when compounded with a verb. The student is advised to master these meanings thoroughly by learning them by heart, and to pick up the derived meanings in the course of his reading, remembering what has been stated above as to the importance of the meaning of the case in deciding the meaning of a Prepositional phrase.

It may be well to add that it is sometimes difficult to trace the steps by which some of the derived meanings of the Prepositions have been reached : this is especially the case with some of the meanings of κατά with the accusative, and ἐπί with the genitive.

Such peculiar meanings must be learnt as idioms.

3. Prepositions connected with the **Accusative** only.

ἀνά.   UP. Occurs only in the New Testament in such phrases as
ἀνὰ δηνάριον *a penny each,* ἀνὰ μέσον *in the midst.*

εἰς.   INTO (to the interior), *to, with a view to, for.*

4. Prepositions connected with the **Genitive** only.

ἀντί.   OVER AGAINST, *instead of, in return for.*

ἀπό.   AWAY FROM (from the exterior).

ἐκ.   OUT OF (from the interior).

πρό.   IN FRONT OF, *before* of place or time.

5. Prepositions connected with the **Dative** only.

ἐν.   IN of place or time, *among.* In the N.T. *with* or *by* of the
instrument or agent.

σύν.   TOGETHER WITH.

6. Prepositions connected with the **Accusative** and **Genitive**.

διά.   THROUGH.   With Accusative *on account of, owing to*.
                               With Genitive *through, throughout, by means of*.

κατά.   DOWN.   With Accusative *down along, through, during, with
                               regard to, according to*, also distributively as κατ'
                               ἔτος *year by year*.
                               With Genitive *down from, down upon, against*.

μετά.   AMONG.   With Accusative *after*.
                               With Genitive *with, among*.

περί.   AROUND.   With Accusative *about, around* of place or time.
                               With the Genitive *about, concerning, on account of*.

ὑπέρ.   OVER.   With Accusative *above, beyond*.
                               With Genitive *on behalf of, for the sake of, con-
                               cerning*.

ὑπό.   UNDER.   With the Accusative *under*.
                               With the Genitive *under the influence of*, hence *by*
                               of the agent after passive verbs.

7. Prepositions connected with the **Accusative, Genitive** and **Dative**.

ἐπί.   UPON.   With Accusative *Upon* (placed on), *up to, as far as*.
                               With Genitive *on, in the presence of, in the time of*.
                               With Dative *on, at, on account of, in addition to*.

παρά.   BESIDE.   With Accusative *to the side of, beside, beyond,
                               contrary to*.
                               With Genitive *from beside, from* (of persons).
                               With Dative *near* (generally of persons),

πρός.   TOWARDS,   With Accusative *towards, up to, in reference to,
        NEAR.   with regard to, with* in the sense of *near*.
                               With Genitive *from* (only once in N.T. in sense
                               of *for*, Acts xxvii. 34).
                               With Dative *at, close to* (rare in N.T.).

APPENDIX TO SECTION I

PREPOSITIONS IN COMPOSITION : FOR REFERENCE ONLY

The meaning of prepositions when compounded with verbs, nouns, etc. is not always the same as that which they have when they are connected with the case of a noun. Examples of some important compound words are given below.

In cases where the meaning of the compound word is very different from that of the simple word it is printed in capitals.

ἀμφί : Root meaning **around.** Only occurs in composition in N.T.

ἀμφιβάλλειν　　to throw round.

ἀνά : (1) Root meaning **up.**

ἀναβαίνειν	to go up.
ἀνέχειν	to hold up, Mid. to hold one's self firm, bear with, TO ENDURE.
ἀνιστάναι	to cause to stand up.
ἀνάκεισθαι	to lie up, recline, sit at table.

(2) Over again, anew, thoroughly.

ἀναγιγνώσκειν	TO READ.
ἀναπαύειν	to give rest to thoroughly, to refresh.
ἀνασταυροῦν	to crucify afresh.

(3) Back, backwards, to and fro.

ἀνακρίνειν	to judge by looking through a series of particulars, to examine, to interrogate.
ἀναπίπτειν	to fall back, to lean back, to recline.
ἀναστρέφειν	to turn back, to walk to and fro, to pass one's time, TO DWELL, TO BEHAVE ONE'S SELF.
ἀναστροφή	CONDUCT.

ἀντί . (1) Root meaning **opposite, against, over against.**

ἀντίδικος	an opponent in a law suit.
ἀντέχειν	to hold before or against. Mid. to keep one's self opposite anyone, TO CLEAVE TO.
ἀντιλέγειν	to speak against.
ἀντίκεισθαι	to be set over against, oppose.
ἀντίχριστος	Antichrist.

(2) Requital.

ἀνταποδιδόναι	to repay, requite.

(3) Substitution.

ἀνθύπατος	a Proconsul.

ἀπό : (1) Root meaning **away from.**

ἀπέρχομαι	to depart from.
ἀποκαλύπτειν	to withdraw a cover from, uncover.
ἀποκρίνειν	to give a decision from one's self, Mid. and Pass. Aor. TO ANSWER.

ἀπολογεῖσθαι   to talk one's self off from a charge, defend one's self.

(2) In an intensive sense.

ἀπέχειν   to have to the full, also in sense (1) to be away, to be distant, Mid. to hold one's self off from, abstain.

ἀποκτείνειν   to kill.

ἀπολλύναι   to destroy.

(3) In the sense of the Latin *re*, back again.

ἀποδιδόναι   to give back, Mid. to give away for one's own advantage, TO SELL.

ἀπολαμβάνειν   to take back, recover.

διά: (1) Root meaning **through**.

διέρχεσθαι   to go through.

(2) Continuity of time or completeness of action.

διαμένειν   to remain or continue.

διακαθαρίζειν   to cleanse throughly.

(3) Distribution or separation.

διακρίνειν   to separate, make distinctions, learn by discrimination, decide, Mid. be at variance with one's self, HESITATE, DOUBT, to distribute.

(4) Transition or change.

διαβάλλειν   to throw across, TO SLANDER.

διαλογεῖσθαι   to think different things, argue, discuss.

διαλλάσσειν   to change, reconcile.

εἰς: Root meaning **into**.

εἰσέρχεσθαι   to go into.

ἐκ: (1) Root meaning **out of, from inside**.

ἐκβάλλειν   to cast out.

ἐξέρχεσθαι   to come out.

ἐκκλησία   a body of men called out from their homes, an assembly, a church.

ἐκλέγεσθαι   to choose out.

ἐξιστάναι   to throw out of position, to astonish.

(2) Removal, separation.

ἐκδύειν   to strip off.

ἐν: (1) Root meaning **in**.

ἐνεργεῖν   to work in, effect.

N.   3

| ἐνοικεῖν | to dwell in. |
| ἐνέχειν | to have in, to hold in, c. dat. to have a grudge against any one, TO BE ENRAGED WITH. |

(2) Motion into or towards.

| ἐμβαίνειν | to go into. |
| ἐνδύειν | to put on. |

ἐπί: (1) Root meaning **on or upon.**

ἐπαγγέλλεσθαι	to announce concerning one's self, TO PROMISE.
ἐπικαλεῖν	to put a name upon, to surname, Mid. to call upon for one's self, appeal to.
ἐπέχειν	to hold on or upon, apply, observe, give attention to, hold forth, present.
ἐπιθυμεῖν	to keep the θυμός turned upon a thing, set one's heart on, desire.
ἐφιστάναι	to place at or over, Mid. to stand by.
ἐπίστασθαι	perhaps Ionic form of Mid. of ἐφιστάναι, to place one's attention on, TO UNDERSTAND.

(2) Motion towards.

| ἐπέρχεσθαι | to come upon, to be coming on, to be at hand, to be future. |

(3) Upwards.

| ἐπαίρειν | to lift up. |

(4) Superintendence.

| ἐπίσκοπος | an overseer or bishop. |
| ἐπιστάτης | one who is set over, a master. |

κατά: (1) Root meaning **down from, down.**

καταβαίνειν	to go down.
καταφρονεῖν	to look down on, despise.
καθίζειν	to make to sit down, to sit down.
καθιστάναι	to set down, appoint.

(2) In succession, in order.

| καταρτίζειν | to set in order, to mend. |
| καθεξῆς | in succession. |

(3) Under.

| κατέχειν | to hold under, hold fast, restrain. |

(4) Thoroughly.

| κατεργάζεσθαι | to work out thoroughly, accomplish. |
| κατεσθίειν | to eat up. |

καταχρᾶσθαι	to use to the full.
καταλύειν	to dissolve, undo, from loosing garments and loads at the end of a journey, TO LODGE.

(5) Opposition.

καταρᾶσθαι	to pray against, curse.
κατακρίνειν	to give judgment against, condemn.

μετά: (1) Root meaning **among**.

μετέχειν	to share, partake of.

(2) Change, alteration.

μεταβαίνειν	to pass from one place to another, remove, depart.
μετανοεῖν	to change one's mind, repent.

(3) After, in search of.

μεταπέμπειν	to send for.

παρά: (1) Root meaning **beside, along, near.**

παραγγέλλειν	to transmit a message along a line, TO COMMAND.
παραβάλλειν	to put one thing beside another for the sake of comparison, to compare.
παραβολή	a comparison, a parable.
παρέχειν	to hold beside, offer, show.
παρακαλεῖν	to call to one's side, summon, admonish, exhort, entreat, comfort, encourage.
παράκλητος	one called in to one's aid, one who pleads one's cause before a judge, an advocate, a helper, the Comforter.

(2) Aside.

παραιτεῖσθαι	to avert by entreaty, refuse, beg pardon, excuse one's self.

(3) Transgression or neglect.

παρακούειν	to hear amiss, disobey.
παραβαίνειν	to go by the side of, violate, transgress.

περί: Root meaning **in a circuit about, around.**

περιβάλλειν	to throw round, to clothe.
περιπατεῖν	to walk about, to conduct one's self.
περιτέμνειν	to circumcise.

πρό: Root meaning **before of place or time, forth.**

προάγειν	to lead before or go before.
προγιγνώσκειν	to know before.
προφητεύειν	to foretell, to speak forth.

πρός: (1) Root meaning **towards**.

    προσέρχεσθαι   to come to, approach.

    προσέχειν   to bring near to, attend, προσέχειν ἑαυτῷ to attend to one's self, beware.

    προσκαλεῖν   to call to one's self.

    προσκυνεῖν   (*with the dative*) to kiss the hand to, fall down before, worship.

  (2)   On or at.

    προσκόπτειν   to strike on, to stumble.

σύν: (1) Root meaning **together with**.

    συνάγειν   to gather together.

    συνεργός   a fellow-worker.

    συνέχειν   to hold together, to constrain, oppress.

    συνιέναι   to bring together in the mind, TO UNDERSTAND.

  (2)   Thoroughly.

    συντηρεῖν   to keep safe.

ὑπέρ: Root meaning **over, above, beyond**.

    ὑπερέχειν   to have or hold over, to excel.

ὑπό: Root meaning **under**, hence of subjection or inferiority.

    ὑπάγειν   to lead under, withdraw one's self, depart.

    ὑπακούειν   to listen to, obey, submit to.

    ὑπάρχειν   to begin below, to begin, to commence, TO BE.

    ὑπομένειν   to remain under, to endure.

Special attention should be paid to the meanings of the compounds of ἔχειν, ἀγγέλλειν, κρίνειν.

Note on the "perfective action" of certain prepositions.

Certain prepositions such as ἀπό, διά, κατά, σύν sometimes practically lose their local meaning in composition, and denote that the action of the verb with which they are connected is to be regarded as fully accomplished, see examples given above.

This is especially the case with verbs which in their simple form denote incomplete action, such as θνήσκειν to be dying, φεύγειν to be fleeing.

Compare *to eat up, to knock in, to hear out, to follow up* in English, and *devorare, efficere, consequi* in Latin.

For a full discussion of the question see Dr J. H. Moulton's *Prolegomena*, pp. 113—118.

SUBJECT AND PREDICATE

8. The Subject of a Finite verb is in the **Nominative** Case.

(A verb is said to be Finite unless it is in the Infinitive Mood.)

Example: The crowd hears. Turba audit. ὁ ὄχλος ἀκούει.

9. The Subject of a verb in the Infinitive mood is put in the **Accusative** Case.

Example: They say that the men know. Dicunt viros noscere. λέγουσι τοὺς ἀνθρώπους γιγνώσκειν.

10. The verb agrees with its subject in number and person.

EXCEPTION. In Classical Greek a noun or pronoun in the neuter plural is regularly followed by a verb in the singular number; but in N.T. Greek there are many exceptions to this rule, especially when the neuter noun denotes persons.

Example: The names of the twelve Apostles are these.

τῶν δὲ δώδεκα ἀποστόλων τὰ ὀνόματά ἐστιν ταῦτα.

Matt. x. 2.

but: Children shall rise up against parents.

ἐπαναστήσονται τέκνα ἐπὶ γονεῖς.

Matt. x. 21.

Compare Jas. ii. 19, John x. 8.

11. Some verbs cannot form a complete predicate by themselves. They require to be supplemented by a noun or adjective which is called the **predicative noun** or **adjective** or the **complement.**

Such verbs, the most important of which is the verb *to be,* are called **copulative** verbs. Generally speaking, they are such verbs as signify *to become, to appear, to be chosen, to be named,* and the like.

The Predicative Noun or Adjective must be in the **same case** as the subject.   Predicative Adjectives agree with the subject in **number** and **gender** as well as in case.

Example : The kingdom becomes great.   Regnum magnum fit. ἡ βασιλεία γίγνεται μεγάλη.

CASES AND THEIR MEANINGS

12. **Inflection** is a change made in the form of a word to denote a modification of its meaning, or to show the relationship of the word to some other word in the sentence.

Examples: *bird* becomes *birds* in the plural : in the same way *man* becomes *men.*

The pronoun *he* is used when it is the subject of a sentence ; but it is changed into *him* when it is the object.

Inflections are comparatively rare in English.

Latin and Greek **nouns,** pronouns and adjectives have inflections to show number and case: adjectives and some pronouns have inflections to show gender as well.

To give a list of these inflections is called giving a **Declension**, or Declining a word, because the cases other than the Nominative are considered to fall away (*declinare*) from the form of the Nominative. For the same reason the cases other than the Nominative are sometimes called **oblique** or slanting cases.

Hence also the origin of the term **Case** from the Latin *casus, falling*.

The cases actually in use are seven in number.

Their names are Nominative, Vocative, Accusative, Genitive, Dative, Ablative[1], Locative (not given in the tables of declensions in grammars).

The commonest uses of these cases are as follows.

The **nominative** is used to express the subject of a finite verb.

The **vocative** is used in addressing a person or thing.

The **accusative** is used to express the direct object of a transitive verb.

The **genitive** is used to limit the meaning of another noun, and to denote various relations, most of which are expressed in English by the use of the preposition *of* or by the possessive case.

The **dative** is used to express that to or for which anything is done. This includes the dative of the indirect object after transitive verbs which is generally rendered into English by the preposition *to*.

The **ablative**[1] is used to express separation, or motion from.

The **locative** is used to express the place at which anything happens.

In English we express the various relationships of words to one another, which are expressed in Greek and Latin by the use of case-endings, by means of Prepositions, or by changing the order of words in a sentence.

Consider the following sentence :

The man showed the way to the son of the farmer with a stick.

Nom.		acc.	dat.	gen.	abl. (in Latin).
Homo	monstravit	viam	filio	agricolae	baculo.

ὁ ἄνθρωπος ἔδειξεν τὴν ὁδὸν τῷ υἱῷ τοῦ γεωργοῦ ῥάβδῳ.

---

[1] In Greek the Ablative case has the same form as the Genitive and is not given as a separate case in the tables of declensions in most Greek Grammars. (See page 28.)

Here we see the use of Prepositions in English, and Cases in Latin and Greek. In English we show that the word *way* is the object of the sentence by putting it after the verb. In Latin and Greek we show that it is the object by putting it in the Accusative Case.

NOTES ON THE USE OF THE OBLIQUE CASES

13. The **vocative** case is used in addressing a person or thing.

Example : Jesus, Master, have mercy upon us.

Jesu, praeceptor, miserere nostri.

'Ιησοῦ ἐπιστάτα, ἐλέησον ἡμᾶς.   Lk. xvii. 13.

In N.T. Greek the Nominative case, generally with the article, is often used instead of the Vocative.

Example : Yea, Father, because it thus seemed good to Thee.

ναί, ὁ πατήρ, ὅτι οὕτως εὐδοκία ἐγένετο ἔμπροσθέν σου.

Lk. x. 21.

14. The root idea of the **accusative** case is that of **extension** and so of **motion towards.**

The Object is the name of that towards which the action of the verb goes forth.

This is also clearly seen from the fact that all prepositions which denote *motion towards*, such as ad, contra, εἰς, πρός, are followed by an Accusative.

In Latin the Accusative without a preposition is used to denote the place towards which one is going, if the place is a town or a small island.—I am going to Rome. Eo Romam.

15. The Accusative is used to express the **direct object** of a transitive verb.

Example : We beheld his glory. Spectavimus gloriam ejus.
ἐθεασάμεθα τὴν δόξαν αὐτοῦ.   Jn. i. 14.

In English there is no means of distinguishing the subject from the object of a sentence by changing the form of the words (except in the case of personal and relative pronouns). The only way in which they can be distinguished is by the order of the words in the sentence :— the subject comes before the verb, and the object after.

16. The subject of a verb in the Infinitive mood is put in the Accusative case.

Example : The crowd......said that it thundered.
Turba dicebat tonitruum esse factum.
ὁ ὄχλος...ἔλεγεν βροντὴν γεγονέναι. Jn. xii. 29.

17. Cognate Accusative. Any verb whose meaning permits it may take after it an Accusative of cognate or kindred meaning: in some cases it takes a direct object as well.

Examples : They rejoiced with great joy.
ἐχάρησαν χαρὰν μεγάλην. Mt. ii. 10.
Ye load men with loads difficult to be borne.
φορτίζετε τοὺς ἀνθρώπους φορτία δυσβάστακτα.
Lk. xi. 46.
I fed you with milk.
γάλα ὑμᾶς ἐπότισα. 1 Cor. iii. 2.
The same construction occurs in Latin.
I have lived a long life. Longam vitam vixi.

18. The Accusative may also denote extent of time or space.

Examples : They remained not many days.
Manserunt non multos dies. (Beza.)
ἔμειναν οὐ πολλὰς ἡμέρας. Jn. ii. 12.
He withdrew from them about a stone's cast.
καὶ αὐτὸς ἀπεσπάσθη ἀπ' αὐτῶν ὡσεὶ λίθου βολήν
Lk. xxii. 41.
So in Latin—A wall ten feet high.
Murus decem pedes altus.

19. Two accusatives with one verb. Verbs meaning to ask questions, to demand, to teach, and (Greek only) to clothe and unclothe, and to remind, may take two object accusatives.

Examples : I too will ask you one question
Interrogabo vos et ego unum sermonem.
ἐρωτήσω ὑμᾶς κἀγὼ λόγον ἕνα. Mt. xxi. 24.
And he began to teach them many things.
Et coepit illos docere multa.
καὶ ἤρξατο διδάσκειν αὐτοὺς πολλά. Mk. vi. 34.

They took off from him the purple, and put his own garments on him.

ἐξέδυσαν αὐτὸν τὴν πορφύραν, καὶ ἐνέδυσαν αὐτὸν τὰ ἱμάτια αὐτοῦ.

Mk. xv. 20.

Who shall remind you of my ways.

ὃς ὑμᾶς ἀναμνήσει τὰς ὁδούς μου.　　1 Cor. iv. 17.

20. When a verb followed by two Accusatives is put into the passive voice the word in the Accusative denoting a person becomes the subject of the passive verb, and the other word in the accusative remains unchanged.

Examples: And John was clothed with camel's hair.

καὶ ἦν ὁ Ἰωάνης ἐνδεδυμένος τρίχας καμήλου.　Mk. i. 6.

He was instructed in the way of the Lord.

οὗτος ἦν κατηχημένος τὴν ὁδὸν τοῦ κυρίου.

Acts xviii. 25.

When a verb followed by a Dative of the person and an Accusative of the thing is put into the Passive voice, the word denoting the person becomes the subject of the verb and the word in the Accusative remains unaltered.

Example: We have been thought worthy by God to be entrusted with the Gospel[1].　δεδοκιμάσμεθα ὑπὸ τοῦ θεοῦ πιστευθῆναι τὸ εὐαγγέλιον.

1 Thess. ii. 4.

21. Verbs meaning to choose, to call, to appoint, to make, may take a **Predicate Accusative** as well as the Object Accusative.

Example: Why callest thou me good?

Quid me dicis bonum?

τί με λέγεις ἀγαθόν;　　　　　　　Mk. x. 18.

22. **Adverbial Accusative.** The Accusative of certain nouns, pronouns and adjectives is sometimes found in an Adverbial sense.

Examples: And every one that striveth is temperate in all things.

πᾶς δὲ ὁ ἀγωνιζόμενος πάντα ἐγκρατεύεται.

1 Cor. ix. 25.

Hurting him in no wise.

μηδὲν βλάψαν αὐτόν.　　　　　　　Lk. iv. 35.

Under this head may be included such phrases as

τὸ λοιπόν, for the rest.

τὸ καθ' ἡμέραν, daily.

ὃν τρόπον, in like manner.

---

[1] The active form of this clause would be—God entrusted the Gospel to us. ἐπίστευσε ἡμῖν ὁ θεὸς τὸ εὐαγγέλιον.

THE GENITIVE CASE

23. **The Genitive case** is an **adjectival** or **descriptive** case ; a noun in the Genitive case is generally connected with another noun which it qualifies very much in the same way as an adjective. The Genitive case is generally expressed in English by the use of the preposition **of** or by the **Possessive case.**

In Greek the Ablative case has always the same form as the Genitive case ; the two cases are therefore treated as one in most grammars, and the name " Genitive " given to both.

The Ablative case denotes **separation from** and expresses many of the relations which are expressed by the Ablative case in Latin.

To avoid conflicting with established usage the name " Genitive " is used here in its accustomed sense to cover both the Genitive case proper and the Ablative case : but the student should always keep in mind that under this common name there are really included two distinct cases.

The most important uses of the Genitive are as follows :

24. **Possessive Genitive** denoting possession.
Example : The father's house.   Patris domus.   ἡ τοῦ πατρὸς οἰκία.

25. **The Genitive of Source or Material.**
Examples : The righteousness of faith (i.e. that springs from faith).
Justitia fidei.   δικαιοσύνη πίστεως.
A herd of swine (i.e. consisting of swine).
Grex porcorum.   ἀγέλη χοίρων.

26. **Partitive Genitive** expressing the whole after words denoting a part.
Example : Many of the Samaritans.   Multi Samaritanorum.
πολλοὶ τῶν Σαμαρειτῶν.
(This Partitive use of the Genitive explains its use after verbs meaning *to touch, to taste, to partake of,* because only PART of the object is affected by the Action of the verb.)

Subjective and Objective Genitive.

27. The Genitive case is described as **Subjective** when the noun in the Genitive is the name of the subject of the action denoted by the word on which it depends.

Example: Who shall separate us from the love of Christ?

Quis separabit nos a caritate Christi?

τίς ἡμᾶς χωρίσει ἀπὸ τῆς ἀγάπης τοῦ Χριστοῦ;

Rom. viii. 35.

i.e. Who can separate us from the love which Christ feels for us?

28. The Genitive case is described as **Objective** when the noun in the Genitive is the name of the object of the action denoted by the word on which it depends.

Example: For the preaching of the cross is to them that are perishing foolishness.

Verbum enim crucis pereuntibus quidem stultitia est.

ὁ λόγος γὰρ ὁ τοῦ σταυροῦ τοῖς μὲν ἀπολλυμένοις μωρία ἐστίν. 1 Cor. i. 18.

The cross is the object of the preaching.

It is often very difficult to say whether a noun in the Genitive is Subjective or Objective. The context alone can decide the matter.

The possessive pronoun may be used in the sense of an objective genitive.

Example: Do this in remembrance of me.

τοῦτο ποιεῖτε εἰς τὴν ἐμὴν ἀνάμνησιν. Lk. xxii. 19.

See also Rom. xi. 31, 1 Cor. xv. 31.

29. Genitive of Time. The Genitive is used in Greek to express the time within which anything takes place.

Example: He came to Jesus during the night.

Hic venit ad Iesum nocte.

οὗτος ἦλθεν πρὸς τὸν Ἰησοῦν νυκτός. Jn. iii. 2.

In Latin the Ablative is used to express time when.

30. Genitive of Price. The Genitive is used in Greek to express the price at which anything is sold.

Example: Are not two sparrows sold for one farthing?

Nonne duo passeres asse veneunt?

οὐχὶ δύο στρουθία ἀσσαρίου πωλεῖται; Mt. x. 29.

In Latin the Ablative is used to express the price at which anything is sold.

31. The Genitive of Definition limits the meaning of the noun with which it goes just like an adjective. It does not occur in Classical Greek or Latin.

Example: The unjust steward. ὁ οἰκονόμος τῆς ἀδικίας. Lk. xvi. 8.

This is imitated in the Vulgate by *Villicus iniquitatis.*

Under this head may be classed the Genitive of Apposition, where the Genitive takes the place of a word in apposition to the noun on which it depends.

Example : The sign of Circumcision (i.e. consisting in circumcision)
σημεῖον περιτομῆς.   Rom. iv. 11.
This construction is common in English : '*The City of London.*'

The Genitive after Adjectives

32.   A noun in the Genitive case follows many adjectives denoting fullness or want, worthiness or unworthiness, participation.

Examples :   Full of grace and truth.   πλήρης χάριτος καὶ ἀληθείας.
Worthy of death or bonds.   ἄξιος θανάτου ἢ δεσμῶν.
Sharing the sufferings.   μέτοχος τῶν παθημάτων.

ἔνοχος *guilty of* or *subject to* is followed by a Genitive of the penalty or of the crime as well as a Dative of the Tribunal Matt. xxvi. 66, Heb. ii. 15, Mk. iii. 29, 1 Cor. xi. 27, Matt. v. 22.

33.   The Comparative Degree of the adjective is sometimes followed by a noun in the Genitive in Greek.

Example :   Thou shalt see greater things than these.
Majora his videbis.
μείζω τούτων ὄψῃ.   Jn. i. 50.

In Latin the Ablative is used in this construction.

Genitive with Verbs

34.   Some verbs both in Latin and Greek are followed by a noun in the Genitive case instead of in the Accusative case.   Such verbs, and also those which are followed by a noun in the Dative case, are not really exceptions to the rule that all transitive verbs are followed by an object in the Accusative case, for they are not properly transitive when they are followed by a case other than the Accusative.   We have similar verbs in English such as *to think of*, *to laugh at*, which are always followed by a noun preceded by a preposition.

The student must observe the use of each verb as he finds it.   The use varies greatly, even in the case of the same verbs.   Many of those which are followed by a Genitive may be followed by an Accusative as well.

In N.T. Greek the Genitive may follow many verbs of the following meanings.

(1) Verbs where the Partitive meaning is obvious.

Verbs meaning *to partake of, to taste, to touch, to seize, to hold.*
μεταλαμβάνειν, μετέχειν, γεύεσθαι, ἅπτεσθαι, ἐπιλαμβάνεσθαι, κρατεῖν etc.

The partitive sense may be seen by comparing ἐκράτησε τῆς χειρὸς αὐτῆς *He took her by the hand*—a part of the body only—with ἐκράτησεν αὐτόν *He seized him.*

(2) Verbs meaning to be full or to fill.

πιμπλάναι, πληροῦν, γέμειν, γεμίζειν etc.

(3) Verbs denoting perception.

to hear   ἀκούειν (also followed by the accusative case).

(4) Verbs denoting emotion etc.

ἐπιθυμεῖν to desire.	ἐπιμελεῖσθαι to give heed to.
τυγχάνειν to attain.	ἀνέχεσθαι to bear with.

(5) Verbs denoting separation or abstention from or hindering, want or need.

ἀποστερεῖσθαι to deprive of.	δέεσθαι beseech.
παύεσθαι to cease from.	χρῇζειν, ὑστερεῖν, to lack or
ἀπέχεσθαι to abstain from.	λείπεσθαι need.

(6) Verbs meaning to rule or to excel.

ἄρχειν, κυριεύειν etc. to rule.	διαφέρειν to excel.

(7) Verbs meaning to remember or to forget.

⎰ μιμνήσκεσθαι to remember.	ἐπιλανθάνεσθαι to forget.
⎱ μνημονεύειν „	ἀμελέειν to pay no heed to.

(8) Many verbs compounded with κατά are followed by a simple Genitive case.   Such are

καταγελᾶν	to laugh at.
κατακαυχᾶσθαι	to boast oneself against.
καταφρονεῖν	to despise.

The Genitive Absolute

35.   A noun or pronoun and a participle may stand together by themselves in the Genitive case, if the noun or pronoun does not denote the same person or thing as the subject or object of the sentence.

This construction is called the **Genitive Absolute.**

Absolute means *loosed,* from the Latin *Absolutus* : phrases of this kind are called Absolute because they are loosed in construction from the rest of the sentence.

The Genitive Absolute should generally be translated by an Adverbial Clause in English introduced by the conjunctions *when*, *since*, *although* etc. Which of these conjunctions is the proper one to use is determined by the context.

Examples : When the devil was cast out, the dumb man spoke.

καὶ ἐκβληθέντος τοῦ δαιμονίου ἐλάλησεν ὁ κωφός.

Mt. ix. 33.

While the bridegroom tarried they all slumbered and slept.

χρονίζοντος δὲ τοῦ νυμφίου ἐνύσταξαν πᾶσαι καὶ ἐκάθευδον.

Mt. xxv. 5.

N.B. The rule given above as to the noun or pronoun not referring to the same person as the subject or object of the sentence is generally observed in Classical Greek.

But it is frequently broken in N.T. Greek, as the following example shows :

Since he had nothing wherewith to pay, his lord commanded him to be sold.

μὴ ἔχοντος δὲ αὐτοῦ ἀποδοῦναι ἐκέλευσεν αὐτὸν ὁ κύριος πραθῆναι.

Mt. xviii. 25.

The same construction is found in Latin, but the case there used is the Ablative.

A similar construction is also rarely found in English.

Example : This done, he went home.

Here *This done* is a phrase consisting of a pronoun and a participle, but they are in the Nominative case, and not in the Genitive case as in Greek.

THE DATIVE CASE

36. **The Dative case** denotes that **to** or **for** which anything is or is done. In Greek the Dative case also does the work of the **Locative** and **Instrumental** cases which had distinct forms in the language from which it was derived. In Latin the work of the Instrumental case is done by the Ablative, and the Locative still exists as a separate form in certain words.

37. The Dative of the **Indirect Object** is used after verbs of giving, showing, etc.

Example : They promised to give him money.

Promiserunt ei pecuniam se daturos.

καὶ ἐπηγγείλαντο αὐτῷ ἀργύριον δοῦναι. Mk. xiv. 11.

38. The Dative of Interest may be used after any verb to denote the person or thing whose interest is affected by the action of the verb.
Examples : Be not anxious for your life.

Ne solliciti sitis animae vestrae.

μὴ μεριμνᾶτε τῇ ψυχῇ ὑμῶν.   Mt. vi. 25.

To his own master he stands or falls.

Domino suo stat aut cadit.

τῷ ἰδίῳ κυρίῳ στήκει ἢ πίπτει.   Rom. xiv. 4.

39. The Dative of Possession after εἶναι, γένεσθαι.

The Dative is used after these verbs to denote the person to whom the person or thing named as the subject of the verb is said to belong.
Examples : Whose name was John.

Cui nomen Johannes.

ὄνομα αὐτῷ Ἰωάννης.   Jn. i. 6.

If any man should have a hundred sheep...

Si fuerint alicui centum oves...

ἐὰν γένηταί τινι ἀνθρώπῳ ἑκατὸν πρόβατα.   Mt. xviii. 12.

40. Locative uses of the Dative.

The Dative is used very rarely in the N.T. to express place where. See Acts xiv. 8, 16, Romans iv. 12, Jas. ii. 25, Jn. xix. 2.

The Dative is used to express the time at which anything takes place.
Example : On the third day.

Tertia die.

τῇ τρίτῃ ἡμέρᾳ.   Mt. xvi. 21.

Note that in Latin the Ablative is used here.

41. The Dative is used to express the sphere to which a quality is referred.

Examples : The poor in spirit.

οἱ πτωχοὶ τῷ πνεύματι.   Mt. v. 3.

An Alexandrian by descent.

Ἀλεξανδρεὺς τῷ γένει.   Acts xviii. 24.

The Dative is also sometimes used to express duration of time Lk. viii. 29, Jn. ii. 20, Acts viii. 11, xiii. 20, Rom. xvi. 25.

42. The Dative used to denote the Instrument etc.

The Dative is used to express the cause or manner of the action of the verb or the instrument by which it is carried out.

Examples : **Cause.** They were broken off because of their unbelief

τῇ ἀπιστίᾳ ἐξεκλάσθησαν.   Rom. xi. 20.

Manner. I partake with thanks.

$$\chi\acute{a}\rho\iota\tau\iota\ \mu\epsilon\tau\acute{\epsilon}\chi\omega.\qquad\qquad\text{1 Cor. x. 30.}$$

Instrument. But the chaff he will burn with un-
quenchable fire.

$$\tau\grave{o}\ \delta\grave{\epsilon}\ \mathring{a}\chi\upsilon\rho\upsilon\nu\ \kappa\alpha\tau\alpha\kappa\alpha\acute{\upsilon}\sigma\epsilon\iota\ \pi\upsilon\rho\grave{\iota}\ \mathring{a}\sigma\beta\acute{\epsilon}\sigma\tau\omega.\qquad\text{Mt. iii. 12.}$$

Very rarely the Dative expresses the *Agent* after a passive verb. See
Lk. xxiii. 15, Mt. vi. 1, Acts i. 3.

43. The Dative of resemblance or union.

The Dative is used with all words implying resemblance, union or
approach. This includes verbs, adjectives, adverbs, and nouns.

For example verbs meaning *to follow, to meet, to make like* are
followed by a Dative.

The Dative with Verbs

44. The Dative is used after certain verbs which in English are
followed by a direct object in the Accusative case.

These verbs, although transitive in English, are intransitive in
Greek, and cannot therefore have a direct object.

There are also verbs which are transitive in Greek, but intransitive
in English, as for example εὐαγγελίζειν *to preach the Gospel to,* φεύγειν
to flee from.

The following may be taken as examples of verbs which are followed
by a Dative case in Greek.

Certain verbs meaning to worship	προσκυνεῖν.
to serve	δουλεύειν, διακονεῖν, ὑπηρετεῖν.
to obey	πείθεσθαι, ὑπακούειν.
to believe	πιστεύειν.
to rebuke	ἐπιτιμᾶν, ἐμβριμᾶσθαι.
to command	ἐπιτάσσειν, παραγγέλλειν.

See Lk. viii. 24—29 for several examples of the use of some of these
verbs

The Dative also follows verbs compounded with certain prepositions
such as ἐν, σύν, ἐπί, παρά, πρός.

ADJECTIVES

45.   Adjectives agree with the Nouns which they qualify in Number, Gender, and Case.

This rule also applies to Participles, and adjectival Pronouns, and to the Article in Greek.

Examples :

Of the wise men.   Virorum sapientium.   τῶν σοφῶν ἀνδρῶν.

Of these men.   Horum virorum.   τούτων τῶν ἀνδρῶν.

The laws written for the world.   Leges mundo scriptae.   οἱ τῷ κόσμῳ γραφόμενοι νόμοι.

An Adjective may be either **attributive** or **predicative**.

46.   An Attributive Adjective simply qualifies its noun without the intervention of the verb *to be* or any other verb.

Example : The good man.   Bonus vir.   ὁ ἀγαθὸς ἀνήρ.

A Predicative Adjective is connected to its noun by the verb *to be* or some other Copulative verb, and forms with the verb and its subject a complete sentence.

Example : The man is good.   Vir bonus est.   ὁ ἀνὴρ ἀγαθός.
(See further sections 75 and 76.)

47.   The Adjective used as a noun.

An Adjective or Participle (generally with the Article in Greek) may be used as a noun.

Examples :   A resurrection of the just and the unjust.
Resurrectio justorum et iniquorum.
ἀνάστασις δικαίων τε καὶ ἀδίκων.   Acts xxiv. **15.**
Blessed are the poor in spirit.
μακάριοι οἱ πτωχοὶ τῷ πνεύματι.   Mt. v. 3.

48.   The neuter singular of an Adjective preceded by an Article is often used as an abstract noun.

Example : The foolishness of God is wiser than men and the weakness of God is stronger than men.

τὸ μωρὸν τοῦ θεοῦ σοφώτερον τῶν ἀνθρώπων ἐστίν, καὶ τὸ ἀσθενὲς τοῦ θεοῦ ἰσχυρότερον τῶν ἀνθρώπων.   1 Cor. i. 25.

PRONOUNS

49. A Pronoun has been defined as a word which is used instead of a noun ; but many words are classed as Pronouns which are also used as Adjectives to define or point out nouns.

Personal, Reflexive and **Relative** Pronouns can stand only in place of nouns.

Demonstrative, Interrogative, Indefinite and **Possessive** Pronouns can be used either in place of nouns, or adjectivally.

50. **Personal Pronouns.** *I, thou, he, she, me, him* etc.

As the ending of a Greek or Latin verb generally shows what person and number the subject is, the Nominative of the Personal Pronouns is seldom used in these languages except for emphasis.

Thus if we wish to translate *we hear* it is quite sufficient to write *audimus* in Latin and ἀκούομεν in Greek.

Example of the use of the Personal Pronoun in the Nominative for emphasis :

We heard out of the Law that Christ abideth for ever, and how sayest thou that the Son of Man must be lifted up ?

Nos audivimus ex lege, quia Christus manet in aeternum ; et quomodo tu dicis : Oportet exaltari Filium hominis ?

ἡμεῖς ἠκούσαμεν ἐκ τοῦ νόμου ὅτι ὁ Χριστὸς μένει εἰς τὸν αἰῶνα, καὶ πῶς λέγεις σὺ ὅτι δεῖ ὑψωθῆναι τὸν υἱὸν τοῦ ἀνθρώπου ;   Jn. xii. 34.

51. All cases of αὐτός are used in the N.T. for the Personal Pronoun of the **third person**, *he, she, it* etc. But in Attic Greek only the cases other than the Nominative are so used : the Nominative case always means *self.*

Examples : I myself.   ἐγὼ αὐτός.

The man himself.   ὁ ἄνθρωπος αὐτός or αὐτὸς ὁ ἄνθρωπος.

This use is found sometimes in the N.T. In the following example we find the Nominative of αὐτός used in the sense of *self,* and the Genitive used as a Personal Pronoun in the sense of *his* or *of him.*

And John himself had his raiment of camel's hair.

αὐτὸς δὲ ὁ Ἰωάννης εἶχεν τὸ ἔνδυμα αὐτοῦ ἀπὸ τριχῶν καμήλου.
Mt. iii. 4.

52. The personal pronoun of the third person may also be expressed by the demonstrative pronouns οὗτος and ἐκεῖνος.

Examples :   He was in the beginning with God.

οὗτος ἦν ἐν ἀρχῇ πρὸς τὸν θεόν.   Jn. i. 2.

ἐκεῖνος is always used emphatically, generally with reference to God or Christ. It is especially frequent in the writings of St John.

Examples : But he spake of the temple of his body.

ἐκεῖνος δὲ ἔλεγεν περὶ τοῦ ναοῦ τοῦ σώματος αὐτοῦ.

Jn. ii. 21.

He that saith that he abideth in him ought himself also to walk even as he walked.

ὁ λέγων ἐν αὐτῷ μένειν ὀφείλει καθὼς ἐκεῖνος περιεπάτησεν καὶ αὐτὸς οὕτως περιπατεῖν. 1 Jn. ii. 6.

Note that the Feminine Nominative singular and plural forms of οὗτος differ only from the corresponding forms of *αὐτός* in the breathing and accent—αὕτη, αὐτή : αὗται, αὐταί.

The forms αὐτοῦ, αὐτῆς, αὐτοῦ etc. which are found in some texts of the N.T. are contracted forms formed from the Reflexive Pronoun ἑαυτόν etc.

They have generally the same meaning as the simple αὐτοῦ, αὐτῆς, αὐτοῦ.

53. *αὐτός* with the Article before it is used in the sense of *the same*. The man himself, ὁ ἄνθρωπος αὐτός. The same man, ὁ αὐτὸς ἄνθρωπος.

Examples : He prayed the third time saying the same words.

προσηύξατο ἐκ τρίτου, τὸν αὐτὸν λόγον εἰπών.

Mt. xxvi. 44.

For thou doest the same things.

τὰ γὰρ αὐτὰ πράσσεις. Rom. ii. 1.

This use must be carefully distinguished from those given above.

54. The Nominative of the Article followed by μέν or δέ is often used as a Personal Pronoun.

Example : But he, going out, began to publish it much.

ὁ δὲ ἐξελθὼν ἤρξατο κηρύσσειν πολλά. Mk. i. 45.

ὁ μέν followed by ὁ δέ or ἄλλος δέ must be translated by *one... another* : οἱ μέν followed by οἱ δέ or ἄλλοι δέ must be translated *some... others.*

Example :

Some mocked, others said *We will hear thee again about this matter*.

οἱ μὲν ἐχλεύαζον, οἱ δὲ εἶπον Ἀκουσόμεθά σου περὶ τούτου καὶ πάλιν.

Acts xvii. 32.

In N.T. Greek even the Relative Pronoun is used with μέν and δέ in the sense mentioned above.

Example : And the husbandmen taking his slaves beat one and killed another and stoned another.

καὶ λαβόντες οἱ γεωργοὶ τοὺς δούλους αὐτοῦ ὃν μὲν ἔδειραν, ὃν δὲ ἀπέκτειναν, ὃν δὲ ἐλιθοβόλησαν. Mt. xxi. 35.

Compare also Lk. xxiii. 33, Jn. v. 11, Romans xiv. 2, 5.

55. Reflexive Pronouns are used either as objects or after a preposition when the person or thing to which they refer is the same as the person or thing to which the subject refers.

The forms common in the N.T. are:

Myself, ἐμαυτόν ; *Himself,* ἑαυτόν, αὑτόν.

Thyself, σεαυτόν ; *Themselves,* ἑαυτούς, αὑτούς.

(ἑαυτούς is also used for *ourselves* and *yourselves.*)

56. Possessive Pronouns are generally equivalent to the possessive Genitive of the Personal Pronoun.

They are   *My* or *mine,* ἐμός ; *Thy* or *thine,* σός.

Our or *ours,* ἡμέτερος ; *Your* or *yours,* ὑμέτερος.

Our Father may be translated either

ὁ ἡμέτερος πατήρ or ὁ πατὴρ ἡμῶν,

and the same is the case with the other persons and numbers.

The Genitive Singular of αὐτός is used for *his, her, its,* and the Genitive Plural for *their.* When used with nouns these words should be called **Possessive Adjectives.**

57. Demonstrative Pronouns are used to point out something.

They are :

οὗτος   *this* (Latin *hic*), which generally refers to that which is near in place, time or thought.

ἐκεῖνος   *that* (Latin *ille*), which generally refers to that which is more remote.

ὅδε, ἥδε, τόδε, *this,* is rare in the N.T. Lk. x. 39, Jas. iv. 13, Rev. ii. 1.

Examples :

This man went down to his house justified rather than that.

κατέβη οὗτος δεδικαιωμένος εἰς τὸν οἶκον αὐτοῦ παρ᾽ ἐκεῖνον.   Lk. xviii. 14.

Thus saith the Holy Spirit.

τάδε λέγει τὸ πνεῦμα τὸ ἅγιον.   Acts xxi. 11.

When used with nouns these words should be called **Demonstrative Adjectives.**

58. The **Interrogative Pronoun.** τίς may take the place of either a noun or an adjective.

Whom did I see?   τίνας εἶδον;

Which men did I see?   τίνας ἄνδρας εἶδον;

τίς may be used in independent or dependent questions.

What does he want?   τί βούλεται;

He asks what you want.   ἐρωτᾷ τί βούλεσθε.

59. The **Indefinite Pronoun.** τις generally means *some, any.*

Some one says this.   τοῦτο λέγει τις.

Some man.   ἄνθρωπός τις.

It is sometimes equivalent to the English article *a* or *an*.

> There was a rich man.
>
> ἄνθρωπός τις ἦν πλούσιος.   Lk. xvi. 1.

60. The Relative Pronoun *who, that* etc. is used to connect two clauses in a sentence like a conjunction : it always refers back to some noun or pronoun in the first of the two clauses, which word is called its antecedent.

In Latin and Greek Relative Pronouns agree with their antecedent in gender and number, but NOT in case.

The case of the Relative Pronoun depends on the function which it performs in the clause in which it stands.

Examples :   I saw the men who came afterwards.

> Vidi homines qui postea venerunt.
>
> εἶδον τοὺς ἀνθρώπους οἳ ὕστερον ἦλθον.

Here *homines* and ἀνθρώπους are in the Accusative case because they are the objects of the verbs in their respective clauses ; but *qui* and οἳ are in the Nominative case because they are the subjects of the verbs in their respective clauses.

> The men, whom you saw, went away.
>
> Homines, quos vidisti, abierunt.
>
> οἱ ἄνθρωποι οὓς εἶδες ἀπῆλθον.

Here *homines* and ἄνθρωποι are in the Nominative case because they are the subjects of the verbs in their respective clauses ; but *quos* and οὓς are in the Accusative case because they are the objects of the verbs in their respective clauses.

61. The Relative Pronoun also agrees with its Antecedent in person.

No change is made in the form of the pronoun to show that its person is changed, the change is only shown by the personal ending of the verb in cases where the Relative is the subject of a clause.

Examples :

You who do this.	I who did this.
Vos qui hoc FACITIS.	Ego qui hoc FECI.
ὑμεῖς οἳ τοῦτο ποιεῖτε.	ἐγὼ ὃς τοῦτο ἐποίησα.

62. The Antecedent of the Relative may be omitted in cases where it can readily be supplied from the context.

Example : For your Father knoweth what things ye have need of.

> Scit enim Pater vester quibus vobis sit opus.
>
> οἶδεν γὰρ ὁ πατὴρ ὑμῶν ὧν χρείαν ἔχετε.   Mt. vi. 8.

63. When the Relative would naturally be in the Accusative case as the object of the verb in its clause, it is generally assimilated to the case of its Antecedent, if this is in the Genitive or Dative.

Examples :

Of the water which I shall give.

ἐκ τοῦ ὕδατος οὗ ἐγὼ δώσω. Jn. iv. 14.

If there had been no assimilation this would have been—

ἐκ τοῦ ὕδατος ὃ ἐγὼ δώσω.

At the catch of fishes which they had taken.

ἐπὶ τῇ ἄγρᾳ τῶν ἰχθύων ᾗ συνέλαβον. Lk. v. 9.

If there had been no assimilation this would have been—

ἐπὶ τῇ ἄγρᾳ τῶν ἰχθύων ἣν συνέλαβον.

64. In a few instances also where the Relative would naturally be in the Dative it is assimilated to the case of its Antecedent.

Example: Until the day in which he was taken up from us.

ἕως τῆς ἡμέρας ἧς ἀνελήμφθη ἀφ᾽ ἡμῶν. Acts i. 22.

If there had been no assimilation this would have been : ἕως τῆς ἡμέρας ᾗ ἀνελήμφθη ἀφ᾽ ἡμῶν.

Compare also Lk. i. 20.

65. In some cases the Antecedent may be omitted, and the Relative assimilated to the omitted Antecedent.

Examples : And they kept silence, and told no one in those days any of the things which they had seen.

καὶ αὐτοὶ ἐσίγησαν καὶ οὐδενὶ ἀπήγγειλαν ἐν ἐκείναις ταῖς ἡμέραις οὐδὲν ὧν ἑώρακαν. Lk. ix. 36.

If this had been written in full, it would have been—οὐδὲν τούτων ἃ ἑώρακαν.

When Christ comes will he do more signs than these which this man did ?

ὁ Χριστὸς ὅταν ἔλθῃ, μὴ πλείονα σημεῖα ποιήσει ὧν οὗτος ἐποίησεν ; Jn. vii. 31.

If this had been written in full, it would have been—τούτων ἃ οὗτος ἐποίησεν.

66. The Antecedent may be attracted into the Relative clause, while at the same time the Relative is assimilated to it in case.

If the Antecedent has an article, it is omitted.

Examples : The multitude began to praise God for all the mighty works which they had seen.

ἤρξαντο τὸ πλῆθος αἰνεῖν τὸν θεὸν περὶ πασῶν ὧν εἶδον δυνάμεων.

Lk. xix. 37.

If this had been written in full, it would have been—περὶ πασῶν τῶν δυνάμεων ἃς εἶδον.

That thou mightest know the certainty concerning the things wherein thou wast instructed.

ἵνα ἐπιγνῷς περὶ ὧν κατηχήθης λόγων τὴν ἀσφάλειαν.   Lk. i. 4.

If this had been written out in full, it would have been—περὶ τῶν λόγων οὓς κατηχήθης.

Compare Lk. i. 20, iii. 19, Mt. xxiv. 38, Acts xxv. 18.

67. Very rarely the Antecedent is assimilated to the case of the Relative.

Examples : Bringing with them one Mnason of Cyprus, an early disciple, with whom we should lodge.

ἄγοντες παρ᾽ ᾧ ξενισθῶμεν Μνάσωνί τινι Κυπρίῳ, ἀρχαίῳ μαθητῇ.

Acts xxi. 16.

If there had been no assimilation this would have been :

ἄγοντες Μνάσωνά τινα Κύπριον ἀρχαῖον μαθητὴν παρ᾽ ᾧ ξενισθῶμεν.

Ye became obedient to the form of teaching whereunto ye were delivered.

ὑπηκούσατε εἰς ὃν παρεδόθητε τύπον διδαχῆς.   Rom. vi. 17.

Compare also 1 Cor. x. 16, Lk. xii. 48.

When a relative pronoun is the subject of the verb "to be" it may agree with the noun or pronoun in the predicate.

Example : For the temple of God is holy which ye are.

ὁ γὰρ ναὸς τοῦ θεοῦ ἅγιός ἐστιν οἵτινες ἐστε ὑμεῖς.   1 Cor. iii. 17.

See also Acts xvi. 12, Eph. iii. 14, Rev. v. 8.

THE DEFINITE ARTICLE

68. There are in English two words to which the name **Article** is given : the Indefinite Article *a* (or *an*), and the Definite Article *the*.

In Latin there is no Article, Definite, or Indefinite : in Greek there is only a Definite Article ὁ, ἡ, τό.

This word was originally a **demonstrative pronoun**, and it is used even in the New Testament as a personal pronoun of the third person before μέν and δέ, see section 54. A relic of its use as a pronoun is also to be seen in the quotation from an ancient poet in St Paul's speech at Athens in Acts xvii. 28 (τοῦ γὰρ καὶ γένος ἐσμέν).

As ordinarily used the Definite Article retains something of its original demonstrative force. Generally speaking it is used in Greek, as it is in English, to denote that the person or thing, to whose name it is attached, is well known, has just been mentioned, or would naturally be thought of in connection with the subject which is being spoken about.

The difference between the Definite and Indefinite Articles in English is readily shown by examples.

Compare the sentences

> I saw a man in the lane yesterday, and
>
> I saw the man in the lane yesterday.

The first sentence refers to any man ; the second to some particular man already known and thought of both by ourselves and the persons to whom we are speaking. For an example in Greek see Mark ii. 15, 16.

Consider also the sentence in the account of our Lord's visit to the Synagogue at Nazareth. *And having shut the book and given it back to the attendant, he sat down.* The Definite Article is used here before *book* and *attendant* because there would be a book and an attendant in every Synagogue, and they would be thought of at once, by those acquainted with Jewish customs, when a Synagogue was mentioned. In explaining the passage to an English audience, unfamiliar with the customs of the Jews, it would however be necessary to explain why the Definite Article was used before these two words.

Although the Definite Article is generally used in Greek where it would be used in English, this rule is by no means of universal application. The student must therefore pay most careful attention to its use ; he must not think that it is used arbitrarily or without reason, because he finds it difficult to express its force in English.

Many of the mistakes made by the translators of the *Authorised Version* were due to their misunderstanding or neglecting the use of the Definite Article. Compare the translations in the A.V. and the R.V. of such passages as 1 Tim. vi. 5, 10. See how greatly the force of the passage is altered by the omission of the Definite Article in Jn. iv. 27 in the R.V. and by its insertion in the marginal reading in Lk. xviii. 13.

See also Acts ii. 42, James ii. 14. In 1 Pet. iii. 1 even the Revisers have wrongly inserted the Article, and have quite spoilt the sense of the verse by reading *without the word.*

The best general rule that can be given for the use of the Definite Article in Greek is that it is always used when it is desired to mark the person or thing denoted by the word with which it goes as **definite** or **well known**, unless the word is regarded as already definite enough without it, or is made definite in some other way.

For example such words as ἥλιος (Mt. xiii. 6), γῆ (Lk. ii. 14), θάλασσα (Lk. xxi. 25) and many others may be used without a Definite Article, because they are regarded as already definite enough in themselves. We generally use the Definite Article with such words in English, although we too may say *He came to earth.*

Again a word may be made definite by the addition of a defining Genitive or an adjective, and so not need a Definite Article as well.

Examples :   πύλαι ᾅδου.   Mt. xvi. 18.
             εἰς χεῖρας θεοῦ ζῶντος.   Heb. x. 31.

69. Below are enumerated certain classes of words and constructions where the Definite Article is regularly **omitted** in English, but regularly, or frequently, used in Greek.

(1) **Proper nouns** may take the Definite Article, especially if the person or place named is well known, or has just been mentioned.

        Jesus is generally written ὁ Ἰησοῦς.

The Definite Article is generally used before Χριστός in the Gospels in the sense of *the expected Messiah*, the One who is well known by that title, just as we speak of *the Christ.*

But in the Epistles, written at a time when Χριστός was becoming a proper name, the Article is often omitted.

An instance occurs in Acts xix. 13 where we can translate this Article into English :

        I adjure you by the Jesus whom Paul preacheth.

        ὁρκίζω ὑμᾶς τὸν Ἰησοῦν ὃν Παῦλος κηρύσσει.

(2) **Abstract nouns** may take the Definite Article especially when it is desired to lay emphasis on the quality spoken about, or to denote it as one previously mentioned.

Examples : Depart from me, ye that work iniquity.

        ἀποχωρεῖτε ἀπ᾽ ἐμοῦ οἱ ἐργαζόμενοι τὴν ἀνομίαν.

                             Mt. vii. 23.

The following sentence contains an example of the Definite Article used with the name of a quality previously mentioned, i.e. φόβος.

There is no fear in love, but perfect love casteth out fear, because fear has punishment.

φόβος οὐκ ἔστιν ἐν τῇ ἀγάπῃ, ἀλλ᾽ ἡ τελεία ἀγάπη ἔξω βάλλει τὸν φόβον, ὅτι ὁ φόβος κόλασιν ἔχει.   1 Jn. iv. 18.

Note also that ἀγάπη, which is the principal matter under consideration, has the Article every time. See also James ii. 14.

(3) The Definite Article may be used **Generically,** that is to mark the noun with which it goes as the name of the representative or representatives of a class.

Examples : [1]For a workman is worthy of his hire.

ἄξιος γὰρ ὁ ἐργάτης τοῦ μισθοῦ αὐτοῦ.   Lk. x. 7.

Ye load men (as a class) with loads difficult to be borne.

φορτίζετε τοὺς ἀνθρώπους φορτία δυσβάστακτα.   Lk. xi. 46.

God is generally written ὁ θεός, because, especially by the monotheistic Jews, God was regarded as standing in a class by Himself.

(4) Nouns qualified by a **Demonstrative or Possessive Pronoun,** or on which the **Possessive Genitive** of a personal or demonstrative pronoun depends, regularly take the Definite Article.

Examples : This man. οὗτος ὁ ἄνθρωπος.

My father. ὁ ἐμὸς πατήρ.

These men's father. ὁ τούτων πατήρ.

(5) The Definite Article is sometimes used in Greek where in English we use a **Possessive Pronoun** to mark something as belonging to a person or thing mentioned in the sentence.

Example : He washed his hands.

ἀπενίψατο τὰς χεῖρας.   Mt. xxvii. 24.

70. Sometimes a word such as *son, daughter, wife, mother, thing,* or *things* is omitted after a Definite Article where it can easily be supplied from the context, and where a qualifying Genitive follows.

Examples : Mary the (wife) of Clopas.

Μαρία ἡ τοῦ Κλωπᾶ.   Jn. xix. 25.

The (sons) of Zebedee.

οἱ τοῦ Ζεβεδαίου.   Jn. xxi. 2.

The (things) of Caesar.

τὰ τοῦ Καίσαρος.   Mt. xxii. 21.

---

[1] We might use the Definite Article here in English and say *The workman is worthy of his hire.*

71. The Definite Article can turn Adjectives, Participles, Adverbs and even Prepositional phrases into **Noun Equivalents**.

Adjectives : Blessed are the poor in spirit.

μακάριοι οἱ πτωχοὶ τῷ πνεύματι.   Mt. v. 3.

Participles : Blessed are they that mourn.

μακάριοι οἱ πενθοῦντες.   Mt. v. 4.

An Article followed by a Participle is generally best translated into English by a Pronoun followed by a relative clause.

Adverbs : Love worketh no ill to his neighbour.

ἡ ἀγάπη τῷ πλησίον κακὸν οὐκ ἐργάζεται.

Rom. xiii. 10.

Prepositional Phrases : They that are of Italy salute you.

ἀσπάζονται ὑμᾶς οἱ ἀπὸ τῆς Ἰταλίας.

Heb. xiii. 24.

72. For the use of the Article before **Infinitives** see 172.

73. The **Neuter Article** τό can turn any word or collection of words which follow it into a noun equivalent, especially when the words are a quotation of something which has been said before.

Example : But Jesus said to him " If thou canst ! " All things are possible to him that believeth. (See verse 22, where the father of the child says, "If thou canst do anything, have mercy on us and help us.")

τὸ Εἰ δύνῃ, πάντα δυνατὰ τῷ πιστεύοντι.   Mk. ix. 23.

For the whole law is fulfilled in one word, even in this, Thou shalt love thy neighbour as thyself.

ὁ γὰρ πᾶς νόμος ἐν ἑνὶ λόγῳ πεπλήρωται, ἐν τῷ Ἀγαπήσεις τὸν πλησίον σου ὡς σεαυτόν.   Gal. v. 14.

Compare also Eph. iv. 9, Romans xiii. 9, Mt. xix. 18.

The article also introduces **dependent questions**.

Lk. i. 62, xxii. 2, 23, 37. Romans viii. 26.

74. For the use of the Definite Article as a **Pronoun** see 54.

The Position of the Article

75. When a noun with an Article is qualified by an attributive adjective, the adjective generally stands between the Article and the noun.

The wise man. ὁ σοφὸς ἀνήρ.

The Article together with the adjective may follow the noun, in which case the noun itself may have another Article before it.

Thus we may translate *The wise man* in three ways:

ὁ σοφὸς ἀνήρ. ἀνὴρ ὁ σοφός. ὁ ἀνὴρ ὁ σοφός.

The first of these arrangements is the commonest.

Such a position of the adjective with reference to the Article and the noun is called the **attributive position**.

76. When an adjective either precedes the Article or follows the noun WITHOUT TAKING AN ARTICLE BEFORE IT, it is said to be in the **predicative position** and does not qualify the noun as an attribute, but forms part of the predicate of the sentence.

Thus ὁ ἀνὴρ σοφός does NOT mean *The wise man*, but *The man is wise*.

This distinction is of **great importance**, and must be thoroughly mastered.

Note. If however the predicate is identical with the subject or denotes something previously well known, the Definite Article may be used in the predicate.

Examples:

Sin is lawlessness. (i.e. they are identical.)
ἡ ἁμαρτία ἐστὶν ἡ ἀνομία.   1 Jn. iii. **4.**
Art thou the teacher of Israel and knowest not these things?
σὺ εἶ ὁ διδάσκαλος τοῦ Ἰσραὴλ καὶ ταῦτα οὐ γινώσκεις;
                                                                   Jn. iii. **10.**
Art not thou the Egyptian?
οὐκ ἄρα σὺ εἶ ὁ Αἰγύπτιος;   Acts xxi. **38.**

When a **Demonstrative Pronoun** qualifies a noun, it takes the position of a predicative adjective, and either precedes the Article or follows the noun.

This man may be translated either οὗτος ὁ ἀνήρ,
or ὁ ἀνὴρ οὗτος.

THE VERB—MOOD, VOICE, TENSE

77. Many of the names given to the different forms of verbs are by no means accurate descriptions of the functions which they perform.

As a rule they describe one function, and one only.

Thus the **Optative** Mood has other functions besides expressing a wish.

The **Present** Tense often expresses time other than present.

The **Subjunctive** Mood is not always used in subordinate sentences.

These names must therefore be looked upon as being somewhat arbitrary and conventional.

The functions of the various forms must be learnt rather from actual usage than from their names.

In Latin grammars the verbs are arranged under **Moods.**

That is to say all the tenses of the Indicative mood are given together, then those of the Subjunctive, and so on.

In Greek grammars the verbs are often arranged under **Tenses.**

That is to say all the moods of the Present tense are given first, then the moods of the Future, Aorist, etc.

This causes some difficulty to those who have learnt Latin before learning Greek.

MOODS

78. Moods are forms which verbs assume to show the way in which the action expressed by the verb is to be regarded, i.e. if it is to be regarded as a **statement**, a **command**, a **wish**, or a **thought.**

The **Indicative** Mood (generally) makes a statement or asks a question.

The **Imperative** Mood gives a command, or expresses a request or a concession.

The **Subjunctive** Mood expresses a thought or wish rather than a fact. The uses of the Subjunctive Mood are so various, and its use in Latin and Greek is so different from its use in English, that it is impossible to bring it under a more exact definition. The student who knows Latin must be on his guard against supposing that in cases where the Subjunctive Mood is used in Latin, it will also be used in Greek.

The **Optative** Mood expresses a wish, and is also used in dependent statements and questions after a principal verb in past time, and in certain kinds of conditional sentences, and in other ways. It occurs very rarely in the N. T.

The **Infinitive** Mood is really a verbal noun.

The **Participle** is a verbal adjective.

VOICE

79. The **Active Voice** is used when the subject of the verb is spoken of as acting or doing something.

The **Passive Voice** is used when the subject of the verb is spoken of as suffering or being acted upon.

N.B. Only Transitive verbs can have a passive voice.

There are certain verbs, such as *He fell*, *They slipped* etc., which do not speak of the subject as acting : these are however regarded as being in the active voice because they are intransitive.

Examples : Active.   The father loves the boy.

               Pater puerum amat.

               ὁ πατὴρ φιλεῖ τὸν παῖδα.

      Passive.   The boy is loved by the father.

               Puer a patre amatur.

               ὁ παῖς φιλεῖται ὑπὸ τοῦ πατρός.

Both these sentences express the same idea, but they express it in different ways. It will be noticed that when a sentence with an active verb is turned into a sentence with a passive verb, the object of the first sentence (the boy) becomes the subject of the second : while the subject of the first sentence (the father) is introduced in English in the second sentence by the preposition *by*.

80.   Consider the sentence

       Boys are strengthened by labour.

       Pueri labore firmantur.

       οἱ παῖδες πόνῳ ῥώννυνται.

It will be seen that, although the constructions of this sentence and the sentence given above—*The boy is loved by the father*—are just the same in English, the construction of the two sentences is not the same in Latin and Greek.

In Latin *a* with the Ablative is used in the first case, and the Ablative alone in the second.

In Greek ὑπό with the Genitive is used in the first case, and the Dative alone in the second.

This is because the doer of the action in the first sentence is a living person, i.e. *the father* : but the thing that does the action in the second sentence is **not** a living person, but *labour*.

In sentences similar to the first sentence the doer of the action is spoken of as the **Agent**, because it is a living thing.

In sentences similar to the second sentence the doer of the action is spoken of as the **Instrument**, because it is not a living thing.

This distinction must be carefully observed.

General rule : In Latin the Agent of the action of a passive verb is translated by *a* with the Ablative, and the Instrument by the Ablative alone.

In Greek the Agent of the action of a passive verb is translated by ὑπό with the Genitive, and he Instrument by the Dative alone.

The same verb may have both an Agent and an Instrument :
The boy is beaten by his father with a stick.
Puer caeditur a patre virga.
ὁ παῖς τύπτεται ὑπὸ τοῦ πατρὸς ῥάβδῳ.

81. The Middle Voice. (Greek only.)

In the Middle Voice the subject is represented as acting upon himself, or in some way that concerns himself.

(1) The subject is represented as acting **upon himself**. This use, which would seem to be the most natural use of the Middle Voice, is the most uncommon. The Active Voice and a Reflexive Pronoun are generally used instead as in Jn. xvii. 19.

This use of the Middle corresponds to the use of the Active with a direct object.

Examples of the reflexive use of the Middle do however occur.

Rise (rouse yourselves), let us be going.
ἐγείρεσθε ἄγωμεν.   Mt. xxvi. 46.
He went and hanged himself.
ἀπελθὼν ἀπήγξατο.   Mt. xxvii. 5.
Except they wash themselves, they eat not.
ἐὰν μὴ βαπτίσωνται οὐκ ἐσθίουσιν.   Mk. vii. 4.

(2) The subject is represented as acting for himself, or with reference to himself.

This use of the Middle Voice corresponds to the use of the Active with an indirect object.

Examples : Ye know not what ye ask (for yourselves).

οὐκ οἴδατε τί αἰτεῖσθε. Mk. x. 38.

Compare this with the Active :

Ask and ye shall receive.

αἰτεῖτε καὶ λήμψεσθε. Jn. xvi. 24.

The following is an example of the Active and the Middle of the same verb in the same sentence :

Give diligence to make your calling and election sure, for by so doing ye shall never fall.

σπουδάσατε βεβαίαν ὑμῶν τὴν κλῆσιν καὶ ἐκλογὴν ποιεῖσθαι· ταῦτα γὰρ ποιοῦντες οὐ μὴ πταίσητέ ποτε. 2 Pet. i. 10.

(3) The Middle Voice is also used in a causative sense, to denote that the subject allows something to be done, or gets something done.

Examples : To get himself enrolled with Mary.

ἀπογράψασθαι σὺν Μαριάμ. Lk. ii. 5.
They got baptized.
ἐβαπτίσαντο. 1 Cor. x. 2.

82. There is however often no difference in meaning that we can trace between the Active and Middle voices of a verb. Even in the case of the examples given above the exact force of the voice of the verbs is considered doubtful by some grammarians.

The difficulty is increased by the fact that the forms of the Middle are identical with those of the Passive except in the Future and Aorist tenses. Moreover many verbs are Deponent, wholly or in part, that is to say they have Passive or Middle forms, and an Active meaning.

No rule can be given ; the student must observe for himself the voice in the tenses of the various verbs which he comes across.

At first sight it seems curious that we should not be able to decide certainly from the form of a verb whether it is Active or Passive in meaning. This ambiguity is however not unknown in English. The sentences *Goods now showing* and *Goods now being shown* mean practically the same, except that in the second sentence we lay more stress on the thought that the goods will be shown by some person.

TENSES

83. The action denoted by a verb may be defined both as regards its **time**, and as regards its **state** or **progress**.

Its **time** may be defined as **Past, Present, or Future.**

Its **state** or **progress** may be regarded as **Continuous** or **Incompleted,** as **Perfect** or **Complete,** as **Simple** or **Indefinite** without any reference to continuity or completion.

Example: Continuous action.	I am writing this letter.
	I was writing this letter.
	I shall be writing this letter.
Complete action.	I have written this letter.
	I had written this letter.
	I shall have written this letter.
Simple action.	I write this letter.
	I wrote this letter.
	I shall write this letter.

The combination of these ideas of time and state should produce nine different tenses.

Past {Continuous / Perfect / Simple}   Present {Continuous / Perfect / Simple}   Future {Continuous / Perfect / Simple}

Different tense forms to express all these ideas exist in English, but not in Latin and Greek. (See page 11.)

Some of the tenses in Latin and Greek perform the functions of more than one English tense, and therefore care is often necessary in translating them; generally speaking however the Greek **Present** corresponds to the English Present Continuous or Present Simple: the Greek **Imperfect** corresponds to the English Past Continuous: the Greek **Future** corresponds to the English Future Continuous or Future Simple: the Greek **Perfect** corresponds to part of the uses of the English Present Perfect: the Greek **Aorist** corresponds to the English Past Simple and to certain uses of the English Present Perfect.

N B. The above remarks only apply to the tenses of the **Indicative Mood** in the Greek verb: the use of the tenses of the other moods is different.

Great care should be devoted to the translation of the tenses in the Greek Testament, as the translators of the A.V. often went wrong on this point, and familiarity with their version is apt to mislead the student.

84. It is somewhat unfortunate that we are compelled to use the name *tense* in connection with the forms of the Greek verb. It directs our attention too much to the **time** of the action of the verb, whereas it was the state of the action, rather than the time, that was most prominently before the mind of a Greek. The time of the action of the verb is often left to be inferred from the context, and cannot always be certainly told from the form of the verb. This is almost invariably the case with the moods other than the Indicative, and is sometimes the case in the Indicative mood itself.

To the Greek mind the forms to which we give the names "Present" and "Imperfect" denoted duration, or repeated action.

The forms to which we give the name "Perfect" or "Pluperfect" denoted action **complete** at the time of speaking, the results of which were regarded as still existing.

The forms to which we give the name "Aorist" denoted a **simple, indefinite** action, and were always used where no stress was laid on the continuity, completion, or incompletion of the action denoted by the verb.

As a rule the Indicative mood of the Aorist refers to an action in past time. The idea of time is however quite secondary, and does not enter at all into the meaning of the moods of the Aorist other than the Indicative. The idea of Past time is only to be found in the forms of the verb which have an **Augment**, that is to say the Imperfect, the Pluperfect, and the Aorist Indicative.

The Future tense in Greek, as in English, refers to **future time in** all its moods, and is thus an exception to the principle that the tenses of the moods other than the Indicative do not denote time in Greek.

85. The use of the **Present Indicative** in Greek generally denotes action in progress or customary or repeated action in present time.

Examples : Lord, save, we are perishing.

Κύριε, σῶσον, ἀπολλύμεθα.   Mt. viii. 25.

Our lamps are going out.

αἱ λαμπάδες ἡμῶν σβέννυνται   Mt. xxv. 8.

Every tree that bringeth not forth good fruit is hewn down and cast into the fire.

πᾶν δένδρον μὴ ποιοῦν καρπὸν καλὸν ἐκκόπτεται καὶ εἰς πῦρ βάλλεται.

Mt. vii. 19.

I die daily.

καθ' ἡμέραν ἀποθνήσκω.   1 Cor. xv. 31.

86. As the Present Tense denotes action in progress, and hence incomplete, it may be used to express action which is attempted or desired, but not performed. This use of the Present is called the **Present of Incompleted Action**, or the **Conative Present**.

Example : Many good works have I shown you from my Father: on account of which of them do ye desire to stone me?

πολλὰ ἔργα ἔδειξα ὑμῖν καλὰ ἐκ τοῦ πατρός· διὰ ποῖον αὐτῶν ἔργον ἐμὲ λιθάζετε;   Jn. x. 32.

See also Rom. ii. 4, 1 Cor. vii. 28, Gal. v. 4.

87. The Present tense is occasionally used in an **Aoristic** sense to denote a simple event in present time, without any thought of action in progress.

Examples : Thy sins are forgiven thee.

ἀφίενταί σοι αἱ ἁμαρτίαι σου.   Mk. ii. 5.

Jesus Christ maketh thee whole.

ἰᾶταί σε Ἰησοῦς Χριστός.   Acts ix. 34.

In these cases the context alone can decide whether the Greek Present is to be translated by the English Present Continuous or Present Simple.

88. The Present Tense may be used for the sake of vividness to describe an event in the **Past** or **Future**.

When it is used to denote an event in the Past, it is generally called the **Historic Present**.

Examples : Present to describe an event in Past time :

And they came again to Jerusalem.

καὶ ἔρχονται πάλιν εἰς Ἱεροσόλυμα.   Mk. xi. 27.

Present to describe an event in Future time :

My time is at hand : I will take the Passover with my disciples at thy house.

ὁ καιρός μου ἐγγύς ἐστιν· πρὸς σὲ ποιῶ τὸ πάσχα μετὰ τῶν μαθητῶν μου.   Mt. xxvi. 18.

See also Lk. xix. 8, 1 Cor. xv. 32, Jn. xxi. 23.

89. The use of the **Imperfect Indicative** denotes action in progress or customary or repeated action in past time.

Examples : And many that were rich were casting in much.

καὶ πολλοὶ πλούσιοι ἔβαλλον πολλά.　　　Mk. xii. 41.

Behold how he loved him.

ἴδε πῶς ἐφίλει αὐτόν.　　　Jn. xi. 36.

Whom they used to lay daily at the gate of the Temple.

ὃν ἐτίθουν καθ' ἡμέραν πρὸς τὴν θύραν τοῦ ἱεροῦ.　　　Acts iii. 2.

See also Mk. xv. 6, Lk. xvii. 27.

90. The Imperfect is sometimes used to denote that an action was attempted or desired, but not performed. (**Conative Imperfect.**)

Example: And they wished to call him by the name of his father Zacharias.

καὶ ἐκάλουν αὐτὸ ἐπὶ τῷ ὀνόματι τοῦ πατρὸς αὐτοῦ Ζαχαρίαν.

Lk. i. 59.

See also Mt. iii. 14, Mk. ix. 38, xv. 23, Acts vii. 26, xxvi. 11.

The Imperfect may also be used to express an impossible wish. See Rom. ix. 3, Gal. iv. 20.

91. The use of the **Aorist Indicative** denotes that the action is regarded simply as an event without any account being taken of its progress or of the existence of its result. Even its time is not always distinctly contemplated ; but, generally speaking, it is regarded as taking place in past time.

The name Aorist means *without boundaries* or *indefinite*, and denotes that the action expressed by the verb is not defined with regard to its time, progress, or result.

92. The Aorist Indicative is most frequently used to describe a past event or series of events, viewed as a whole, without any reference to the progress of the action, or the existence of its result.

The fact so recorded may be

　(*a*)　A momentary action.

　　And having stretched forth his hand, he touched him.

　　καὶ ἐκτείνας τὴν χεῖρα ἥψατο αὐτοῦ.　　　Mt. viii. 3.

　(*b*)　A continued act or state viewed as a single action.

　　He abode two whole years in his own hired dwelling.

　　ἔμεινεν δὲ διετίαν ὅλην ἐν ἰδίῳ μισθώματι.　　　Acts xxviii. 30.

　(*c*)　A series of similar acts viewed as constituting a single event.

　　Thrice I suffered shipwreck.

　　τρὶς ἐναυάγησα.　　　2 Cor. xi. 25.

93.   The Inceptive or Ingressive Aorist.

The Aorist of a verb which denotes a state or condition in the Present or Imperfect often denotes the beginning of the state.

Compare the use of the Imperfect in the first example with that of the Aorist in the two following :

Examples :   But he remained silent and answered nothing.

ὁ δὲ ἐσιώπα καὶ οὐδὲν ἀπεκρίνατο.   Mk. xiv. 61.

And they wondered at his answer and held their peace

καὶ θαυμάσαντες ἐπὶ τῇ ἀποκρίσει αὐτοῦ ἐσίγησαν.

Lk. xx. 26.

And after they held their peace, James answered.

μετὰ δὲ τὸ σιγῆσαι αὐτοὺς ἀπεκρίθη Ἰάκωβος.

Acts xv. 13.

In the first of these examples we have the Imperfect denoting the continuance of a state of silence, in the last two we have the Aorist denoting the beginning of the state.

Consider also the force of the Aorist in the following examples :

And having said this, he fell asleep.

καὶ τοῦτο εἰπὼν ἐκοιμήθη.   Acts vii. 60.

Though he was rich, for your sakes he became poor.

δι᾽ ὑμᾶς ἐπτώχευσεν πλούσιος ὤν.   2 Cor. viii. 9.

See Lk. xv. 32, Jn. iv. 52, Rom. xiv. 9.

94.   The Resultative Aorist.

The Aorist of a verb which denotes effort or intention in the Present or Imperfect often denotes the success of the effort.

Compare the use of the tenses in the following examples :

Hinder them not to come to me.

μὴ κωλύετε αὐτὰ ἐλθεῖν πρός με.   Mt. xix. 14.

But the centurion kept them from their purpose.

ὁ δὲ ἑκατοντάρχης...ἐκώλυσεν αὐτοὺς τοῦ βουλήματος.

Acts xxvii. 43.

In the first of these examples we have the Present denoting the attempted but unsuccessful action of the Disciples, in the second the Aorist denoting the successful action of the centurion.

See also Mt. xxvii. 20.

95. Special uses of the Aorist.

The Gnomic Aorist[1]. The Aorist is used in proverbial sayings (γνῶμαι), to express what generally happens. The Present is used in English.

Example: The grass withereth, and the flower falleth.

ἐξηράνθη ὁ χόρτος καὶ τὸ ἄνθος ἐξέπεσεν.   1 Pet. i. 24.

See also Jas. i. 11, 24.

The Epistolary Aorist. The writer of a letter sometimes puts himself in the place of his readers, and describes as past an action which is present to himself, but which will be past to his readers when they receive the letter. The Present is used in English.

Example: I think it necessary to send to you Epaphroditus my brother.

ἀναγκαῖον δὲ ἡγησάμην Ἐπαφρόδιτον τὸν ἀδελφὸν πέμψαι.
Phil. ii. 25.

See also Acts xxiii. 30, 1 Cor. v. 11, Eph. vi. 22, Phil. ii. 28, Col. iv. 8, Philemon 12.

The Dramatic Aorist. The Aorist is used to express vividly the state of mind which a person has just reached. The Present is used in English.

Example: I know what to do.

ἔγνων τί ποιήσω.   Lk. xvi. 4.

96. The use of the **Perfect Indicative** in Greek denotes that the action of the verb is regarded as complete at the time of speaking, and that its results are regarded as still existing.

When it is said that the action is regarded as " complete " this does not mean that it is regarded as ended ; but only that it is regarded as brought to its appropriate conclusion in such a way that its effects remain in action. The Perfect has therefore really as much to do with present as with past time, since it describes the present result of a past action.

97. The main uses of the Perfect in the New Testament are as follows :

(1) The Perfect of Completed Action denoting an action completed in past time the results of which still remain.

Examples : Ye have filled Jerusalem with your teaching.

πεπληρώκατε τὴν Ἱερουσαλὴμ τῆς διδαχῆς ὑμῶν.   Acts v. 28.

I have fought the good fight, I have finished the course, I have kept the faith.

τὸν καλὸν ἀγῶνα ἠγώνισμαι, τὸν δρόμον τετέλεκα, τὴν πίστιν
τετήρηκα.   2 Tim. iv. 7.

---

[1] " The Gnomic Aorist gives a more vivid statement of general truths, by employing a distinct case or several distinct cases in the past to represent (as it were) all possible cases, and implying that what has occurred is likely to occur again under similar circumstances." Goodwin, *Moods and Tenses* 155.

(2) **The Perfect of Existing State.** The Perfect is sometimes used to denote a present existing state, the past action of which it is the result being left out of account.

Such Perfects are generally found in certain verbs which use the Perfect in this sense only, for example μέμνημαι, πέποιθα, οἶδα, γέγραπται, ἔγνωκα.

The Perfect of Existing State is generally best translated by the English Present.

Examples : He trusteth in God.

πέποιθεν ἐπὶ τὸν θεόν. Mt. xxvii. 43.

We believe and know that thou art the Holy One of God.

ἡμεῖς πεπιστεύκαμεν καὶ ἐγνώκαμεν ὅτι σὺ εἶ ὁ ἅγιος τοῦ θεοῦ.

Jn. vi. 69.

98. The use of the **Pluperfect** in Greek denotes that the action of the verb is regarded as complete at a point in past time implied in the context. Unless the completion of the action in past time is distinctly emphasized the Pluperfect must not be used. It is not used, as in English, to denote that the action simply occurred before a certain point in past time ; in this case the Aorist or Imperfect would be used, and the fact that the action denoted was antecedent to another action in past time would be left to be inferred from the context, and not made plain by the use of a special tense.

99. The uses of the Pluperfect in the New Testament are as follows :

(1) Pluperfect of Completed Action.

Examples : For it had been founded upon the rock.

τεθεμελίωτο γὰρ ἐπὶ τὴν πέτραν. Mt. vii. 25.

For the Jews had agreed already that if anyone should confess that he was the Christ he should be put out of the Synagogue.

ἤδη γὰρ συνετέθειντο οἱ Ἰουδαῖοι ἵνα ἐάν τις αὐτὸν ὁμολογήσῃ Χριστόν, ἀποσυνάγωγος γένηται. Jn. ix. 22.

(2) **The Pluperfect of Existing State.**

Verbs which denote a present state in the Perfect denote a past state in the Pluperfect. They must be translated by a simple past tense in English.

In the following example a Pluperfect of Existing State and a Pluperfect of Completed Action are seen side by side.

And the more part knew not why they had come together.

καὶ οἱ πλείους οὐκ ᾔδεισαν τίνος ἕνεκα συνεληλύθεισαν.

Acts xix. 32.

100. The following are examples of the use of the Aorist or Imperfect to denote an event which is spoken of as taking place before another past event. In these cases the Greek Aorist and Imperfect must be translated by the English Pluperfect, not because there is any confusion in meaning between the tenses, but because the Greeks stated the action simply as a past event, and left it to the context to make plain that it took place before some other past event, whereas the English prefer to make the order of the events clear by the use of a special tense.

Examples: And they had forgotten to take bread, and they had none with them in the boat except one loaf.

καὶ ἐπελάθοντο λαβεῖν ἄρτους, καὶ εἰ μὴ ἕνα ἄρτον οὐκ εἶχον μεθ᾽ ἑαυτῶν ἐν τῷ πλοίῳ. Mk. viii. 14.

Shewing coats and garments which Dorcas had made.

ἐπιδεικνύμεναι χιτῶνας καὶ ἱμάτια, ὅσα ἐποίει ἡ Δορκάς.

Acts ix. 39.

See also Mt. xiv. 3, 4, Lk. viii. 27, Jn. xii. 17, xiii. 12, xix. 30.

101. It is most important to distinguish clearly between the meanings of the Imperfect, the Aorist, and the Perfect.

The difference between them is best learnt by the study of examples such as those given below, but it may help the student to regard the meaning of the Imperfect as graphically represented by a line (——) or by a series of points (· · · · ·), and that of the Aorist as graphically represented by a point (·). In the examples given in section 92, where the Aorist denotes a continued act or state or a series of acts, the line or series of points is reduced to a single point by perspective.

The Perfect is not used in Greek unless stress is laid on the fact that the action denoted by the verb has been brought to its appropriate conclusion, and that its results remain.

102. Examples of the difference between the **Imperfect** and the **Aorist**.

I used to sit daily with you in the Temple teaching, and ye did not lay hands upon me.

Quotidie apud vos sedebam docens in templo, et non me tenuistis.

καθ᾽ ἡμέραν πρὸς ὑμᾶς ἐκαθεζόμην ἐν τῷ ἱερῷ διδάσκων, καὶ οὐκ ἐκρατήσατέ με.   Mt. xxvi. 55.

But he remained silent, and answered nothing.

Ille autem tacebat, et nihil respondit.

ὁ δὲ ἐσιώπα καὶ οὐδὲν ἀπεκρίνατο.   Mk. xiv. 61.

And he sat down (single action) over against the treasury, and beheld (continued action) how the multitude cast money into the treasury (repeated action): and many that were rich cast in much (repeated action). And there came a certain poor widow, and she cast in two mites (single action)—for they all cast in of their superfluity (viewing the action as a whole).

Et sedens Jesus contra gazophylacium, aspiciebat quomodo turba jactaret aes in gazophylacium, et multi divites jactabant multa. Cum venisset autem vidua una pauper, misit duo minuta—omnes enim ex eo, quod abundabat illis, miserunt.

καὶ καθίσας κατέναντι τοῦ γαζοφυλακίου ἐθεώρει πῶς ὁ ὄχλος βάλλει χαλκὸν εἰς τὸ γαζοφυλάκιον· καὶ πολλοὶ πλούσιοι ἔβαλλον πολλά· καὶ ἐλθοῦσα μία χήρα πτωχὴ ἔβαλεν λεπτὰ δύο—πάντες γὰρ ἐκ τοῦ περισσεύοντος αὐτοῖς ἔβαλον.   Mk. xii. 41.

It will be observed that in these examples the Greek Imperfect corresponds to the Latin Imperfect, and the Greek Aorist to the tense which is generally called the "Perfect" in Latin grammars.

As will be seen from the following examples this tense does the work both of the Greek Aorist, and of the Greek Perfect; but, although there was only one form to express these two ideas in Latin, yet the meanings were quite distinct, as is shown by the fact that the "Perfect" in Latin is followed by a Primary or Secondary tense according as it has a true Perfect or an Aorist meaning.

103. The following are examples of the difference between the **Aorist** and the **Perfect**.

Go to thy house and to thy friends and tell them what the Lord hath done for thee (completed action with abiding result), and how he had mercy on thee (single action).

Vade in domum tuam ad tuos, et annuntia illis quanta tibi Dominus fecerit, et misertus sit tui.

ὕπαγε εἰς τὸν οἶκόν σου πρὸς τοὺς σούς, καὶ ἀπάγγειλον αὐτοῖς ὅσα ὁ Κύριός σοι πεποίηκεν καὶ ἠλέησέν σε.   Mk. v. 19.

And further he brought Greeks into the Temple (single action), and hath defiled (completed action with abiding result) this holy place.

Insuper et Gentiles induxit in templum, et violavit sanctum locum istum.

ἔτι τε καὶ Ἕλληνας εἰσήγαγεν εἰς τὸ ἱερὸν καὶ κεκοίνωκεν τὸν ἅγιον τόπον τοῦτον.   Acts xxi. 28.

And that he was buried (single action), and that he was raised again (completed action with abiding result) the third day according to the Scriptures.

Et quia sepultus est, et quia resurrexit tertia die secundum Scripturas.

καὶ ὅτι ἐτάφη, καὶ ὅτι ἐγήγερται τῇ τρίτῃ ἡμέρᾳ κατὰ τὰς γραφάς.
                                                              1 Cor. xv. 4.

We have no form in English that will give a satisfactory rendering of the Greek Perfect in this case.

104. Generally speaking the Greek Aorist should be translated by the English Past, and the Greek Perfect by the English Perfect ; but this rule cannot be universally applied, as the tenses do not correspond exactly to one another in meaning. The Greek Aorist is wider in meaning than the English Past, and the Greek Perfect is narrower in meaning than the English Perfect.

It is therefore often necessary to translate an Aorist by a Perfect or even by a Present.

The English Past Tense denotes an action which took place at a definite past time, or an action between which and the time of speaking the speaker wishes to suggest an interval.

The English Perfect Tense denotes an action which took place at an indefinite past time, and also an action between which and the time of speaking the speaker does not wish to suggest an interval.

If we say *Did you go to London last week?* we use the Past tense, because we are speaking of an action which took place at a definite time.

If we were not thinking of any definite time, we should say *Have you been to London?*

A boy may shut his book and say *I have finished my lessons.* He would not say *I finished my lessons,* unless he meant to suggest that they were finished some time before : *I finished my lessons an hour ago.*

As the Greek Aorist denotes a single action without any regard to its time or progress, it is used in all these cases, and must be translated into English by the Past or the Perfect according to the general sense of the passage.

This is not because there is any confusion between the Aorist and the Perfect in Greek, but because the English Past is not wide enough in meaning to translate all the meanings of the Greek Aorist. The English Perfect supplies the forms necessary to express the meanings of the Aorist which the Past cannot express.

The English Perfect is not confined, as the Greek Perfect is, to the expression of events complete at the time of speaking whose results continue. As has been shown above, it can denote events which happened at some indefinite time in the past, and also events which have just taken place.

The following table may make the relationship of the tenses clearer.

The English Past tense expresses an action which took place at a definite time in the past, or an action between which and the time of speaking the speaker wishes to suggest an interval.

The English Perfect tense expresses an action which took place at an indefinite past time, or an action between which and the time of speaking the speaker does not wish to suggest an interval.

The Greek Aorist denotes an action regarded simply as an event without any account being taken of its progress or result.

The English Perfect tense expresses an action regarded as complete at the time of speaking whose results are regarded as still existing.

The Greek Perfect expresses an action regarded as complete at the time of speaking whose results are regarded as still existing.

Examples from the New Testament

105. The Greek Aorist denoting an event which happened in **indefinite past time** translated by an English Perfect.

I thank thee, O Father, Lord of heaven and earth, that thou hast hid these things from the wise and understanding, and hast revealed them unto babes.

ἐξομολογοῦμαί σοι, πάτερ, κύριε τοῦ οὐρανοῦ καὶ τῆς γῆς, ὅτι ἀπέ-
κρυψας ταῦτα ἀπὸ σοφῶν καὶ συνετῶν, καὶ ἀπεκάλυψας αὐτὰ νηπίοις.

Mt. xi. 25.

Have ye not read what David did when he was hungry and those that were with him ?

οὐκ ἀνέγνωτε τί ἐποίησεν Δαυείδ, ὅτε ἐπείνασεν καὶ οἱ μετ' αὐτοῦ;

Mt. xii. 3.

Note that in this example the Aorist is used both to denote indefinite action (have ye not read), and definite action (what David did when he was hungry).

The Greek Aorist denoting an event between which and the time of speaking **no interval** is suggested translated by an English Perfect.

We have seen strange things to-day.

εἴδομεν παράδοξα σήμερον.

Lk. v. 26.

Therefore that field has been called the field of blood until this day.

διὸ ἐκλήθη ὁ ἀγρὸς ἐκεῖνος ἀγρὸς αἵματος ἕως τῆς σήμερον.

Mt. xxvii. 8.

See also Acts vii. 52, 53.

106. In certain cases we are compelled to translate the Aorist by an English Present or by an English Perfect which has its full sense of complete action with abiding result. From the point of view of the Greek we seem to have to do with one of the most ancient uses of the Aorist in which it is used to express what has just happened. See Dr J. H. Moulton's *Prolegomena*, page 135.

Examples: This is my beloved Son, in whom I am well pleased.

οὗτός ἐστιν ὁ υἱός μου ὁ ἀγαπητός, ἐν ᾧ εὐδόκησα.

Matt. iii. **17.**

See also the parallel passages Mk. i. 11, Lk. iii. 22.

For this thy brother was dead and is alive again, he was lost and is found.

ὅτι ὁ ἀδελφός σου οὗτος νεκρὸς ἦν καὶ ἀνέζησεν, ἀπολωλὼς καὶ εὑρέθη.

Lk. xv. 32.

See also Jn. xv. 6.

The Aorists ἔγνων and ἔγνω in Jn. xvii. 25 and ἔγνω in 2 Tim. ii. 19 must be explained as gathering up the whole process denoted by the Present γιγνώσκειν into a single moment. They must be translated by a Present in English.

In the following instance the verb is Present in form in English, but Perfect in meaning.

He is risen, he is not here.

ἠγέρθη, οὐκ ἔστιν ὧδε. Mk. xvi. 6.

See also Mk. v. 39, Lk. xxiv. 34.

In the following instances the Perfect is the best translation.

I have married a wife.

γυναῖκα ἔγημα. Lk. xiv. 20.

Behold the world has gone after him.

ἴδε ὁ κόσμος ὀπίσω αὐτοῦ ἀπῆλθεν. Jn. xii. 19.

See also Mt. xii. 28, Lk. vii. 16, Jn. xiii. 1, 1 Thess. ii. 16.

107. The use of the **Future Indicative** in Greek denotes that the action is expected to take place in future time.

The context decides whether the state of the action is to be regarded as simple or progressive.

Examples : (1) Simple future action.

And she shall bear a son, and thou shalt call his name Jesus.

τέξεται δὲ υἱόν, καὶ καλέσεις τὸ ὄνομα αὐτοῦ Ἰησοῦν.

Mt. i. 21.

(2) Action in progress in future time.

And therein I rejoice, yea and will continue to rejoice.

καὶ ἐν τούτῳ χαίρω· ἀλλὰ καὶ χαρήσομαι. Phil. i. 18.

THE TENSES OF THE DEPENDENT MOODS

108. (1) **Not in Reported Speech.**

The tenses of the moods other than the Indicative, with the exception of the Future, do not denote the time of the action of the verb, but only its state, that is to say they represent the action as continuous, completed, or simply as an event.

The time of the action is denoted by the context.

It is quite a mistake to suppose that the Aorist Subjunctive in Greek corresponds with the Imperfect Subjunctive in Latin, or that the Aorist or Perfect Infinitive in Greek is equivalent to the Perfect Infinitive in Latin.

N.B. The Augment is the only decisive mark of past time in the Greek verb, and this does not of course occur in the Dependent moods[1].

[1] Except when used instead of the reduplication in certain Perfects.

109. The **Present** tense of the dependent moods denotes action in progress or repeated action.

Examples : Infinitive,

To be writing the same things to you to me indeed is not irksome...

τὰ αὐτὰ γράφειν ὑμῖν ἐμοὶ μὲν οὐκ ὀκνηρόν, ὑμῖν δὲ ἀσφαλές.

Phil. iii. 1.

Subjunctive,

If therefore thou shalt be offering thy gift at the altar.

ἐὰν οὖν προσφέρῃς τὸ δῶρόν σου ἐπὶ τὸ θυσιαστήριον.

Mt. v. 23.

Imperative,

Give us day by day our daily bread.

τὸν ἄρτον ἡμῶν τὸν ἐπιούσιον δίδου ἡμῖν τὸ καθ᾽ ἡμέραν.

Lk. xi. 3.

Participle,

We are ambassadors on behalf of Christ, as though God were entreating by us.

ὑπὲρ Χριστοῦ οὖν πρεσβεύομεν ὡς τοῦ θεοῦ παρακαλοῦντος δι᾽ ἡμῶν.

2 Cor. v. 20.

110. The **Aorist** tense of the dependent mood denotes action represented as a simple event or fact without reference either to its progress or the existence of its result.

Examples : Infinitive,

I came not to destroy the law, but to fulfil.

οὐκ ἦλθον καταλῦσαι τὸν νόμον ἀλλὰ πληρῶσαι.   Mt. v. 17.

Subjunctive,

And if he sin against thee seven times in the day—thou shalt forgive him.

καὶ ἐὰν ἑπτάκις τῆς ἡμέρας ἁμαρτήσῃ εἰς σὲ—ἀφήσεις αὐτῷ.

Lk. xvii. 4.

Imperative,

Give us this day our daily bread.

τὸν ἄρτον ἡμῶν τὸν ἐπιούσιον δὸς ἡμῖν σήμερον.   Mt. vi. 11.

Participle,

And taking her by the hand he raised her up.

ἤγειρεν αὐτὴν κρατήσας τῆς χειρός.   Mk. i. 31.

111. The Perfect tense of the dependent moods denotes complete action the results of which remain.

Examples: Infinitive and participle,

And the jailor being roused out of sleep, and seeing the prison doors open, drew his sword, and was about to kill himself, supposing that the prisoners had escaped.

ἔξυπνος δὲ γενόμενος ὁ δεσμοφύλαξ καὶ ἰδὼν ἀνεῳγμένας τὰς θύρας τῆς φυλακῆς σπασάμενος τὴν μάχαιραν ἤμελλεν ἑαυτὸν ἀναιρεῖν, νομίζων ἐκπεφευγέναι τοὺς δεσμίους. Acts xvi. 27.

Imperative,

Peace, be still. (Literally, "be muzzled.")

σιώπα, πεφίμωσο. Mk. iv. 39.

Compare Acts xiv. 19, xxvii. 13, Rom. xv. 14, 2 Tim. iv. 8.

112. The Future tense of the dependent moods represents an action as future from the point of view of the time of the principal verb.

It is thus an exception to the rule that the tenses of the dependent moods do not express time.

Examples: Infinitive,

And when it was shewn me that there would be a plot against the man...

μηνυθείσης δέ μοι ἐπιβουλῆς εἰς τὸν ἄνδρα ἔσεσθαι.

Acts xxiii. 30.

Participle:

Thou sowest not that body that shall be...

οὐ τὸ σῶμα τὸ γενησόμενον σπείρεις. 1 Cor. xv. 37.

The use of the tenses of the Imperative and Participle will be treated further in paragraphs 125, 259—266.

(2) In Reported Speech

113. The term Reported Speech includes all object clauses depending on a verb of saying or thinking which contain the words or thoughts of any person stated indirectly, and also all indirect quotations and questions.

See 145, 159, 160.

When the Infinitive and (in Classical Greek) the Optative stand in Indirect Discourse, each tense represents the corresponding tense of the same verb in Direct Discourse. See 151—157.

Periphrastic Forms of Tenses

114. In N.T. Greek Periphrastic forms of the tenses, that is tenses made up of a participle and part of the verb *to be,* often occur.

The Periphrastic Present is made up of the Present Participle and the Present of the verb εἶναι (rare).

Example:

For we are not, as many, making merchandise of the word of God.

οὐ γάρ ἐσμεν ὡς οἱ πολλοὶ καπηλεύοντες τὸν λόγον τοῦ θεοῦ.

2 Cor. ii. 17.

The Periphrastic Imperfect is made up of the Present Participle and the Imperfect of the verb εἶναι.

Example: And Jesus was going before them.

καὶ ἦν προάγων αὐτοὺς ὁ Ἰησοῦς.   Mk. x. 32.

See also Lk. i. 21, 22.

The Periphrastic Perfect is made up of the Perfect Participle and the Present of the verb εἶναι.   Lk. xx. 6.

The Periphrastic Pluperfect is made up of the Perfect Participle and the Imperfect of the verb εἶναι.   Mt. xxvi. 43, Lk. ii. 26.

The Periphrastic Future is made up of the Present Participle and the Future of the verb εἶναι. The force is that of the Future continuous with the thought of continuity emphasized.

Examples: Thou shalt catch men.

ἀνθρώπους ἔσῃ ζωγρῶν.   Lk. v. 10.

Jerusalem shall be trodden underfoot.

Ἰερουσαλὴμ ἔσται πατουμένη.   Lk. xxi. 24.

μέλλειν with the Infinitive is also used with a force akin to that of the Future Indicative. It usually denotes an action which one intends to do or which is certain to take place.

Example: For Herod will seek the young child to destroy him.

μέλλει γὰρ Ἡρῴδης ζητεῖν τὸ παιδίον τοῦ ἀπολέσαι αὐτό.

Mt. ii. 13.

SENTENCES—SIMPLE, COMPOUND, AND COMPLEX

115. A **Simple Sentence** is a sentence which contains a single subject and a single predicate.

Compound and Complex Sentences are sentences which contain more than one subject and predicate.

In dealing with sentences it will be found convenient to keep carefully to the following terminology:

The name **Sentence** should be applied only to a complete statement, command, or question occurring between two full-stops.

Groups of words forming part of a Compound or Complex Sentence, and having a subject and predicate of their own, should be called **Clauses**.

Groups of words forming an equivalent to some part of speech, and not having a subject or predicate of their own, should be called **Phrases**.

116. Two or more clauses, none of which depends on any of the others, but which all make equally important and independent statements, are said to be combined by coordination, and to form a **Compound Sentence**.

Such clauses are generally joined together by the coordinating conjunctions καί, ἀλλά, δέ, ἤ, γάρ.

Example : And he went forth again by the sea side ; and all the multitude resorted unto him, and he taught them.

καὶ ἐξῆλθεν πάλιν παρὰ τὴν θάλασσαν · καὶ πᾶς ὁ ὄχλος ἤρχετο πρὸς αὐτόν, καὶ ἐδίδασκεν αὐτούς.   Mk. ii. 13.

This simple form of sentence construction is very common in the N.T.

117. A **Complex Sentence** is a sentence which contains a principal clause, and one or more subordinate clauses depending on it, or on one another, as noun, adjective, or adverb equivalents.

The verb in the principal clause of a complex sentence is nearly always in the Indicative or Imperative Mood, and it should be looked for first in translating the sentence.

Example of a Complex Sentence :

If any man willeth to do his will, he shall know of the doctrine, whether it is of God, or whether I speak from myself.

ἐάν τις θέλῃ τὸ θέλημα αὐτοῦ ποιεῖν, γνώσεται περὶ τῆς διδαχῆς, πότερον ἐκ τοῦ θεοῦ ἐστὶν ἢ ἐγὼ ἀπ᾽ ἐμαυτοῦ λαλῶ.   Jn. vii. 17.

118. Subordinate clauses are divided into three classes :

Noun clauses which take the place of a noun.
Adverbial clauses which take the place of an adverb.
Adjectival clauses which take the place of an adjective.

THE USE OF THE SUBJUNCTIVE IN INDEPENDENT SENTENCES OR IN PRINCIPAL CLAUSES

119. The Hortatory Subjunctive. The Subjunctive is used in the 1st person plural when the speaker is exhorting others to join him in the doing of an action.

Example : Beloved, let us love one another.

Dilecti, diligamus alii alios.

ἀγαπητοί, ἀγαπῶμεν ἀλλήλους.   1 Jn. iv. 7.

120. The 1st person singular is also used with ἄφες prefixed.

Example : Let me cast out the mote out of thine eye.

ἄφες ἐκβάλω τὸ κάρφος ἐκ τοῦ ὀφθαλμοῦ σου.   Mt. vii. 4.

121. Deliberative Subjunctive. The Subjunctive is used in deliberative questions, when a person asks himself or another what he is to do.

Example : What shall we do ?

Quid faciamus ?

τί ποιήσωμεν;   Lk. iii. 10.

122. The Subjunctive is often used to ask a question after θέλεις, θέλετε, βούλεσθε, without a conjunction between.

Example : Where wilt thou that we prepare for thee to eat the Passover?

ποῦ θέλεις ἑτοιμάσωμέν σοι φαγεῖν τὸ πάσχα;   Mt. xxvi. 17.

This use even occurs when words are inserted between θέλεις etc. and the Subjunctive.

Example : What will ye that I should do for you?

τί θέλετέ με ποιήσω ὑμῖν;   Mk. x. 36.

123. The use of οὐ μή.

The Future Indicative and the Aorist Subjunctive are used in Classical Greek with οὐ μή in the sense of the Future Indicative with οὐ but with more emphasis.

In the New Testament οὐ μή occurs frequently with the Aorist Subjunctive, and occasionally with the Future Indicative.

When it occurs in a quotation from the Septuagint or in the words of Christ it is often used as a simple negative future without any special emphasis. This seems to be due to the fact that these passages are translations from a Hebrew or Aramaic original[1].

When it occurs elsewhere it generally has an emphatic sense.

[1] The use of οὐ μή in these passages is not accounted for by the fact that there was a double negative in Aramaic: but by the feeling of the translators that "inspired language was fitly rendered by words of a peculiarly decisive tone."

Examples.　(1)　Of the emphatic sense :

Him that cometh to me I will in no wise cast out.

τὸν ἐρχόμενον πρός με οὐ μὴ ἐκβάλω ἔξω.　　　Jn. vi. 37.

If I must die with thee, I will not deny thee.

ἐὰν δέῃ με συναποθανεῖν σοι, οὐ μή σε ἀρνήσομαι.　Mk. xiv. 31.

(2)　Of the unemphatic sense :

The cup which my Father has given me, shall I not drink it ?

τὸ ποτήριον ὃ δέδωκέν μοι ὁ Πατήρ, οὐ μὴ πίω αὐτό;　Jn. xviii. 11.

See also Mt. xxv. 9, Mk. xiii. 2.

For a full discussion of the question see Dr J. H. Moulton's *Prolegomena*, pages 187—192.

THE IMPERATIVE MOOD

124.　The **Imperative Mood** is used to express commands, exhortations and entreaties, and, in some cases, permission.

Examples.　**Command.**　Give to him that asketh thee.
　　　　　　　　　　Qui petit a te, da ei.
　　　　　　　　　　τῷ αἰτοῦντί σε δός.　　　Mt. v. 42.

　　　　　　Entreaty.　But, if thou canst do anything, help us.
　　　　　　　　　　Sed, si quid potes, adjuva nos.
　　　　　　　　　　ἀλλ', εἴ τι δύνῃ, βοήθησον ἡμῖν.
　　　　　　　　　　　　　　　　Mk. ix. 22.

　　　　　　Permission.　If need so require, let him do what he
　　　　　　　　　　will; he sinneth not; let them marry.
　　　　　　　　　　ἐὰν οὕτως ὀφείλει γίνεσθαι, ὃ θέλει ποιείτω·
　　　　　　　　　　οὐχ ἁμαρτάνει· γαμείτωσαν.
　　　　　　　　　　　　　　　　1 Cor. vii. 36.

125.　The tenses of the Imperative which are in general use are the **Present** and the **Aorist**.

The Present Imperative, in accordance with the use of the Present Tense in moods other than the Indicative, denotes action **in Progress, or Habitual** action.

The Aorist Imperative, in accordance with the use of the Aorist Tense in moods other than the Indicative, denotes that the action is regarded as a **Single Event.**

Examples : Compare together the use of the Imperatives in the two forms of the Lord's Prayer.

Give us (keep on giving us) day by day our daily bread.

τὸν ἄρτον ἡμῶν τὸν ἐπιούσιον δίδου ἡμῖν τὸ καθ' ἡμέραν.　Lk. xi. 3.

Give us to-day our daily bread.

τὸν ἄρτον ἡμῶν τὸν ἐπιούσιον δὸς ἡμῖν σήμερον.　　　Mt. vi. 11.

The Pres. Imperative denotes a continuous act of giving—day after day.

The Aor. Imperative denotes a single act of giving—for to-day. Compare also Mt. v. 42 with Lk. vi. 30; and consider carefully the exact force of the Imperatives in the examples given below.

PROHIBITIONS

126. **Prohibitions** are negative commands or petitions.

They are expressed in Greek by the **Present Imperative** or the **Aorist Subjunctive** (not Imperative) with the negative μή and its compounds.

The distinction in meaning between the Pres. Imperative and the Aor. Subjunctive is the same as that between the Pres. Imperative and Aor. Imperative in affirmative commands.

The Pres. Imperative forbids the **Continuance** of an action already in progress, or sometimes the **Habitual Doing** of an action, or even the attempt to do it.

The Aor. Subjunctive forbids the doing of an action without any regard to its progress or frequency, and it is most generally used with regard to an action **not already begun.**

These distinctions of meaning are carefully observed by the writers of the N.T. and must not be neglected in translating because we have no corresponding niceties of phrase in English.

(In Latin the Perfect Subjunctive with *ne* is used to express a Prohibition.)

127. Examples of the use of the **Present Imperative** to denote the prohibition of an action **in progress,** or in the sense of a command to cease to do the action.

It is I, be not afraid (do not continue to be afraid).

ἐγώ εἰμι, μὴ φοβεῖσθε.　　　　　　　　　　　　Mk. vi. 50.

Thy daughter is dead, do not trouble the Master any further.

τέθνηκεν ἡ θυγάτηρ σου, μηκέτι σκύλλε τὸν Διδάσκαλον.

Lk. viii. 49.

Compare the expression used in Mk. v. 35—ἡ θυγάτηρ σου ἀπέθανεν· τί ἔτι σκύλλεις τὸν Διδάσκαλον;

Daughters of Jerusalem, weep not for me (cease to weep for me).

θυγατέρες Ἱερουσαλήμ, μὴ κλαίετε ἐπ' ἐμέ.   Lk. xxiii. 28.

Take these things hence, do not continue to make my Father's house a house of merchandise.

ἄρατε ταῦτα ἐντεῦθεν, μὴ ποιεῖτε τὸν οἶκον τοῦ Πατρός μου οἶκον ἐμπορίου.   Jn. ii. 16.

(Notice the use of the Aor. Imperative—commanding the immediate removal of the doves.)

Behold thou art made whole: do not go on sinning, lest a worse thing come upon thee.

ἴδε ὑγιὴς γέγονας· μηκέτι ἁμάρτανε, ἵνα μὴ χεῖρόν σοί τι γένηται.

Jn. v. 14.

128. In the following example the Present Imperative appears to be used to forbid the repeated doing of an action.

Do not keep going from house to house.

μὴ μεταβαίνετε ἐξ οἰκίας εἰς οἰκίαν.   Lk. x. 7.

(The command cannot mean *cease to go from house to house*, because the disciples had not yet started on their mission.)

Let not sin continue to reign in your mortal body...neither keep on presenting your members unto sin as instruments of unrighteousness ; but present yourselves (once for all) to God.

μὴ οὖν βασιλευέτω ἡ ἁμαρτία ἐν τῷ θνητῷ ὑμῶν σώματι...μηδὲ παριστάνετε τὰ μέλη ὑμῶν ὅπλα ἀδικίας τῇ ἁμαρτίᾳ, ἀλλὰ παραστήσατε ἑαυτοὺς τῷ θεῷ.   Rom. vi. 12, 13.

Notice the contrast in the use of the Aorist Imperative παραστήσατε. See also Mk. xiii. 21, Jn. x. 37, Eph. iv. 26, 1 Tim. iv. 14, v. 22, 1 Jn. iv. 1.

For the possible use of the Present Imperative in the sense of *do not attempt to do the action* (conative) see 1 Cor. xiv. 39, Gal. v. 1, and Dr J. H. Moulton's *Prolegomena*, p. 125.

129. The use of the **Aorist Subjunctive** in the sense of a command not to **begin** the action.

Do not get gold...for your purses.

μὴ κτήσησθε χρυσὸν...εἰς τὰς ζώνας ὑμῶν.   Mt. x. 9.

Do not therefore begin to be ashamed of the testimony of our Lord nor of me his prisoner.

μὴ οὖν ἐπαισχυνθῇς τὸ μαρτύριον τοῦ κυρίου ἡμῶν, μηδὲ ἐμὲ τὸν δέσμιον αὐτοῦ.   2 Tim. i. 8.

130. The following are examples of the use of both the Pres. Imperative and the Aor. Subjunctive in the same sentence.

Do not carry (continue to carry) a purse, nor a scrip, nor shoes, and do not salute any man by the way.

μὴ βαστάζετε βαλλάντιον, μὴ πήραν, μὴ ὑποδήματα, καὶ μηδένα κατὰ τὴν ὁδὸν ἀσπάσησθε.   Lk. x. 4.

Then spake the Lord to Paul in the night by a vision, "Do not fear (as you have already begun to), but go on speaking, and do not begin to hold thy peace."

εἶπεν δὲ ὁ κύριος ἐν νυκτὶ δι' ὁράματος τῷ Παύλῳ· μὴ φοβοῦ, ἀλλὰ λάλει καὶ μὴ σιωπήσῃς.   Acts xviii. 9.

Compare also Lk. xiv. 8 with verse 12.

THE OPTATIVE MOOD

131. The **Optative Mood** has almost disappeared from use in N.T. Greek. When used it generally expresses a wish.

Example : May it be unto me according to thy word.

γένοιτό μοι κατὰ τὸ ῥῆμά σου.   Lk. i. 38.

See also Philemon 20, 2 Tim. iv. 16.

132. The Potential Optative with ἄν is used to express what would happen on the fulfilment of a supposed condition.

It is to be translated by the English Auxiliaries *would*, *should*, *could*, and it is very rare in the N.T.   See Acts viii. 31, xvii. 18.

The Optative in Dependent Questions and in Conditional Sentences is also very rare, and will be treated under those heads.

THE INFINITIVE AND ITS EQUIVALENTS IN NOUN CLAUSES AND IN CERTAIN ADVERBIAL CLAUSES

133. The so-called **Infinitive Mood** had its origin in the **Dative** and **Locative** cases of a verbal noun.

λύειν meant originally *for loosing* or *in loosing*.

This Dative or Locative force can still be seen in some of the uses of the Infinitive, especially when it is used in Adverbial clauses denoting purpose or result.

But, generally speaking, the Infinitive is regarded as an indeclinable verbal noun which can be made declinable by the addition of the article.

The Infinitive partakes of the nature both of a verb and a noun.

As a verb it has a subject expressed or understood, and it may have an object, it is qualified by adverbs, and has tense and voice.

As a noun it may stand as the subject or object of another verb, it may be in apposition to another noun or pronoun, or it may be governed by a preposition.

The subject of the Infinitive is properly in the Accusative case.

The use of the Greek Infinitive is much wider than that of the English Infinitive. It is sometimes translated by the English Infinitive, or by the English verbal noun in *ing*, and sometimes by the English Indicative, Subjunctive, or even Imperative mood.

The fact that the Infinitive was in its origin a verbal noun has caused it to be employed in a great variety of subordinate clauses.

It is used, naturally, in **Noun clauses**, as being a noun, and it is also used in **Adverbial** clauses expressing purpose or result, because it retains something of its old Dative sense.

134. Clauses introduced by ἵνα or ὅτι frequently take the place of the Infinitive in New Testament Greek just as clauses introduced by *that* frequently do in English.

For example we can say

  I declare him to be innocent.

Or *I declare that he is innocent.*

  He commanded bread to be set before them.

Or *He commanded that bread should be set before them.*

It is sufficient for the servant to be as his master.
Or *It is sufficient for the servant that he should be as his master.*
I am going to buy bread.
Or *I am going that I may buy bread.*

A clause introduced by ὅτι may take the place of an Infinitive in a Noun clause after a verb of saying or thinking in both Classical and New Testament Greek.

In New Testament Greek a clause introduced by ἵνα may take the place of the Infinitive in almost every other kind of clause where a simple infinitive might be used, but in Classical Greek this construction is only used in Adverbial clauses expressing purpose.

135. The student must never be surprised to find a clause introduced by ἵνα in the New Testament where an Infinitive might have been expected. The two uses are practically parallel.

The Infinitive and a clause introduced by ἵνα occur side by side in 1 Cor. xiv. 5 :

θέλω δὲ πάντας ὑμᾶς λαλεῖν γλώσσαις μᾶλλον δὲ ἵνα προφητεύητε.

I wish all of you to speak with tongues, but more that ye may prophesy.

Observe the exact parallel of the English use of an Infinitive and a clause introduced by *that*.

The Infinitive occurs in one Gospel, and a clause introduced by ἵνα in the parallel passage in another Gospel.

Example : The latchet of whose shoes I am not worthy to stoop down and unloose. οὗ οὐκ εἰμὶ ἱκανὸς κύψας λῦσαι τὸν ἱμάντα τῶν ὑποδημάτων αὐτοῦ.　　　　Mk. i. 7.

The latchet of whose shoe I am not worthy to unloose. οὗ οὐκ εἰμὶ ἐγὼ ἄξιος ἵνα λύσω αὐτοῦ τὸν ἱμάντα τοῦ ὑποδήματος.　　　　Jn. i. 27.

See sections 180—196 for a fuller treatment of this subject.

136. Clauses and phrases which take a verb in the Infinitive mood may be arranged under four heads :

(1) **Principal clauses** where the Infinitive is used in the sense of an Imperative to express a command or exhortation.

(2) **Adverbial clauses.**
   (*a*) Final clauses, denoting purpose.
   (*b*) Consecutive clauses, denoting result.
   (*c*) Temporal clauses after πρίν.

(3) **Noun clauses** standing as
   (*a*) Subject.
   (*b*) Object.
   (*c*) In apposition to a noun or pronoun.

(4) **Explanatory phrases** limiting the meaning of a noun, or adjective, or even of a verb.

(1) The Imperative Infinitive

137. The Infinitive is sometimes used to express a command or exhortation. This is an ancient use of the Infinitive in Greek, and has parallels in modern languages, but it is very rare in the New Testament.

Example : Rejoice with them that do rejoice, and weep with them that weep.

    χαίρειν μετὰ χαιρόντων, κλαίειν μετὰ κλαιόντων.

Rom. xii. 15.

See also Acts xxiii. 26, Phil. iii. 16, Titus ii. 2.

(2) The use of the Infinitive in Adverbial Clauses

138.   (*a*) **The Infinitive of Purpose.**
The Infinitive is used in Greek, as in English, to denote the purpose of the action of the principal verb.

The original Dative force of the Infinitive, expressing that to or for which anything is done, comes out plainly in this use.

Compare together the English sentences :

    I am going to the Temple to pray.   (Infinitive.)
And I am going to the Temple for prayer.   (Noun in the Dative.)

Examples : I am going to fish, or I go a fishing.

      ὑπάγω ἁλιεύειν.   Jn. xxi. 3.

      For Christ sent me not to baptise, but to preach the gospel.

      οὐ γὰρ ἀπέστειλέν με Χριστὸς βαπτίζειν, ἀλλὰ εὐαγγελί-
      ζεσθαι.   1 Cor. i. 17.

A clause introduced by ἵνα is, however, more generally used in this sense. See 184, 198.

139. (b) The Infinitive of Result.

The Infinitive may also be used to express the result or consequence of the action of the principal verb.

It is generally introduced by ὥστε, but is occasionally found standing alone. See further 230—232.

Example : And the waves beat into the boat, so that the boat was now filling.

> καὶ τὰ κύματα ἐπέβαλλεν εἰς τὸ πλοῖον, ὥστε ἤδη γεμίζε-
> σθαι τὸ πλοῖον.   Mk. iv. 37.

Example of an Infinitive without ὥστε denoting result :

For God is not unrighteous so as to forget your work.

> οὐ γὰρ ἄδικος ὁ Θεὸς ἐπιλαθέσθαι τοῦ ἔργου ὑμῶν.   Heb. vi. 10.

See also Acts v. 3, Col. iv. 6, Heb. v. 5.

140. (c) The Infinitive in Temporal clauses after πρίν.

When the verb in the principal clause is affirmative, a temporal clause introduced by πρίν has its verb in the Infinitive.

Example : Verily I say to thee that, in this night, before the cock crow, thou shalt deny me thrice.

> ἀμὴν λέγω σοι ὅτι ἐν ταύτῃ τῇ νυκτὶ πρὶν ἀλέκτορα φωνῆσαι
> τρὶς ἀπαρνήσῃ με.   Mt. xxvi. 34.

See also section 216.

(3) The use of the Infinitive in Noun Clauses

141. A Noun clause is a clause that stands in the relationship of a noun to the principal clause or some other clause in a complex sentence.

The Infinitive, as being a verbal noun, is regularly used in Noun clauses in Greek and Latin.

142. (a) Noun clauses standing as the Subject of a verb.

In these clauses the verb is put in the Infinitive mood, and its subject in the Accusative case.

Examples : For it is easier for a camel to go through the eye of a needle than for a rich man to enter into the kingdom of God.

> εὐκοπώτερον γάρ ἐστιν κάμηλον διὰ τρήματος βελόνης εἰσελθεῖν ἢ
> πλούσιον εἰς τὴν βασιλείαν τοῦ θεοῦ εἰσελθεῖν.   Lk. xviii. 25.

Is it lawful for us to give tribute to Caesar or not?

ἔξεστιν ἡμᾶς Καίσαρι φόρον δοῦναι ἢ οὔ;　　　　Lk. xx. 22.

And it came to pass that he was sitting at meat in his house.

καὶ γίγνεται κατακεῖσθαι αὐτὸν ἐν τῇ οἰκίᾳ αὐτοῦ.　　Mk. ii. 15.

143. A clause introduced by *ὅτι* may take the place of the Infinitive as the subject of a verb.

Example: Carest thou not that we perish?

οὐ μέλει σοι ὅτι ἀπολλύμεθα;　　　　Mk. iv. 38.

See also Lk. x. 40.

144. (*b*) **Noun clauses standing as the Object of a verb.**

The verb in these clauses may be nearly always in the Infinitive mood, but a clause introduced by *ὅτι* is often substituted for the Infinitive in both Classical and New Testament Greek, and in New Testament Greek a clause introduced by *ἵνα* is often found as a substitute for the Infinitive after certain verbs.   See 188—190.

145. Object Clauses after verbs denoting saying or thinking, or **Dependent Statements.**

A Dependent Statement, or the **Oratio Obliqua**, as it is often called, repeats the thoughts or sayings of a person, not in the words in which they were originally conceived or spoken, but in the words of the reporter, or, to put it in another way, it is an **Object Clause** depending on a verb of saying, thinking, or feeling.

Example: Mr Smith said that he was very pleased to be there that evening, and to see them all sitting round that table.

These words are a **report** of what Mr Smith said, and **not** the words which he actually uttered.

The words which he did say were: *I am very pleased to be here this evening, and to see you all sitting round this table.*

In the first example his words are **incorporated** into the structure of the sentence, and made into a Noun Clause, which is the Object of the verb *said.*

The whole passage has been remodelled to suit the position of the reporter instead of the position of the speaker.

The verb *I am very pleased* has been put into the third person and so have the Personal Pronouns *I* and *you.*

The tense of the verb is changed from Present to Past.

Here has been changed to *there*, and *this* to *that.*

146. Object Clauses of this kind *may* be translated into Greek, and *must* be translated into Classical Latin, by the **Accusative** and **Infinitive** construction, that is, the principal verbs are put into the Infinitive mood, and their Subjects are put into the Accusative Case.

A clause introduced by ὅτι followed by a verb in the Indicative or Optative Mood is however frequently substituted for the Accusative and Infinitive construction in Greek.

147. We have these two parallel constructions also in English :

We can say *I declare him to be a criminal.*
　　　　Or *I declare that he is a criminal.*
　　　　　We believe them to be here.
　　　　Or *We believe that they are here.*

The first of these constructions is an Accusative and Infinitive construction, just like the Greek or Latin construction.

The second corresponds to the clause introduced by ὅτι in Greek.

The second of these two constructions is far the most common in English ; the first can only be used after a few verbs.

148. The following are examples of Dependent Statements in the Accusative and Infinitive construction taken from the New Testament.

　　Ye say that I cast out devils by Beelzebub.
　　Dicitis per Beelzebul ejicere me daemonia. (Beza.)
　　λέγετε ἐν Βεελζεβοὺλ ἐκβάλλειν με τὰ δαιμόνια.　　Lk. xi. 18.

　　How do they say that Christ is the son of David ?
　　Quomodo dicunt Christum esse filium David ?
　　πῶς λέγουσιν τὸν Χριστὸν εἶναι Δαυεὶδ υἱόν ;　　Lk. xx. 41.

　　The crowd therefore that stood by and heard said that it had thundered.

　　Turba ergo quae stabat et audierat dicebat tonitruum esse factum.
　　ὁ οὖν ὄχλος ὁ ἑστὼς καὶ ἀκούσας ἔλεγεν βροντὴν γεγονέναι.
　　　　　　　　　　　　　　　　　　　　　　　Jn. xii. 29.

　　I do not think that even the world itself would contain the books which should be written.

　　Ne mundum quidem ipsum opinor capturum esse eos qui scribe-
rentur libros. (Beza.)
　　οὐδ᾽ αὐτὸν οἶμαι τὸν κόσμον χωρήσειν τὰ γραφόμενα βιβλία.
　　　　　　　　　　　　　　　　　　　　　　　Jn. xxi. 25.

149. When the **subject** of the principal clause is **the same** as the subject of the infinitive it is generally omitted and, if the infinitive is connected with a predicate noun or adjective, this is made to agree with the subject of the principal clause.

Saying that they were wise they became foolish.

φάσκοντες εἶναι σοφοὶ ἐμωράνθησαν.   Rom. i. 22.

See also Rom. ix. 3, 2 Cor. x. 2.

But if the subject of the infinitive is expressed for the sake of emphasis it is put in the accusative case.

Thou art confident that thou art a guide of the blind.

πέποιθάς τε σεαυτὸν ὁδηγὸν εἶναι τυφλῶν.   Rom. ii. 19.

See also Phil. iii. 13, Rev. ii. 2.

Even when the articular infinitive is used after a preposition the subject (if expressed) is put in the accusative case.

After I have risen from the dead I will go before you.

μετὰ τὸ ἐγερθῆναί με προάξω ὑμᾶς.   Mk. xiv. 28.

See also Mt. xxvii. 12, Lk. ii. 4, Acts i. 8.

150. After verbs of **feeling, seeing** or **knowing** (perception as opposed to statement) the Accusative and the **Participle** is preferred to the Accusative and the Infinitive, especially in Classical Greek.   (Not in Latin.)

I see that thou art in the gall of bitterness and in the bond of iniquity.

εἰς γὰρ χολὴν πικρίας καὶ σύνδεσμον ἀδικίας ὁρῶ σε ὄντα.   Acts viii. 23.

See also Lk. viii. 46.   **For the Genitive and** Participle after ἀκούειν see Jn. vii. 32.

Tense of the Infinitive

151. In Latin and Greek the tense of the Infinitive in a dependent statement is always the same as that used by the original speaker when he uttered the words.

The use in English is different.

In English, when the verb of saying or feeling is in a **Primary** tense (that is, in the Present or Future tense) the tense of the verbs in the dependent statement is **unchanged.**

If the original speaker said *I see the city,* this becomes in indirect speech *He says that he sees the city* : the person of the verb only is changed and the tense remains the same.

If the original speaker said *I saw the city,* this becomes in indirect speech *He says that he saw the city.*

If the original speaker said *I shall see the city,* this becomes in indirect speech *He says that he will see the city.*

After a verb of saying or feeling in a future tense these sentences would be—*He will say that he sees the city, He will say that he saw the city, He will say that he will see the city.*

But when the verb of saying or feeling is in a **Secondary** tense (that is, a Past tense) the tense of the verbs in the dependent statement is **put one stage further in the past** than the time of the tense used by the original speaker.

If the original speaker said *I see the city*, this becomes in indirect speech *He said that he* **saw** *the city*.

If the original speaker said *I saw the city*, or *I have seen the city*, this becomes in indirect speech *He said that he* **had seen** *the city*.

If the original speaker said *I shall see the city*, this becomes in indirect speech *He said that he* **would see** *the city*.

We see in these examples that the present tense of independent statement becomes the past tense in dependent statement.

The past tense of independent statement becomes the pluperfect (or doubly past) tense, in dependent statement.

The future tense of independent statement becomes the second future or future in the past[1] tense in dependent statement.

152. But in Latin and Greek the infinitives in dependent statements are always put in the **same tense** as that used by the original speaker, both when the principal verb is in a Primary tense, and when it is in a Secondary tense.

If the original speaker said *I see the city*,

This will become *He says that he sees the city* in English.

Dicit se urbem videre in Latin.

λέγει τὴν πόλιν ὁρᾶν in Greek.

The tense used by the original speaker is kept in all three languages because the principal verb is in a Primary tense.

But if the principal verb is in a Secondary tense the sentence will be as follows :

English :   He said that he saw the city.

Latin :   Dixit se urbem videre.

Greek :   ἔλεγε τὴν πόλιν ὁρᾶν.

In these examples the tense used by the original speaker is retained in the dependent statement in Latin and Greek, but not in English.

In the same way if the original speaker said *I saw the city*, after a principal verb in a Primary tense this will become

He says that he saw the city.

Dicit se urbem vidisse.

λέγει τὴν πόλιν ἰδεῖν.

[1] This name has been adopted by the Joint Committee on Grammatical Terminology.

But after a principal verb in a Secondary tense the sentence will be as follows :

> He said that he **had seen** the city
> Dixit se urbem vidisse.
> ἔλεγε τὴν πόλιν ἰδεῖν.

If the original speaker said *I shall see the city*, after a principal verb in a Primary tense this will become

> He says that he will see the city.
> Dicit se urbem visurum esse.
> λέγει τὴν πόλιν ὄψεσθαι.

But after a principal verb in a Secondary tense the sentence will be as follows :

> He said that he **would see** the city.
> Dixit se urbem visurum esse.
> ἔλεγε τὴν πόλιν ὄψεσθαι.

It is good practice to read over the report of a speech in a news-paper, where most speeches are reported in the Oratio Obliqua, and to put it into direct speech by restoring in thought the words which the speaker actually used.

153. As has been mentioned above, there is in Greek another way of expressing dependent statements besides the Accusative and Infinitive construction. This way is almost exactly similar to the English way of expressing dependent statements, for the clause is introduced by ὅτι (*that*) and the verbs are in a Finite mood (that is, they are in some mood other than the Infinitive).

As is the case in the Infinitive construction explained above, the tense used by the original speaker must in no case be altered in expressing his words as a dependent statement.

This point deserves special attention, because it is entirely opposed to the English use, where, as we have seen above, the tense of all verbs in dependent statements is altered after a principal verb in a Second-ary tense.

If the original speaker said *I see the city*, this will become after a principal verb in a Primary tense

> He says that he sees the city.
> λέγει ὅτι τὴν πόλιν ὁρᾷ.

But after a principal verb in a Secondary tense it will be

He said that he saw the city.

ἔλεγεν ὅτι τὴν πόλιν ὁρᾷ.

If the original speaker said *I saw the city*, this will become after a principal verb in a Primary tense

He says that he saw the city.

λέγει ὅτι τὴν πόλιν εἶδεν.

But after a principal verb in a Secondary tense it will be

He said that he had seen the city.

ἔλεγεν ὅτι τὴν πόλιν εἶδεν.

If the original speaker said *I shall see the city*, this will become after a principal verb in a Primary tense

He says that he will see the city.

λέγει ὅτι τὴν πόλιν ὄψεται.

But after a principal verb in a Secondary tense it will be

He said that he would see the city.

ἔλεγεν ὅτι τὴν πόλιν ὄψεται.

The following are examples of this construction taken from the New Testament :

Supposing that she was going to the tomb to weep there.

δόξαντες ὅτι ὑπάγει εἰς τὸ μνημεῖον ἵνα κλαύσῃ ἐκεῖ.   Jn. xi. 31.

They supposed that they would have received more.

ἐνόμισαν ὅτι πλεῖον λήψονται.   Mt. xx. 10.

154. After a principal verb in a Secondary tense the **Same Tense** of the **Optative** mood as that used in the Indicative mood by the original speaker is frequently employed in Classical Greek in dependent statements introduced by ὅτι.   This construction is never found in the New Testament.

Examples : He said that he saw the city.   ἔλεγεν ὅτι τὴν πόλιν ὁρῴη.
(The original speaker said ὁρῶ τὴν πόλιν.)

He said that he had seen the city.   ἔλεγεν ὅτι τὴν πόλιν ἴδοι.
(The original speaker said εἶδον τὴν πόλιν.)

He said that he would see the city.   ἔλεγεν ὅτι τὴν πόλιν ὄψοιτο.
(The original speaker said ὄψομαι τὴν πόλιν.)

155. N.B.   A verb is **never** put into the **Subjunctive mood** in Greek, as it is in Latin, because it is the verb in a dependent statement.

The chief thing to remember in Greek is never to change the tense used by the original speaker when putting his words into the Oratio Obliqua.

Subordinate Clauses in Dependent Statements

156. The rules given above apply to verbs in principal clauses in Dependent Statements.

As however a whole speech may be expressed as a dependent statement, it is obvious that complex sentences which contain subordinate as well as principal clauses may occur in a statement of this kind.

Example : Mr Smith said that *although he had been their member for twenty years,* he had never known *how much they appreciated his services, until he entered the hall that evening.*

Here all the clauses in italics are subordinate clauses in a dependent statement.

In English after a verb of saying or feeling in a Secondary tense all the verbs in such subordinate clauses are put into past tenses, just as the verb in the principal clause is.

But in New Testament Greek all verbs in Subordinate clauses in a dependent statement are kept in the same tense and mood as that used by the original speaker. This is the case both when the Accusative and Infinitive construction is used in the principal clause of the dependent statement and also when it is introduced by ὅτι.

Dependent statements made up of complex sentences are however very rare in the N.T.

Example : They came saying that they had seen a vision of angels who said that he was alive.

ἦλθον λέγουσαι καὶ ὀπτασίαν ἀγγέλων ἑωρακέναι, οἳ λέγουσιν αὐτὸν ζῆν. Lk. xxiv. 23.

The words which the women said were *We have seen a vision of angels who say that he is alive.*

157. In Classical Greek after a verb of saying or feeling in a Secondary tense all verbs in the Subordinate clauses of a dependent statement, whether they are in the Indicative or Subjunctive mood, may be put in the same tense of the Optative mood.

158. ὅτι is frequently used in the New Testament to introduce a **direct quotation** of the speaker's actual words; it is of course redundant, and can only be expressed in English by the use of Inverted Commas.

Example :   He said "I am he."

ἐκεῖνος ἔλεγεν ὅτι ἐγώ εἰμι.   Jn. ix. 9.

The redundant ὅτι may even be used before a direct question.   See Mk. iv. 21.

159. Object clauses after verbs meaning *to entreat, to exhort, to command,* or **Dependent Commands or Petitions.**

Dependent Commands or Petitions follow verbs of commanding or entreating to tell us the command that was given or the request that was made, not in the words of the original speaker, but in the words of the reporter.

Examples :   He commanded them to go away.

(The words used by the original speaker were *Go away.*)
     He requested them to follow him.

(The words of the original speaker were *Follow me.*)

Dependent commands or petitions are generally expressed in Greek, as in English, by the use of the **Infinitive mood.**

Examples :   He commanded them not to depart from Jerusalem.

παρήγγειλεν αὐτοῖς ἀπὸ Ἱεροσολύμων μὴ χωρίζεσθαι.

Acts i. 4.

Master, I beseech thee to look upon my son.

διδάσκαλε, δέομαί σου ἐπιβλέψαι ἐπὶ τὸν υἱόν μου.

Lk. ix. 38.

In New Testament Greek a clause introduced by ἵνα often takes the place of the Infinitive construction in dependent commands or petitions. See **189.**

Subordinate clauses in Dependent Commands follow the same rule as subordinate clauses in Dependent Statements ; see section 156.

For an example see Mt. xviii. 25.

160. Object clauses after verbs meaning *to ask a question etc.* or **Dependent Questions.**

Dependent Questions follow verbs meaning to ask a question etc., to tell us the question that was asked, not in the words of the original speaker, but in the words of the reporter.

Example :   He asked if they were going away.

(The words used by the original speaker were *Are you going away ?*)

The rules for translating dependent questions into N.T. Greek are exactly the same as those for translating dependent statements in a clause beginning with ὅτι. **The mood and tense** used by the original speaker are retained, whether the verb on which they depend is in a Primary or Secondary tense.

Examples : They asked if Simon lodged there.

ἐπυθάνοντο εἰ Σίμων ἐνθάδε ξενίζεται.   Acts x. 18.

The question which they asked was *Does Simon lodge here?*

Calling the centurion he asked him if he had been long dead.

προκαλεσάμενος τὸν κεντυρίωνα ἐπηρώτησεν εἰ πάλαι ἀπέθανεν.

Mk. xv. 44.

161. But in the writings of St Luke we often find the **Optative** substituted for an Indicative or Subjunctive used by the original speaker when the main verb is in a Secondary tense.

This is also the usage of Classical Greek.

And they began to question among themselves which of them it was that should do this thing.

καὶ αὐτοὶ ἤρξαντο συζητεῖν πρὸς ἑαυτοὺς τὸ τίς ἄρα εἴη ἐξ αὐτῶν ὁ τοῦτο μέλλων πράσσειν.   Lk. xxii. 23.

See also Lk. xviii. 36, Acts xvii. 11, xxi. 33.

162. Any Object clause introduced by any **Interrogative word** is regarded as a Dependent Question, and is constructed in accordance with the rules given above. The main verb need not have the meaning of asking a question at all.

Examples : If the good man of the house had known at what hour the thief would come, he would have watched.

εἰ ᾔδει ὁ οἰκοδεσπότης ποίᾳ φυλακῇ ὁ κλέπτης ἔρχεται, ἐγρηγόρησεν ἄν.   Mt. xxiv. 43.

They saw where he dwelt.

εἶδον ποῦ μένει.   Jn. i. 39.

N.B. The **Subjunctive Mood is never used** in Greek, as in Latin, as the proper mood for dependent questions.

If it is ever found in them, it is because it was in the question as asked by the original speaker, as for example in Acts xxv. 26, Lk. xii. 5.

163. Dependent Exclamations follow the same rules as Dependent Questions. See Mk. iii. 8, xv. 4, Gal. vi. 11.

164. The following classes of verbs call for special mention because of the peculiarity of the constructions in the object clauses which follow them.

165. Object clauses after verbs meaning *to strive, to plan, to take heed, to effect.*

The usual construction in an object clause after these verbs in Classical Greek is ὅπως followed by a Future Indicative.

In the New Testament an Infinitive is sometimes found, and sometimes a clause introduced by ἵνα. See 190.

Examples of the use of the Infinitive after such verbs are found in Lk. xiii. 24, Gal. ii. 10, 2 Tim. iv. 9.

166. Object clauses after verbs denoting *fear* or *danger.*

These verbs are followed by an object clause introduced by μή both in Classical and New Testament Greek. See 192.

167. Verbs meaning *to rejoice, to wonder, to be vexed, to grieve* are generally followed by an object clause introduced by ὅτι with a verb in the Indicative mood.

In Mk. xv. 44 and 1 Jn. iii. 13 a verb meaning *to wonder* is followed by a clause introduced by εἰ, as is often the case in Classical Greek.

168. Verbs meaning *to hope, to promise, and to swear* are generally followed by an Aorist Infinitive.

169. (c) **Noun clauses standing in apposition to a noun or pronoun.**

Example: Pure religion and undefiled before our God and Father is this, to visit the fatherless and widows in their affliction, and to keep himself unspotted from the world.

θρησκεία καθαρὰ καὶ ἀμίαντος παρὰ τῷ θεῷ καὶ πατρὶ αὕτη ἐστίν, ἐπισκέπτεσθαι ὀρφανοὺς καὶ χήρας ἐν τῇ θλίψει αὐτῶν, ἄσπιλον ἑαυτὸν τηρεῖν ἀπὸ τοῦ κόσμου. James i. 27.

See also Acts xv. 28, 29, 1 Thess. iv. 3.

(4) The Epexegetic or Explanatory Infinitive

170. The Infinitive may be used after a noun or adjective, especially those which denote ability, fitness, readiness, or need, in an explanatory sense, just as in English.

Examples : Whose shoes I am not worthy to bear.

οὗ οὐκ εἰμὶ ἱκανὸς τὰ ὑποδήματα βαστάσαι. Mt. iii. 11.

He that hath ears to hear, let him hear.

ὁ ἔχων ὦτα ἀκούειν, ἀκουέτω.   Lk. viii. 8.

Opportunity to return.

καιρὸν ἀνακάμψαι.   Heb. xi. 15.

Time for you to awake out of sleep.

ὥρα ἤδη ὑμᾶς ἐξ ὕπνου ἐγερθῆναι.   Rom. xiii. 11.

171. This Explanatory Infinitive is found even after verbs. See Acts xv. 10.

The Infinitive with the Article

172. The prefixing of an article to the Infinitive emphasises its character as a noun. When preceded by an article it becomes a declinable neuter noun, varying in case as the case of the article varies.

The Infinitive may have a subject, object, or other limiting words attached to it. These words generally come between the article and the Infinitive, and form with it a phrase equivalent to a noun.

Examples : Phrase containing Infinitive with Article as **subject** of a sentence :

But to eat with unwashed hands does not defile the man.

τὸ δὲ ἀνίπτοις χερσὶν φαγεῖν οὐ κοινοῖ τὸν ἄνθρωπον.   Mt. xv. 20.

Infinitive phrase as **object.**

I refuse not to die.

οὐ παραιτοῦμαι τὸ ἀποθανεῖν.   Acts xxv. 11.

Infinitive phrase in **apposition.**

I determined this for myself not to come again to you with sorrow

ἔκρινα γὰρ ἐμαυτῷ τοῦτο τὸ μὴ πάλιν ἐν λύπῃ πρὸς ὑμᾶς ἐλθεῖν.
       2 Cor. ii. 1.

173. Infinitive phrase governed by a **Preposition.**

Examples : And because it had no root it withered away.

καὶ διὰ τὸ μὴ ἔχειν ῥίζαν ἐξηράνθη.   Mk. iv. 6.

But take heed that ye do not your righteousness before men to be seen of them.

προσέχετε δὲ τὴν δικαιοσύνην ὑμῶν μὴ ποιεῖν ἔμπροσθεν τῶν ἀνθρώπων πρὸς τὸ θεαθῆναι αὐτοῖς.   Mt. vi. 1.

And as he sowed some fell by the wayside.

καὶ ἐν τῷ σπείρειν αὐτὸν ὃ μὲν ἔπεσεν παρὰ τὴν ὁδόν.   Lk. viii. 5.

The Infinitive with τοῦ

174. The Infinitive with the Genitive Article has a peculiar series of uses in which it "retains its Genitive force almost as little as the Genitive Absolute[1]." (J. H. Moulton.)

It is used in the Septuagint and the New Testament **exactly as if it were a simple Infinitive** to express purpose, or consequence, or epexegetically, or even as the subject or object of a Finite verb.

175. (1) **Purpose.**

Example: For Herod will seek the young child to destroy him.

μέλλει γὰρ Ἡρῴδης ζητεῖν τὸ παιδίον τοῦ ἀπολέσαι αὐτό.

Mt. ii. 13.

In Lk. ii. 22, 24 the simple Infinitive and the Infinitive with τοῦ are used side by side with exactly the same force.

See also Lk. i. 76, 77 and 79. Compare Phil. iii. 10.

This is the most common use of this construction.

176. (2) **Consequence or Result.**

Example: And ye, when ye saw it, did not repent afterwards so as to believe him.

ὑμεῖς δὲ ἰδόντες οὐδὲ μετεμελήθητε ὕστερον τοῦ πιστεῦσαι αὐτῷ.

Mt. xxi. 32.

See also Acts xviii. 10; Rom. vi. 6, vii. 3.

177. (3) **As Subject or Object** of a Finite verb just like the simple Infinitive.

Example: And when it was determined that we should sail into Italy.

ὡς δὲ ἐκρίθη τοῦ ἀποπλεῖν ἡμᾶς εἰς τὴν Ἰταλίαν. Acts xxvii. 1.

See also Lk. xvii. 1, Acts x. 25, xx. 3.

And when we heard these things, we, and they that were there, besought him not to go up to Jerusalem.

ὡς δὲ ἠκούσαμεν ταῦτα παρεκαλοῦμεν ἡμεῖς τε καὶ οἱ ἐντόπιοι τοῦ μὴ ἀναβαίνειν αὐτὸν εἰς Ἰερουσαλήμ. Acts xxi. 12.

See also Acts iii. 12, xv. 20, xxiii. 20; James v. 17.

178. (4) The Infinitive with τοῦ is also used **epexegetically** (that is, in such a way as to explain the meaning) with nouns, adjectives, and verbs just like the simple Infinitive. See 170.

Examples: And he sought a suitable time to betray him to them without a tumult.

[1] This construction is rarely found in Classical authors in the sense of purpose. Thuc. i. 4. It is freely used in such illiterate authors as Hermas and is even found in Justin, *Dialogue*, 67.

καὶ ἐζήτει εὐκαιρίαν τοῦ παραδοῦναι αὐτὸν ἄτερ ὄχλου αὐτοῖς.
Lk. xxii. 6.

And seeing that he had faith to be healed....
καὶ ἰδὼν ὅτι ἔχει πίστιν τοῦ σωθῆναι.   Acts xiv. 9.

O foolish and slow of heart to believe....
Ὦ ἀνόητοι καὶ βραδεῖς τῇ καρδίᾳ τοῦ πιστεύειν.... Lk. xxiv. 25

He...evil entreated our fathers by casting out their children.
οὗτος...ἐκάκωσεν τοὺς πατέρας τοῦ ποιεῖν τὰ βρέφη ἔκθετα αὐτῶν.
Acts vii. 19.

See also Acts xxiii. 15, Rom. viii. 12, 1 Pet. iv. 17.

179. (5) It is also used normally in its proper **Genitive sense** with nouns and adjectives, and also after verbs governing a genitive.

Examples : In hope of partaking.
ἐπ' ἐλπίδι τοῦ μετέχειν.   1 Cor. ix. 10.

Wherefore also I was hindered these many times from coming to you.
διὸ καὶ ἐνεκοπτόμην τὰ πολλὰ τοῦ ἐλθεῖν πρὸς ὑμᾶς. Rom. xv. 22.

See also Lk. i. 9; 1 Cor. xvi. 4; 2 Cor. i. 8, viii. 11 ; Phil. iii. 21.

THE USE OF CLAUSES INTRODUCED BY ἵνα AND OTHER FINAL PARTICLES AS SUBSTITUTES FOR THE INFINITIVE

180. As has been already stated a clause introduced by ἵνα or ὅπως is frequently found in New Testament Greek where an Infinitive might have been expected, and where an Infinitive would have been used in Classical Greek. Even in New Testament Greek an Infinitive can be used with exactly the same force as the ἵνα clause in nearly every case.

At the time when the New Testament was being written, clauses introduced by ἵνα were gradually taking the place of the Infinitive in familiar speech, and in modern Greek the Infinitive has entirely disappeared and νά with a Subjunctive taken its place.

Many of the older Commentators and Grammarians deny that ἵνα can have any other meaning than that which it has in the Classical writers, namely that of purpose, and put forced interpretations on every passage where it occurs, to bring in this meaning. This position is now abandoned as the result of modern research into the history of the language and the discovery of the Egyptian papyri, where the use of ἵνα in senses other than that of purpose is common. The student should not try to force the meaning of purpose on ἵνα unless the context obviously demands it.

The uses of clauses introduced by ἵνα and the other Final Particles, ὅπως and μή, are here grouped together for convenience of reference : the difference between New Testament and Classical Greek is so marked in this respect as to make the subject worthy of special study.

181. The exact force of a clause introduced by ἵνα must be inferred from the context, and not from the form of the clause. As in English, it is the natural meaning and not the form of a clause that we must consider before we try to analyse a complex sentence.

Take for example Jn. ix. 2 :

ῥαββεί, τίς ἥμαρτεν, οὗτος ἢ οἱ γονεῖς αὐτοῦ, ἵνα τυφλὸς γεννηθῇ;

Rabbi, who did sin, this man or his parents, so that he was born blind ?

It is obvious that, although the clause ἵνα τυφλὸς γεννηθῇ is in form a clause expressing purpose, it cannot be so in reality, as it is unthinkable that the parents of the man would have sinned in order that he might be born blind. The clause must express result and be described as a Consecutive clause.

The verb in clauses introduced by ἵνα, ὅπως and μή in the New Testament is nearly always in the Subjunctive Mood, but in certain cases the Future Indicative is used instead.

182. Clauses introduced by Final Particles may be arranged under four heads, just as the clauses which take a Verb in the Infinitive Mood, see 136.

(1) **Principal clauses** where the ἵνα clause is used as a substitute for an Imperative Infinitive.

(2) **Adverbial clauses** where the ἵνα clause is used as a substitute for an Infinitive retaining something of its old Dative sense :

    (*a*) Final clauses.

    (*b*) Consecutive clauses.

(3) **Noun clauses** where the ἵνα clause is used as a substitute for an Infinitive used as a caseless verbal noun. Such clauses may stand

    (*a*) As Subject.

    (*b*) As Object.

    (*c*) In Apposition.

(4) **Explanatory clauses** used as a substitute for an Explanatory Infinitive.

(1) Clauses introduced by ἵνα standing in the place of an Imperative Infinitive

183. This construction is rare and not Classical. The verb is in the Subjunctive Mood.

Examples : Nevertheless do ye also severally love each one his own wife even as himself, and let the wife fear her husband.

πλὴν καὶ ὑμεῖς οἱ καθ᾽ ἕνα ἕκαστος τὴν ἑαυτοῦ γυναῖκα οὕτως ἀγαπάτω ὡς ἑαυτόν, ἡ δὲ γυνὴ ἵνα φοβῆται τὸν ἄνδρα.   Eph. v. 33.

But as ye abound in everything...see that ye abound in this grace also.

ἀλλ᾽ ὥσπερ ἐν παντὶ περισσεύετε...ἵνα καὶ ἐν ταύτῃ τῇ χάριτι περισσεύητε.   2 Cor. viii. 7.

See also Mk. v. 23, 1 Cor. vii. 29, Gal. ii. 10, Rev. xiv. 13.

For the use of the simple Infinitive in this sense see 137.

(2) Adverbial clauses introduced by ἵνα, etc.

184. (a) **Final clauses** denoting the purpose of the action of the verb in the principal clause. (Quite Classical.)

These clauses are introduced by ἵνα or ὅπως if affirmative, and by μή or ἵνα μή if negative.

The verb is generally in the Subjunctive in New Testament Greek, and occasionally in the Future Indicative. (In Classical Greek the Optative is used after ἵνα if the verb in the principal clause is in a past tense, but this does not occur in the New Testament.)

Examples : He came that he might bear witness to the light.

οὗτος ἦλθεν ἵνα μαρτυρήσῃ περὶ τοῦ φωτός.   Jn. i. 7.

And their eyes have they closed ; lest haply they should perceive with their eyes.

καὶ τοὺς ὀφθαλμοὺς αὐτῶν ἐκάμμυσαν, μή ποτε ἴδωσιν τοῖς ὀφθαλμοῖς.
          Acts xxviii. 27.

Judge not that ye be not judged.

μὴ κρίνετε ἵνα μὴ κριθῆτε.   Mt. vii. 1.

For the use of the simple Infinitive in this sense see 138.

185. (b) **Consecutive clauses** denoting the result of the action of the verb in the principal clause. (Rare and not Classical.)

Introduced by ἵνα followed by the Subjunctive.

Examples :

Rabbi, who did sin, this man or his parents, so that he was born blind ?

    ῥαββεί, τίς ἥμαρτεν, οὗτος ἢ οἱ γονεῖς αὐτοῦ, ἵνα τυφλὸς γεννηθῇ ;
Jn. ix. 2.

But ye, brethren, are not in darkness, so that that day should overtake you as thieves.

    ὑμεῖς δέ, ἀδελφοί, οὐκ ἐστὲ ἐν σκότει, ἵνα ἡ ἡμέρα ὑμᾶς ὡς κλέπτας κατελάβῃ.
1 Thess. v. 4.

See also Lk. ix. 45; I Jn. i. 9; Rev. iii. 9, viii. 12. Compare the use of the Infinitive in Heb. vi. 10.

For the use of the Infinitive in this sense see 139.

(3) Noun clauses introduced by ἵνα, etc.

186. Standing as **Subject** of a Verb. (Not Classical.)

These clauses are introduced by ἵνα followed by a Subjunctive, or rarely by a Future Indicative.

Examples : So it is not the will of your Father which is in Heaven that one of these little ones should perish.

    οὕτως οὐκ ἔστιν θέλημα ἔμπροσθεν τοῦ πατρὸς ὑμῶν τοῦ ἐν οὐρανοῖς ἵνα ἀπόληται ἐν τῶν μικρῶν τούτων.   Mt. xviii. 14.

My meat is to do the will of him that sent me.

    ἐμὸν βρῶμά ἐστιν ἵνα ποιῶ τὸ θέλημα τοῦ πέμψαντός με.
Jn. iv. 34.

Ye have a custom that I should release one unto you at the Passover.

    ἔστι δὲ συνήθεια ὑμῖν ἵνα ἕνα ἀπολύσω ὑμῖν ἐν τῷ πάσχα.
Jn. xviii. 39.

Here moreover it is required in stewards that a man be found faithful.

    ὧδε λοιπὸν ζητεῖται ἐν τοῖς οἰκονόμοις ἵνα πιστός τις εὑρεθῇ.
1 Cor. iv. 2.

See also Mk. ix. 12, Acts xxvii. 42, Rev. ix. 4, 5.

187. This construction is used especially as the subject of predicates meaning *it is profitable*, *it is sufficient* and the like.

Example : It is profitable for you that one man die for the people.

    συμφέρει ὑμῖν ἵνα εἷς ἄνθρωπος ἀποθάνῃ ὑπὲρ τοῦ λαοῦ.
Jn. xi. 50.

See also Mt. v. 29, 30, x. 25, xviii. 6; Lk. xvii. 2; 1 Cor. iv. 3.
For the use of the simple Infinitive in this sense see 142.

188. Noun clauses standing as an **Object** of a verb. (Not Classical, except in certain cases mentioned below.)

(a) Object clauses after verbs meaning *to entreat, to exhort, to command, to wish.*

These clauses are introduced by ἵνα[1] or ὅπως followed by the Subjunctive. (Very rare in the Classics.)

Examples : He asked that he would come down and heal his son.

> ἠρώτα ἵνα καταβῇ καὶ ἰάσηται αὐτοῦ τὸν υἱόν.   Jn. iv. 47.

If thou be the Son of God, command that these stones become bread.

> εἰ υἱὸς εἶ τοῦ θεοῦ, εἰπὲ ἵνα οἱ λίθοι οὑ.ͅοι ἄρτοι γένωνται.
>
> Mt. iv. 3.

Pray ye therefore the Lord of the harvest that he send forth labourers into his harvest.

> δεήθητε οὖν τοῦ κυρίου τοῦ θερισμοῦ ὅπως ἐργάτας ἐκβάλῃ εἰς τὸν θερισμὸν αὐτοῦ.   Lk. x. 2.

Therefore whatsoever ye would that men should do unto you do also unto them.

> πάντα οὖν ὅσα ἐὰν θέλητε ἵνα ποιῶσιν ὑμῖν οἱ ἄνθρωποι, οὕτως καὶ ὑμεῖς ποιεῖτε αὐτοῖς.   Mt. vii. 12.

190. (β) Object clauses after verbs meaning *to strive, to plan, to take heed, to effect.*

These clauses are introduced by ἵνα rarely by ὅπως, the verb is generally in the Subjunctive.

(In Classical Greek the usual construction after these verbs is ὅπως followed by the Future Indicative.)

Examples : And the chief priests took counsel that they might kill Lazarus also.

> ἐβουλεύσαντο δὲ οἱ ἀρχιερεῖς ἵνα καὶ τὸν Λάζαρον ἀποκτείνωσιν.
>
> Jn. xii. 10.

And when this letter has been read among you, cause that it be read also in the church of the Laodiceans.

> καὶ ὅταν ἀναγνωσθῇ παρ᾽ ὑμῖν ἡ ἐπιστολή, ποιήσατε ἵνα καὶ ἐν τῇ Λαοδικέων ἐκκλησίᾳ ἀναγνωσθῇ.   Col. iv. 16.

191. When the Object clause after a verb meaning *to care for* or *to take heed* is negative, μή is generally used instead of ἵνα μή.

---

[1] A clause introduced by ἵνα may also follow θέλω, Mk. vi. 25; Lk. vi. 31.

Example : Beware lest anyone deceive you.

βλέπετε μή τις ὑμᾶς πλανήσῃ.   Mt. xxiv. 4.

Verbs meaning to strive etc. are often followed by a simple Infinitive, see 165.

192. (γ) Object clauses after verbs denoting *fear* or *danger*. (Classical.)

These clauses are introduced by μή followed by the Subjunctive. They are negatived by οὐ.

Examples : The chief captain fearing lest Paul should be torn in pieces by them.

φοβηθεὶς ὁ χιλίαρχος μὴ διασπασθῇ ὁ Παῦλος ὑπ' αὐτῶν.

Acts xxiii. 10.

For I fear lest, when I come to you, I shall find you not as I wish.

φοβοῦμαι γὰρ μή πως ἐλθὼν οὐχ οἵους θέλω εὕρω ὑμᾶς.

2 Cor. xii. 20.

193. When the object of fear is conceived as already past or present, and, as such, already decided, although the result is unknown to the speaker, the Indicative is used in these clauses both in Classical and New Testament Greek.

Example : I am afraid of you lest by any means I have bestowed labour upon you in vain.

φοβοῦμαι ὑμᾶς μή πως εἰκῇ κεκοπίακα εἰς ὑμᾶς.   Gal. iv. 11.

See also Gal. ii. 2, 1 Thess. iii. 5.

194. (c) Noun clauses introduced by ἵνα standing in apposition to a noun or pronoun and containing an explanation of the meaning of the noun or pronoun.

This construction is very common in the writings of St John. The verb is always in the Subjunctive mood. (Not Classical.)

Examples : And whence is this to me, that the mother of my Lord should come unto me ?

καὶ πόθεν μοι τοῦτο ἵνα ἔλθῃ ἡ μήτηρ τοῦ κυρίου μου πρὸς ἐμέ ;

Lk. i. 43.

Greater love hath no man than this, that a man lay down his life for his friends.

μείζονα ταύτης ἀγάπην οὐδεὶς ἔχει, ἵνα τις τὴν ψυχὴν αὐτοῦ θῇ ὑπὲρ τῶν φίλων αὐτοῦ.   Jn. xv. 13.

For this is the love of God, that we should keep his commandments.

αὕτη γάρ ἐστιν ἡ ἀγάπη τοῦ θεοῦ, ἵνα τὰς ἐντολὰς αὐτοῦ τηρῶμεν.

1 Jn. v. 3.

What then is my reward? That, when I preach the gospel, I may make the gospel without charge.

τίς οὖν μού ἐστιν ὁ μισθός; ἵνα εὐαγγελιζόμενος ἀδάπανον θήσω τὸ εὐαγγέλιον.   1 Cor. ix. 18.

See also Jn. vi. 29, 39, 40, xv. 8, 12, xvii. 3; 1 Jn. iii. 1, 11, 23, iv. 21; 2 Jn. 6; 3 Jn. 4; perhaps Acts viii. 19. For the simple Infinitive used in this sense see 169 and compare James i. 27.

(4) Explanatory clauses introduced by ἵνα

195. Closely connected with this last use is another where a clause introduced by ἵνα takes the place of an **Epexegetic Infinitive** to explain or limit the use of a noun or adjective.

This construction is used with words denoting authority, power, fitness or set time.

Example: Or who gave thee this authority to do these things?

ἢ τίς σοι ἔδωκεν τὴν ἐξουσίαν ταύτην ἵνα ταῦτα ποιῇς;   Mk. xi. 28.

Note how this construction is altered in the parallel passages (Mt. xxi. 23, Lk. xx. 2) as if it were felt to be a barbarism.

Compare also Jn. i. 27 with Mt. iii. 11. This construction is found in Mt. viii. 8 and Lk. vii. 6, but both these passages come from Q.

196. Dr Burney thinks that when ἵνα introduces a clause used after words denoting a set time it is a mistranslation of the Aramaic particle 'דְ or דְ which can mean *when* as well as *in order that*.

This is shown by the fact that ὅτε is sometimes used with such words in the Fourth Gospel.

Compare: The time has come when the Son of Man shall be glorified.

ἐλήλυθεν ἡ ὥρα ἵνα δοξασθῇ ὁ υἱὸς τοῦ ἀνθρώπου.   Jn. xii. 23.

with The time is coming when neither in this mountain nor in Jerusalem shall ye worship the Father.

ἔρχεται ὥρα ὅτε οὔτε ἐν τῷ ὄρει τούτῳ οὔτε ἐν Ἱεροσολύμοις προσκυνήσετε τῷ πατρί.   Jn. iv. 21.

ἵνα is used in this sense in Jn. xiii. 1, xvi. 2, 32.

ὅτε is used in this sense in Jn. iv 23, v. 25, 28, xvi. 25.

The difficult text: Ἀβραὰμ ὁ πατὴρ ὑμῶν ἠγαλλιάσατο ἵνα ἴδῃ τὴν ἡμέραν τὴν ἐμήν.   Jn. viii. 56.

may be translated, "Your father Abraham rejoiced *when* he saw my day", if this theory is correct.

197. ὅτι also seems to be used in this sense in Jn. ix. 8 and xii. 41.

Dr Burney thinks that, as the word 'דְ can also be used as a relative pronoun, the following difficult passages are made more intelligible by taking ἵνα as a mistranslation of the Aramaic Relative: Jn. i. 8, v. 7, vi. 30, 50, ix. 36, xiv. 1.

ἵνα is used in Mk. iv. 22 where it makes little sense, but in the parallel passages in Mt. x. 26 and Lk. viii. 17 a Relative is used and makes excellent sense. See also Mk. iv. 12 and compare Mt. xiii. 13.

ὅτι also seems to be used as a mistranslation of the Aramaic Relative in Jn. i. 16, viii. 45 and ix. 17 and it is quite possible that the same mistake in translation has been made in Mk. iv. 41 and viii. 24. In the latter passage a Relative would give much better sense than the ordinary translation.

These strained or incorrect usages seem to be due rather to a desire to make a perfectly literal translation of an Aramaic document than to ignorance of Greek.

See Dr Torrey's *Four Gospels*, pp. 237, 241, 245, and his *Our Translated Gospels*, pp. lv and lix.

ADVERBIAL CLAUSES

198. Adverbial clauses are clauses that stand in the relationship of an adverb to some verb in another clause.

Adverbial clauses may be divided into eight classes. (See page 22.)

(1) Final clauses or clauses denoting Purpose

199. A final clause denotes the purpose of the action of the verb in the clause on which it depends.

Final clauses are introduced by the final particles ἵνα or ὅπως if affirmative, and by μή or ἵνα μή if negative, followed by a verb in the subjunctive mood in N.T. Greek.

Examples : He came that he might bear witness to the light.

ἦλθεν ἵνα μαρτυρήσῃ περὶ τοῦ φωτός.　　　Jn. i. 7.

Judge not that ye be not judged.

μὴ κρίνετε ἵνα μὴ κριθῆτε.　　　Mt. vii. 1.

And their eyes have they closed ; lest haply they should perceive with their eyes.

καὶ τοὺς ὀφθαλμοὺς αὐτῶν ἐκάμμυσαν, μή ποτε ἴδωσιν τοῖς ὀφθαλμοῖς.
Acts xxviii. 27.

200. A simple Infinitive, as might be expected from the fact that the infinitive was originally the dative case of a verbal noun, is sufficient by itself to form the verb in a final clause. See 138.

We have similar parallel uses in English of a clause introduced by *that* and a simple infinitive to express purpose.

We may say either *I sent my servant to call the guests.*

　　　or　　　*I sent my servant that he might call the guests.*

Example : And he sent his slaves to call them that were bidden to the marriage.

καὶ ἀπέστειλεν τοὺς δούλους αὐτοῦ καλέσαι τοὺς κεκλημένους εἰς τοὺς γάμους.　　　Matt. xxii. 3.

201. Purpose may even be expressed by ὥστε or ὡς with the inf. Matt. xxiv. 24, xxvii. 1, Lk. ix. 52.

202. The Infinitive with an article preceded by the prepositions εἰς or πρός or even an Infinitive preceded by the Genitive of the article may be used as the verb in a final clause.

Examples will be found in Matt. vi. 1, xx. 19, Lk. i. 77.
See 175.

203. The Present or Future Participle may also be used to form a final clause.

Examples : Unto you first God having raised up his Servant sent him to bless you.

ὑμῖν πρῶτον ἀναστήσας ὁ θεὸς τὸν Παῖδα αὐτοῦ ἀπέστειλεν αὐτὸν εὐλογοῦντα ὑμᾶς.　　　Acts iii. 26.

...I journeyed to Damascus to bring them also that were there unto Jerusalem in bonds.

...εἰς Δαμασκὸν ἐπορευόμην, ἄξων καὶ τοὺς ἐκεῖσε ὄντας δεδεμένους εἰς Ἱερουσαλήμ... Acts xxii. 5.

204. A Final clause may also be expressed by a relative clause with the verb in the Future Indicative. This construction is very rare.

See Matt. xxi. 41, Acts vi. 3.

(2) Temporal clauses or clauses denoting Time

205. A temporal clause denotes the time of the action of the verb in the clause on which it depends.

Temporal clauses are introduced by ὅτε or ὡς meaning *when*, ἕως etc. meaning *while* or *until*, πρίν meaning *before*.

206. Temporal clauses are divided into two classes :

(1) Those that refer to a definite event occurring at a definite time are called **definite** temporal clauses.

Example : *I saw him when I went to town.*

(2) Those that refer to an event or a series of events occurring at an indefinite time are called **indefinite** temporal clauses.

Examples : *I saw him whenever I went to town.*

That is to say *I went to town often and saw him every time.*

I will see him whenever I go to town.

That is to say *I have not been to town yet, and I do not know when I shall go ; but, when I do go, I will see him.*

It will be seen that these sentences have a conditional force.

The first might be expressed as follows.

If I went to town I saw him.

The second might be expressed as follows.

If I go to town I will see him.

207. In Greek these two kinds of clauses have quite distinct constructions.

(1) **Definite Temporal Clauses** are introduced by ὅτε or ὡς followed by the Indicative as in English.

Example : And it came to pass when Jesus had finished these words, he departed from Galilee.

καὶ ἐγένετο ὅτε ἐτέλεσεν ὁ Ἰησοῦς τοὺς λόγους τούτους, μετῆρεν ἀπὸ τῆς Γαλιλαίας. Matt. xix. 1.

208. (2) **Indefinite Temporal Clauses** are introduced by ὅτε followed by a verb in the **imperfect or aorist indicative** with ἄν or ἐάν when the clause refers to an indefinite number of actions in **past time.**

ὅτε and ἄν join together to form ὅταν.

Example : And the unclean spirits whenever they beheld him fell down before him.

καὶ τὰ πνεύματα τὰ ἀκάθαρτα ὅταν αὐτὸν ἐθεώρουν, προσέπιπτον αὐτῷ.　　　　　　　　　　　　　　　　　Mk. iii. 11.

209. Indefinite Temporal Clauses are introduced by ὅτε followed by a verb in the **subjunctive** with ἄν when the clause refers to **future time.**

Example : And whenever they lead you to judgement, and deliver you up, be not anxious beforehand what ye shall speak.

καὶ ὅταν ἄγωσιν ὑμᾶς παραδιδόντες, μὴ προμεριμνᾶτε τί λαλήσητε.
　　　　　　　　　　　　　　　　　Mk. xiii. 11.

It will be noticed that ἄν is used in Greek when the word *ever* can be attached to *when* in English.

210. There are a few instances in the N.T. where Temporal clauses are Indefinite in form, but Definite in meaning.

Example : But days will come when the bridegroom shall be taken away from them.

ἐλεύσονται δὲ ἡμέραι ὅταν ἀπαρθῇ ἀπ' αὐτῶν ὁ νυμφίος.　　Mk. ii. 20.
See also Lk. v. 35, xiii. 28 ; Rev. viii. 1.

211. Temporal Clauses introduced by ἕως *while* or *until.*

When ἕως means *while,* and the clause which it introduces refers to the same time as the verb in the clause on which it depends, it takes the **Indicative mood,** just as in English.

Example : We must work the works of him that sent me while it is day.

ἡμᾶς δεῖ ἐργάζεσθαι τὰ ἔργα τοῦ πέμψαντός με ἕως ἡμέρα ἐστίν.
　　　　　　　　　　　　　　　　　Jn. ix. 4.

212. When ἕως means *until,* and the clause which it introduces refers to an actual past fact, it takes a past tense of the Indicative mood, as in English.

Example : The star which they saw in the East went before them, till it came and stood over where the young child was.

ὁ ἀστήρ, ὃν εἶδον ἐν τῇ ἀνατολῇ, προῆγεν αὐτοὺς ἕως ἐλθὼν ἐπεστάθη ἐπάνω οὗ ἦν τὸ παιδίον.　　　　　　　　Mt. ii. 9.

213. When the clause introduced by ἕως depends on a verb denoting future or habitual action, and refers to the **future**, it takes the Subjunctive, generally with ἄν.

Examples : There abide until ye depart thence.

ἐκεῖ μένετε ἕως ἂν ἐξέλθητε ἐκεῖθεν.   Mk. vi. 10.

And goeth after that which is lost, until he find it.

καὶ πορεύεται ἐπὶ τὸ ἀπολωλὸς ἕως εὕρῃ αὐτό.   Lk. xv. 4.

214. When the clause introduced by ἕως depends on a verb in **past time** and refers to an event which was thought of as **future** at the time when the action of the principal verb took place, it takes the Subjunctive without ἄν (Optative in Classical Greek).

Example : He cast him into prison until he should pay the debt.

ἔβαλεν αὐτὸν εἰς φυλακὴν ἕως ἀποδῷ τὸ ὀφειλόμενον.

Mt. xviii. 30.

215. ἕως οὗ, ἕως ὅτου have the same meaning as ἕως, but are never used with ἄν.

Clauses introduced by ἄχρι, ἄχρι οὗ, ἄχρι ἧς ἡμέρας, μέχρι, μέχρις οὗ have in general the same construction as clauses introduced by ἕως.

216. Clauses introduced by πρίν or πρίν ἤ, before.

When the verb in the principal clause is **affirmative** the clause introduced by πρίν takes the **accusative and infinitive** construction.

Example : Verily I say to thee that, in this night, before the cock crow, thou shalt deny me thrice.

ἀμὴν λέγω σοι ὅτι ἐν ταύτῃ τῇ νυκτὶ πρὶν ἀλέκτορα φωνῆσαι τρὶς ἀπαρνήσῃ με.   Matt. xxvi. 34.

217. When the principal clause is **negative** the clause introduced by πρίν takes the same constructions as clauses introduced by ἕως.

But there are only two examples of such clauses in the N.T., Lk. ii. 26, Acts xxv. 16.

In the second of these examples the Optative is Classical, as often in the writings of St Luke.

218. Temporal clauses may also be expressed by a **Participle**, especially in the Genitive Absolute.

Examples : And when he came out, he saw a great multitude.

καὶ ἐξελθὼν εἶδεν πολὺν ὄχλον.   Mt. xiv. 14.

And when they got up into the boat, the wind ceased.

καὶ ἀναβάντων αὐτῶν εἰς τὸ πλοῖον ἐκόπασεν ὁ ἄνεμος.

Mt. xiv. 32.

N.   8

219. Temporal clauses may also be expressed by **Prepositions** with the **Infinitive** and an article.

ἐν τῷ = ἕως, Matt. xiii. 25 ; Lk. i. 21 ; Acts viii. 6.

πρὸ τοῦ = πρίν, Matt. vi. 8 ; Lk. ii. 21 ; Gal. ii. 12, iii. 23.

μετὰ τό = after, Matt. xxvi. 32 ; Acts i. 3.

(3) Local clauses or clauses denoting Place

220. **Local Clauses** denote the place where the action of the verb in the clause on which they depend is said to take place.

They are introduced by οὖ, ὅπου *where*, ὅθεν *whence* etc.

221. Local clauses are divided into two classes just as Temporal clauses are.

(1) **Definite Local Clauses** referring to a single definite place.

(2) **Indefinite Local Clauses** referring to a series of places, or to some indefinite place.

222. In the first class the verb is in the **Indicative** mood.

Example : Lay not up for yourselves treasures upon the earth, where moth and rust do consume.

μὴ θησαυρίζετε ὑμῖν θησαυροὺς ἐπὶ τῆς γῆς, ὅπου σὴς καὶ βρῶσις ἀφανίζει.   Matt. vi. 19.

223. In the second class the verb is in a past tense of the **Indicative mood with** ἄν when the clause refers to a series of places where an act occurred in past time.

Example : And wheresoever he entered into villages...they laid the sick in the market places...

καὶ ὅπου ἂν εἰσεπορεύετο εἰς κώμας...ἐν ταῖς ἀγοραῖς ἐτίθεσαν τοὺς ἀσθενοῦντας.   Mk. vi. 56.

224. When the clause refers to an indefinite place where an act is expected to occur in future time the verb is in the **Subjunctive mood with** ἄν or ἐάν.

Example : Wheresoever this gospel shall be preached in the whole world, that also which this woman hath done shall be told for a memorial of her.

ὅπου ἐὰν κηρυχθῇ τὸ εὐαγγέλιον τοῦτο ἐν ὅλῳ τῷ κόσμῳ, λαληθή-σεται καὶ ὃ ἐποίησεν αὕτη εἰς μνημόσυνον αὐτῆς.   Mt. xxvi. 13.

(4) Causal clauses or clauses denoting the Reason for the action of the verb in the clause on which they depend

225. Causal clauses are introduced by ἐπεί, ὅτι, ἐφ᾽ ᾧ, διότι, ἐπειδή etc. with a verb in the **Indicative mood** just as in English.

Example: I forgave thee all that debt because thou besoughtest me.

πᾶσαν τὴν ὀφειλὴν ἐκείνην ἀφῆκά σοι, ἐπεὶ παρεκάλεσάς με.

Matt. xviii. 32.

226. A causal clause may also be expressed by

(a) **A Genitive Absolute.**

Example: And since he had nothing wherewith to pay...

μὴ ἔχοντος δὲ αὐτοῦ ἀποδοῦναι.   Matt. xviii. 25.

227. (b) **A Participle** agreeing with some word in the main clause.

Example: Since he saw that it pleased the Jews he proceeded to take Peter also.

ἰδὼν δὲ ὅτι ἀρεστόν ἐστιν τοῖς Ἰουδαίοις προσέθετο συλλαβεῖν καὶ Πέτρον.   Acts xii. 3.

228. (c) An Infinitive with διά and an article, or an Infinitive with an article in the Dative case. Matt. xxiv. 12, 2 Cor. ii. 13.

229. (d) When ὡς is prefixed to a Causal participle it implies that the action denoted by the participle is supposed or asserted to be the cause of the action of the principal verb.

Whether it is the real cause or not is left doubtful, but it is generally implied that it is not the real cause of the action.

See also Acts xxiii. 20, xxvii. 30.

(5) Consecutive clauses or clauses denoting Result

230. **A Consecutive Clause** denotes the Result of the action of the verb in the clause on which it depends.

Consecutive Clauses are introduced by ὥστε followed by the **Infinitive or Indicative.**

231. ὥστε followed by the **Infinitive** expresses the result which the action of the verb in the principal clause is **calculated** to produce. This is the commoner form in the N.T.

Example: Becometh a tree, so that the birds come...

γίνεται δένδρον ὥστε ἐλθεῖν τὰ πετεινά,...

Matt. xiii. 32.

232. ὥστε with the **Indicative** expresses the result which **actually does follow** on the action of the verb in the principal clause.

Example : For God so loved the world that he gave his only begotten Son.

οὕτως γὰρ ἠγάπησεν ὁ θεὸς τὸν κόσμον, ὥστε τὸν Υἱὸν τὸν μονογενῆ ἔδωκεν....   Jn. iii. 16.

See also Gal. ii. 13.

But this distinction is not exactly observed in the N.T.

233. ὥστε often begins an independent clause with the meaning *and so* or *therefore*. Matt. xix. 6.

234. Sometimes an Infinitive is used without ὥστε to express consequence. See sections 139 and 176.

See Acts v. 3 ; Col. iv. 6; Heb. v. 5, vi. 10.

(6) Conditional clauses

235. A Conditional Clause and the principal clause with which it is connected make up a sentence which is commonly called a Conditional Sentence.

In such a sentence the conditional clause states a **supposition** and the principal clause states the **result** of the fulfilment of this supposition.

The conditional clause is generally spoken of as the **Protasis**, and the principal clause as the **Apodosis**[1].

Example : If you do this you will become rich.

Here *If you do this* is the Protasis and *you will become rich* is the Apodosis.

236. The Protasis is introduced by εἰ, *if*.

The particle ἄν is regularly joined to εἰ in the Protasis when the verb in the Protasis is in the **Subjunctive** Mood, εἰ combined with ἄν forms ἐάν, ἤν, ἄν.

The negative of the Protasis is μή and that of the Apodosis is οὐ. This is the rule in Classical Greek, but in N.T. Greek οὐ is often found in the Protasis when the verb is in the Indicative mood, especially in conditions of the first class given below.

237. The construction of Conditional sentences varies according as the time of the supposition is **Past, Present,** or **Future.**

[1] The Committee of Grammatical Terminology suggests the names "if clause" and "then clause" instead of Protasis and Apodosis.

Present or Past Suppositions

238. (1) Present or Past particular suppositions, implying **nothing** as to the **fulfilment** of the condition.

When the Protasis simply states a present or past particular supposition, implying nothing as to the fulfilment or non-fulfilment of the condition, a **present or past tense of the Indicative** is used in the Protasis : **any part** of the finite verb may stand in the Apodosis.

Examples. **Present time :**

If thou art the Son of God, command this stone...

εἰ υἱὸς εἶ τοῦ θεοῦ, εἰπὲ τῷ λίθῳ τούτῳ...   Lk. iv. 3.

Past time :

For if Abraham was justified by works, he hath whereof to glory.

εἰ γὰρ Ἀβραὰμ ἐξ ἔργων ἐδικαιώθη, ἔχει καύχημα.   Rom. iv. 2.

239. (2) **Supposition contrary to fact.**

When the Protasis states a present or past supposition implying that the condition **is not or was not fulfilled**, the **secondary tenses** of the **indicative** are used both in the protasis and the apodosis.

The verb in the apodosis nearly always has the adverb ἄν.

The Imperfect denotes continued action.

The Aorist simple fact.

The Pluperfect (rare) completed action.

The time of the action is implied in the **context** rather than expressed by the tense of the verb[1].

Examples. **Present Time :**

This man, if he were a prophet, would know who and what the woman is...

οὗτος εἰ ἦν προφήτης, ἐγίνωσκεν ἂν τίς καὶ ποταπὴ ἡ γυνή...
    Lk. vii. 39.

If thou knewest the gift of God, and who it is that speaketh with thee, thou wouldst have asked him...

εἰ ᾔδεις τὴν δωρεὰν τοῦ θεοῦ, καὶ τίς ἐστιν ὁ λέγων σοι,...σὺ ἂν ᾔτησας αὐτόν...   Jn. iv. 10.

If ye believed Moses ye would believe me.

εἰ γὰρ ἐπιστεύετε Μωυσεῖ, ἐπιστεύετε ἂν ἐμοί.   Jn. v. 46.

[1] But as a rough rule it may be said that the Imperfect expresses an unfulfilled condition in present time, and the Aorist expresses an unfulfilled condition in past time.

Past time :

For if they had known, they would not have crucified the Lord of Glory.

εἰ γὰρ ἔγνωσαν, οὐκ ἂν τὸν κύριον τῆς δόξης ἐσταύρωσαν.

1 Cor. ii. 8.

This construction is so unlike the English or Latin that it requires special attention.

The form which such sentences take in English is no help whatever to translating them into Greek.

The rule must be mastered and remembered.

Future Suppositions

240.   There are two forms of Future conditional sentences:

(1) The more vivid form.
(2) The less vivid form.

241.   (1)   In the more vivid form the **Subjunctive** with ἐάν is used in the Protasis, and the **Future Indicative** or some other form expressing future time is used in the Apodosis.

Example: If ye have faith as a grain of mustard seed, ye shall say...

ἐὰν ἔχητε πίστιν ὡς κόκκον σινάπεως, ἐρεῖτε τῷ ὄρει τούτῳ....

Matt. xvii. 20.

242.   The **Future Indicative** is sometimes used in the Protasis for greater vividness.

Example: If we deny him, he will deny us.

εἰ ἀρνησόμεθα, κἀκεῖνος ἀρνήσεται ἡμᾶς.   2 Tim. ii. 12.

243.   (2)   In the less vivid form the **Optative** is used in both Protasis and Apodosis, ἄν in Apodosis.

Example : If you were to do this, you would be a good man.

εἰ τοῦτο ποιοίης, ἀγαθὸς ἂν εἴης.

N.B.   This construction does not occur in its full form in the N.T In the following example the Protasis only occurs.

Example: But even if ye should suffer for righteousness sake, happy are ye.

ἀλλ' εἰ καὶ πάσχοιτε διὰ δικαιοσύνην, μακάριοι.   1 Pet. iii. 14.

General Suppositions

244. If the supposition refers to the occurrence of an act of a certain general class and the Apodosis states what is wont to happen if this act takes place at any time, the sentence is called a GENERAL SUPPOSITION.

If it is a supposition in present time the Protasis takes ἐάν with the Subjunctive, and the Apodosis takes the Present Indicative.

Example : If any man walk in the day, he stumbleth not.

ἐάν τις περιπατῇ ἐν τῇ ἡμέρᾳ, οὐ προσκόπτει.   Jn. xi. 9.

If the supposition is in past time the Protasis takes εἰ with the Optative and the Apodosis takes the Imperfect Indicative.

Example: If at any time he had anything, he used to give it.

εἰ τί ἔχοι, ἐδίδου.

This construction does not occur in the N.T.

The Conditional Participle

245. A Participle may be used as an equivalent to a Conditional clause.

It should generally be translated by a Conditional clause in English.

Example : How shall we escape, if we neglect so great salvation?

πῶς ἡμεῖς ἐκφευξόμεθα τηλικαύτας ἀμελήσαντες σωτηρίας;

Heb. ii. 3.

See also Lk. ix. 25; 1 Cor. xi. 29; Gal. vi. 9; 1 Tim. iv. 4.

245 *a*.   **Mixed Conditional Sentences.**

Certain cases occur in which conditional sentences are made up of a Protasis belonging to one of the classes enumerated above and an Apodosis belonging to another.

See Lk. xvii. 6; Jn. viii. 39; Acts viii. 31, xxiv. 19; 1 Cor. vii. 28.

(7) Concessive clauses

246. A Concessive clause denotes some fact which is regarded as likely to prevent or to have prevented the occurrence of the action of the verb in the clause on which it depends.

These clauses are introduced in English by the words *though* or *although*, and in Greek by εἰ καί, ἐὰν καί: καὶ εἰ, καὶ ἐάν with a Finite verb, or by καίπερ followed by a Participle.

Example: For although I am absent in the flesh, I am with you in the spirit.

εἰ γὰρ καὶ τῇ σαρκὶ ἄπειμι, ἀλλὰ τῷ πνεύματι σὺν ὑμῖν εἰμί.

Col. ii. 5.

Though he was a Son, yet he learned obedience by the things which he suffered.

καίπερ ὢν υἱός, ἔμαθεν ἀφ' ὧν ἔπαθεν τὴν ὑπακοήν.

Heb. v. 8.

247. καὶ εἰ and καὶ ἐάν occur but rarely in the N.T. The difference between εἰ (or ἐάν) καί and καὶ εἰ (καὶ ἐάν or κἄν) is that the former pair introduce a clause which states an admitted fact and the latter introduce a clause which makes an improbable suggestion. Compare the example given above with Matt. xxvi. 35:

Even if I must die with thee, I will not deny thee.

κἂν δέῃ με σὺν σοὶ ἀποθανεῖν, οὐ μή σε ἀπαρνήσομαι.

Compare also Jn. viii. 16.

248. A simple Participle may also serve to express a concessive clause.

Example: And though they found no cause of death in him, yet they asked of Pilate that he should be slain.

καὶ μηδεμίαν αἰτίαν θανάτου εὑρόντες ᾐτήσαντο Πειλᾶτον ἀναιρεθῆναι αὐτόν.   Acts xiii. 28.

(8) Comparative clauses

249. A Comparative clause compares the action or state denoted by the verb in the clause on which it depends with some other action or state.

Comparative clauses are introduced by ὡς, ὥσπερ, καθώς, etc. *as* or ἤ *than* followed by the Indicative as in English.

Examples: Shouldst not thou also have had mercy on thy fellow servant even as I had mercy on thee?

οὐκ ἔδει καὶ σὲ ἐλεῆσαι τὸν σύνδουλόν σου, ὡς κἀγὼ σὲ ἠλέησα;
Mt. xviii. 33.

It is easier for a camel to go through a needle's eye than for a rich man to enter into the kingdom of God.

εὐκοπώτερόν ἐστιν κάμηλον διὰ τρήματος ῥαφίδος εἰσελθεῖν ἢ πλούσιον εἰς τὴν βασιλείαν τοῦ θεοῦ.   Mt. xix. 24.

Compare also Mt. xxiv. 27.

ὡς in the sense of "as if" is sometimes followed by a Subjunctive, Mk. iv. 26; 1 Thess. ii. 7.

ADJECTIVAL CLAUSES

250. Adjectival clauses are introduced by the relative pronouns ὅς and ὅστις and the relative adjectives ὅσος and οἷος, and qualify some noun or pronoun in another clause just like an adjective. The noun which the adjectival clause qualifies is called its Antecedent.

For the rules which decide the number, gender and case of a relative pronoun see 60.

251. When an Adjectival, or Relative clause, as it is generally called, refers to an actual event or fact it is called a Definite Relative

Clause, and the verb is in the same mood and tense as it would be in English, except in the case of relative clauses in dependent statements, commands, or questions : see 156, 159.

Examples: After me cometh a man which is become before me.

ὀπίσω μου ἔρχεται ἀνὴρ ὃς ἔμπροσθέν μου γέγονεν.   Jn. i. 30.

The words which I have spoken unto you are spirit and are life.

τὰ ῥήματα ἃ ἐγὼ λελάληκα ὑμῖν πνεῦμά ἐστιν καὶ ζωή ἐστιν.

Jn. vi. 63.

252. When a relative clause refers to a supposed event or instance and hence implies a condition, it is called an **Indefinite or Conditional Relative Clause.** In the New Testament such relative clauses generally take a verb in the Subjunctive mood with ἄν or ἐάν

Example: Whosoever wishes to be great among you shall be your minister.

ἀλλ' ὃς ἂν θέλῃ μέγας γενέσθαι ἐν ὑμῖν ἔσται ὑμῶν διάκονος.

Mk. x. 43.

This might be equally well expressed by a conditional sentence:

If anyone wishes to be great among you he shall be your minister.

253. The Future or Present Indicative with or without ἄν is occasionally found in Indefinite relative clauses referring to the future.

See Mt. v. 41, x. 32, xviii. 4; Mk. xi. 25.

254. Adjectival clauses may also be introduced by the relative adverbs ὅτε, *when*, and οὗ, *whence*. Such clauses are rare in the New Testament. They are distinguished from Adverbial clauses of time and place in that they do not fix the time or place of the action of the main verb.

That is fixed already by some word in the principal clause which is the antecedent to the relative clause.

Examples : And at even, when the sun did set, they brought unto him all that were sick.

ὀψίας δὲ γενομένης, ὅτε ἔδυσεν ὁ ἥλιος, ἔφερον πρὸς αὐτὸν πάντας τοὺς κακῶς ἔχοντας.   Mk. i. 32.

And he came to Nazareth where he had been brought up.

καὶ ἦλθεν εἰς Ναζαρά, οὗ ἦν τεθραμμένος.   Lk. iv. 16.

PARTICIPLES

255. A **Participle** is a verbal adjective, sharing in the characteristics of both verbs and adjectives.

As a **verb** it has a subject, and, if it is the participle of a transitive verb in the active voice, it has an object. It has also tense and voice.

As an **adjective** it agrees with the noun which it qualifies in number, gender, and case.

256. A Participle may be used either **adjectivally** or **adverbially**.

When it is used **adjectivally** it limits the noun with which it agrees, just like an adjective.

It is generally best translated into English by a **relative clause**, especially when it is preceded by an article.

For an example see section 260.

When a participle is used **adverbially** it is equivalent to an adverbial clause modifying some other verb in the sentence.

Such participles are generally best translated into English by a suitable **adverbial clause**.

The context must decide which kind of adverbial clause the participle in question is equivalent to : the participle does not in itself denote purpose, condition, concession or time, etc., but the context implies some such idea and the participle admits it.

257. For the Participle as equivalent to a

Final clause see 203.

Temporal clause see 218

Causal clause see 227, 229.

Conditional clause see 245.

Concessive clause see 248.

258. The Participle may also denote the **means** by which the action of the principal verb is brought about, or the **manner** in which it is effected, or the **circumstances** which attend its performance.

Examples. **Means:**

Which of you by being anxious can add one cubit to his stature ?

τίς δὲ ἐξ ὑμῶν μεριμνῶν δύναται προσθεῖναι ἐπὶ τὴν ἡλικίαν αὐτοῦ πῆχυν ἕνα;   Mt. vi. 27.

Manner : But others mocking said....

ἕτεροι δὲ διαχλευάζοντες ἔλεγον.   Acts ii. 13.

ὡς is often inserted before a participle of Manner.

Example : For he taught them as one having authority and not as the scribes.

ἦν γὰρ διδάσκων αὐτοὺς ὡς ἐξουσίαν ἔχων καὶ οὐχ ὡς οἱ γραμματεῖς.
                                                                Mk. i. 22.

Attendant Circumstances :

And he taught in their synagogues being glorified of all.

καὶ αὐτὸς ἐδίδασκεν ἐν ταῖς συναγωγαῖς αὐτῶν, δοξαζόμενος ὑπὸ πάντων.   Lk. iv. 15.

And they beckoned to their partners in the other boat that they should come and help them.

καὶ κατένευσαν τοῖς μετόχοις ἐν τῷ ἑτέρῳ πλοίῳ τοῦ ἐλθόντας συλλαβέσθαι αὐτοῖς. Lk. v. 7.

Take Mark and bring him with thee.

Μάρκον ἀναλαβὼν ἄγε μετὰ σεαυτοῦ. 2 Tim. iv. 11.

The Participle of attendant circumstances is generally equivalent to a verb in a similar mood and tense to the principal verb joined to it by καί, and, as a rule, it is best to translate it so in English.

See the examples given above: in Lk. iv. 15 the participle is equivalent to an Imperfect Indicative joined to ἐδίδασκεν by καί. In Lk. v. 7 it is equivalent to an Infinitive. In 2 Tim. iv. 11 it is equivalent to an Imperative.

For the Participle in the Genitive Absolute see 35.

The Tenses of the Participle

259. In accordance with the principles mentioned in sections 108—112 the tenses of the participle do not denote time, but **state**.

The time of the action must be gathered from the context.

The Present Participle denotes action in progress.

It may be used to express

(1) Action going on at the same time as the action of the main verb.

Example: And they went forth, and preached everywhere, the Lord working with them, and confirming the word with signs following.

ἐκεῖνοι δὲ ἐξελθόντες ἐκήρυσσαν πανταχοῦ, τοῦ Κυρίου συνεργοῦντος, καὶ τὸν λόγον βεβαιοῦντος διὰ τῶν ἐπακολουθούντων σημείων.

Mk. xvi. 20.

(2) Action **identical** with that of the main verb, but described from a different point of view.

Example: This spake he, signifying by what death he should glorify God.

τοῦτο δὲ εἶπεν σημαίνων ποίῳ θανάτῳ δοξάσει τὸν θεόν.

Jn. xxi. 19.

260. The Present Participle may also be used simply to **define** its subject as belonging to a certain class, that is the class which does or suffers the action denoted by the verb from which it comes. In this case it becomes equivalent to **an adjective.** It is generally preceded by an article, and it is best translated into English by a relative clause.

Example : Blessed are they which do hunger and thirst after righteousness, for they shall be filled.

μακάριοι οἱ πεινῶντες καὶ διψῶντες τὴν δικαιοσύνην, ὅτι αὐτοὶ χορτασθήσονται.   Mt. v. 6.

261. The Present Participle sometimes denotes continued action at a time before the action of the main verb takes place. The time of the action has to be inferred from the context. This use corresponds to that of the Imperfect Indicative.

Example : For they are dead who sought the young child's life.

τεθνήκασι γὰρ οἱ ζητοῦντες τὴν ψυχὴν τοῦ παιδίου.   Mt. ii. 20.
See also Jn. xii. 17 ; Acts iv. 34 ; Gal. i. 23.

262. **The Aorist Participle** does not properly denote an act in past time, but an act regarded as a **simple event** without regard to its progress or completion.

As however it is difficult to conceive of an action as a simple event except in the past, the Aorist Participle generally denotes an action which took place before the action of the main verb : but this past sense is by no means necessarily a part of the meaning of the tense.

263. The Aorist Participle of **antecedent action.**

The Aorist Participle is most frequently used of an action which took place before the action of the main verb.

Examples : And having fasted forty days and forty nights, he afterwards hungered.

καὶ νηστεύσας ἡμέρας τεσσαράκοντα καὶ τεσσαράκοντα νύκτας ὕστερον ἐπείνασεν.   Mt. iv. 2.

But he that had been healed did not know who it was.

ὁ δὲ ἰαθεὶς οὐκ ᾔδει τίς ἐστίν.   Jn. v. 13.

I thank God...for the grace of God that was given you.

εὐχαριστῶ τῷ θεῷ...ἐπὶ τῇ χάριτι τοῦ θεοῦ τῇ δοθείσῃ ὑμῖν.
    1 Cor. i. 4.

264. The Aorist Participle of **identical action.**

The Aorist Participle sometimes denotes action identical with that of the main verb, but described from a different point of view.

In this case the action is obviously not antecedent in time to that of the main verb.

Example : I have sinned in that I betrayed innocent blood.

ἥμαρτον παραδοὺς αἷμα ἀθῷον.   Mt. xxvii. 4.

Compare also the common phrase ἀποκριθεὶς εἶπεν.

The Aorist Participle of identical action most frequently accompanies a verb in the Aorist Indicative, but it also occurs with the Future: Lk. ix. 25;

3 Jn. 6. It is also found with the Present and Imperfect: Mk. viii. 29; and with the Perfect; Acts xiii. 33.

265. The Future Participle represents an action as future with regard to the time of the main verb.

Example : Thou sowest not that body that shall be.

οὐ τὸ σῶμα τὸ γενησόμενον σπείρεις.   1 Cor. xv. 37.

It also denotes purpose :

It is not more than twelve days since I went up to worship at Jerusalem.

οὐ πλείους εἰσίν μοι ἡμέραι δώδεκα ἀφ᾽ ἧς ἀνέβην προσκυνήσων εἰς Ἱερουσαλήμ.   Acts xxiv. 11.

See also Mt. xxvii. 49.

266. The Perfect Participle denotes **completed** action. Like the Perfect Indicative it may have reference to past action and resulting state, or only to the resulting state.

Examples: Behold the men that had been sent by Cornelius...stood before the door.

ἰδοὺ οἱ ἄνδρες οἱ ἀπεσταλμένοι ὑπὸ τοῦ Κορνηλίου...ἐπέστησαν ἐπὶ τὸν πυλῶνα.   Acts x. 17.

Filled with all knowledge.

πεπληρωμένοι πάσης τῆς γνώσεως.   Rom. xv. 14.

But we preach Christ crucified.

ἡμεῖς δὲ κηρύσσομεν Χριστὸν ἐσταυρωμένον.   1 Cor. i. 23.

For the difference between the Present and the Perfect Participles compare together Mt. xxviii. 13 and Mt. xxvii. 52, also Mt. xviii. 12 & 13.

266 a. The difference between the Present, Aorist and Perfect Participles may be illustrated by the following (probably apocryphal) story.

A certain bishop, renowned for his studies in the Greek tenses, is said to have been asked by a certain person whose zeal exceeded his discretion whether he was " saved." The bishop is said to have replied " It all depends whether you mean σωζόμενος, σωθείς or σεσωσμένος. I trust I am σωζόμενος (in a state of salvation), I know I am σωθείς (saved once for all by the death of Christ), I hope to be σεσωσμένος (delivered from all danger of falling by being received into Heaven)[1]."

[1] Examples of the Present and Aorist Participles used in the senses mentioned above are to be seen in Acts ii. 47; 1 Cor. i. 18; 2 Tim. i. 9.

The Perfect Participle is used nearly in the sense given above in Eph. ii. 5.

N.B. The time denoted by a Participle is always relative to that of the main verb of the sentence in which it occurs, and must be inferred from it. It is not relative to the time of speaking.

See Lk. xv. 18 and 20. In the first of these two verses the time of the Participle ἀναστάς is future with regard to the time of speaking, but past with reference to the time of the main verb πορεύσομαι. In the second verse the time of the Participle is past both with regard to the time of speaking and with regard to the time of the main verb.

We translate the first *I will arise and go*, and the second *He arose and went*.

THE USE OF οὐ AND μή

267. The rules for the use of the negatives οὐ and μή and their compounds in the N.T. are as follows :

οὐ is direct and positive and negatives facts.

μή is doubtful and indirect and negatives conceptions and wishes.

οὐ is practically always used to negative verbs in the **Indicative** mood even in the protases of conditional sentences where μή is used in Classical Greek, but protases of conditional sentences denoting an unfulfilled condition generally take μή. See Rom. viii. 9 ; Jn. xviii. 30.

In clauses introduced by μή used as a final particle, and meaning *lest*, οὐ is always used as the negative. 2 Cor. xii. 20. See 192.

μή is always used to negative the **Subjunctive** (with the exception given above), the **Imperative**, and the **Optative**.

μή is regularly used to negative the **Infinitive** even in dependent statements where οὐ is used in Classical Greek. Mt. xxii. 23.

μή is regularly used to negative **Participles** and not confined, as it is in Classical Greek, to participles equivalent to conditional clauses etc.

The use of μή with a participle in the N.T. is not therefore to be taken as a sign that the participle is used in a conditional sense.

There are only about 17 instances of the use of οὐ with a participle in the N.T.

As a rough rule it will suffice to remember that in the New Testament οὐ is used with the Indicative mood and μή with the other moods.

Successive negatives in Greek strengthen the first negative, if the second is a compound negative like οὐδείς.

Example : He did not eat anything.

οὐκ ἔφαγεν οὐδέν.   Lk. iv. 2.

But if the second negative is a simple negative, it retains its force.

Example: It is not therefore not of the body.

οὐ παρὰ τοῦτο οὐκ ἔστιν ἐκ τοῦ σώματος.

1 Cor. xii. 15.

εἰ μή and ἐὰν μή are used as fixed phrases in the sense of *except* or *unless*. εἰ δὲ μήγε means *otherwise*.

When πᾶς is used to qualify the subject of a verb negatived by οὐ it must be translated *no*.

Example: Nothing shall be impossible with God.

οὐκ ἀδυνατήσει παρὰ τοῦ θεοῦ πᾶν ῥῆμα. Lk. i. 37.

See also Eph. v. 5, 1 Jn. ii. 21, Mk. xiii. 20.

MODES OF ASKING QUESTIONS

268. Very often the fact that a sentence is a question is only indicated by the mark of interrogation at the end. It must be remembered that these marks have been put in by the editors of the text, and not by the original writers, as such marks were unknown in their days.

Questions may also be introduced by the interrogative words τίς, εἰ, ποῖος, πότε, πῶς etc. and by οὐ and μή.

269. When οὐ is used to introduce a question it shows that an **affirmative** answer is expected. (Latin *nonne*.)

Example: Is not this the carpenter's son?

Nonne hic est fabri filius?

οὐχ οὗτός ἐστιν ὁ τοῦ τέκτονος υἱός; Mt. xiii. 55.

270. When μή is used to introduce a question it shows that a **negative** answer is expected. (Latin *num*.)

Example: Does our law judge any man, unless it hear first from him?

Numquid lex nostra judicat hominem, nisi prius audierat ab ipso?

μὴ ὁ νόμος ἡμῶν κρίνει τὸν ἄνθρωπον ἐὰν μὴ ἀκούσῃ πρῶτον παρ' αὐτοῦ; Jn. vii. 51.

μή is also used to ask tentative questions to which the answer *No* is expected on the whole.

Example: Can this be the Christ?

Numquid ipse est Christus?

μήτι οὗτός ἐστιν ὁ Χριστός; Jn. iv. 29.

271. For Deliberative questions see 121.

THE USE OF THE PARTICLE ἄν

272. The various uses of the Particle ἄν in the New Testament are collected here for convenience of reference.

We have no English word which corresponds to ἄν, the most that can be said is that it implies vagueness or uncertainty in the sentences where it occurs.

273. Its uses may be divided into two classes.

(1) Where it occurs after εἰ followed by a Subjunctive in the protasis of a conditional sentence, or after the relative words ὅς, οἷος, ὅσος, ὅτε, ἐπεί, οὗ, ὅπου, ἕως in indefinite relative clauses.

εἰ followed by ἄν becomes ἐάν or occasionally ἄν.

ὅτε followed by ἄν becomes ὅταν, ἐπεί becomes ἐπειδάν.

N.B. After relative words, especially ὅς, ἄν is often written ἐάν.

These uses are explained in sections 208, 209, 213, 223, 224, 241, 252.

274. (2) Where it occurs after a verb in a past tense of the Indicative or in the Optative mood in the apodosis of a conditional sentence to express the result of an unfulfilled condition or of a remote future condition. See sections 239, 243.

275. The first part of a conditional sentence is sometimes left out or understood, and ἄν with a past tense of the Indicative or an Optative stands alone. This use is known as the Potential use of ἄν. Such sentences are frequent in Classical Greek, but rare in the New Testament. It is sometimes difficult in such sentences to say what the condition would have been, if it had been expressed.

Examples : Wherefore gavest thou not my money into the bank, and I at my coming should have required it with interest ?

διὰ τί οὐκ ἔδωκάς μου τὸ ἀργύριον ἐπὶ τράπεζαν ; κἀγὼ ἐλθὼν σὺν
τόκῳ ἂν αὐτὸ ἔπραξα.   Lk. xix. 23.

I could pray to God that...all that hear me this day might become such as I am, except these bonds.

εὐξαίμην ἂν τῷ θεῷ...πάντας τοὺς ἀκούοντάς μου σήμερον γενέσθαι
τοιούτους ὁποῖος καὶ ἐγώ εἰμι, παρεκτὸς τῶν δεσμῶν τούτων. Acts xxvi. 29.

See also Acts viii. 31, xvii. 18.

276. ἄν occasionally occurs after ὅπως in the New Testament. This is a relic of a Classical use of which we are unable to express the force in English.

277. It also occurs with the Optative in Indirect Questions in Lk. i. 62, vi. 11, ix. 46 ; Acts v. 24, x. 17.

APPENDIX

The Greek verbs are not, like the Latin, divided into conjugations with various endings. All the verbs in -ω have the same endings, the differences between them being caused by variations in the stem.

The verb λύω which is commonly given as an example in Greek grammars has but one stem λυ- to which the tense endings are added.

Most verbs however have two stems : the Verbal Stem from which most of the tenses of the verb and derived words are formed, and the Present Stem from which the present and imperfect tenses are formed.

The verbs in the following table are divided into classes according to the changes which take place in the verbal stem.

They include all the verbs which occur most frequently in the New Testament.

The verbs in the last class are especially frequent and important.

CLASSES OF VERBS.

Class 1. Verbs in which the verbal stem and the present stem are the same.

Present	Future	Aorist	Perf. Act.	Perf. Pass.	Aorist Pass.	Meaning
ἄγω	ἄξω	ἤγαγον ἦξα			ἤχθην	drive or lead
ἀκούω	ἀκούσομαι also in N.T. ἀκούσω	ἤκουσα	ἀκήκοα		ἠκούσθην	hear
ἀνοίγω	ἀνοίξω	ἤνοιξα (ἀνέῳξα ἠνέῳξα)	ἀνέῳγα		ἠνοίχθην ἀνεῴχθην ἠνεῴχθην	open
ἄρχομαι	ἄρξομαι	ἠρξάμην				begin
βλέπω	βλέψω	ἔβλεψα				see
βούλομαι		ἠβουλόμην			ἐβουλήθην ἠβουλήθην	wish
γράφω	γράψω	ἔγραψα	γέγραφα	γέγραμμαι	ἐγράφθην	write
δέχομαι	δέξομαι	ἐδεξάμην		δέδεγμαι		receive
διδάσκω	διδάξω	ἐδίδαξα			ἐδιδάχθην	teach
δύναμαι	δυνήσομαι	ἠδυνάμην (Attic Imperfect)			ἠδυνήθην	am able
θέλω	θελήσω	ἠθέλησα				will
πείθω	πείσω	ἔπεισα	πέποιθα	πέπεισμαι	ἐπείσθην	persuade
πέμπω	πέμψω	ἔπεμψα			ἐπέμφθην	send
πιστεύω	πιστεύσω	ἐπίστευσα	πεπίστευκα	πεπίστευμαι	ἐπιστεύθην	believe
ἀγαπάω	ἀγαπήσω	ἠγάπησα	ἠγάπηκα			love

Most verbs in αω are conjugated like ἀγαπάω.

Present	Future	Aorist	Perf. Act. Present Ind. ζῶ, ζῇς, ζῇ, Inf. ζῆν	Perf. Pass.	Aorist Pass.	Meaning
ζάω	ζήσω	ἔζησα				live
ποιέω	ποιήσω	ἐποίησα	πεποίηκα	πεποίημαι	ἐποιήθην	make or do

Most verbs in εω are conjugated like ποιέω.

Present	Future	Aorist	Perf. Act.	Perf. Pass.	Aorist Pass.	Meaning
δοκέω		ἔδοξα				seem
καλέω	καλέσω	ἐκάλεσα	κέκληκα	κέκλημαι	ἐκλήθην	call
πληρόω	πληρώσω	ἐπλήρωσα	πεπλήρωκα	πεπλήρωμαι	ἐπληρώθην	fill

Verbs in οω are conjugated like πληρόω.

Class 2. Verbs with mute stems which have a diphthong or long vowel ε, ευ in all tenses except the second aorist where the vowels are short ι, υ.

Present	Future	Aorist				Meaning
φεύγω	φεύξομαι	ἔφυγον (2nd Aor.)				flee
καταλείπω	καταλείψω	κατέλειψα / κατέλιπον (2nd Aor.)				leave

Class 3. Verbs which add τ to the verbal stem in order to form the present stem.

Present	Future	Aorist	Perf. Act.	Perf. Pass.	Aorist Pass.	Meaning
ἀποκαλύπτω	ἀποκαλύψω	ἀπεκάλυψα			ἀπεκαλύφθην	reveal
ἐκκόπτω	ἐκκόψω	ἐξέκοψα			ἐξεκόπην	cut out
κρύπτω	κρύψω	ἔκρυψα	κέκρυφα	κέκρυμμαι	ἐκρύφθην / ἐκρύβην	hide
πίπτω	πεσοῦμαι	ἔπεσον	πέπτωκα			fall
τίκτω	τέξομαι	ἔτεκον			ἐτέχθην	bring forth

Class 4. Verbs in which the verbal stem ends in a guttural κ, γ, χ which is softened to σσ in the present stem.

Present	Future	Aorist	Perf. Act.	Perf. Pass.	Aorist Pass.	Meaning
κηρύσσω	κηρύξω	ἐκήρυξα	κεκήρυχα	κεκήρυγμαι	ἐκηρύχθην	proclaim
πράσσω	πράξω	ἔπραξα	πέπραχα	πέπραγμαι	ἐπράχθην	make or do

Class 5. Verbs ending in ζω in the present, these are formed from stems ending in δ with futures in σω, or from stems ending in γ or γγ with futures in ξω.

Present	Future	Aorist	Perf. Act.	Perf. Pass.	Aorist Pass.	Meaning
βαπτίζω	βαπτίσω	ἐβάπτισα		βεβάπτισμαι	ἐβαπτίσθην	baptise
σώζω	σώσω	ἔσωσα	σέσωκα	σέσωσμαι	ἐσώθην	save
κράζω	κεκράξομαι κράξω	ἔκραξα	κέκραγα			cry

Most verbs in ζω in the N.T. are conjugated like βαπτίζω.

Class 6. Verbs in which the verbal stem ends in a liquid λ, μ, ν, ρ.

Division 1, stems ending in λ which becomes λλ in the present.

ἀγγέλλω	ἀγγελῶ	ἤγγειλα	ἤγγελκα	ἤγγελμαι	ἠγγέλθην	announce
βάλλω	βαλῶ	ἔβαλον	βέβληκα	βέβλημαι	ἐβλήθην	throw
στέλλω	στελῶ	ἔστειλα	ἔσταλκα	ἔσταλμαι	ἐστάλην	send

Division 2, presents in αυνω and αμω formed from verbal stems in αυ- and αρ-.

αἴρω	ἀρῶ	ἦρα	ἦρκα	ἦρμαι	ἤρθην	take away
κερδαίνω	κερδανῶ	ἐκέρδανα				gain
	κερδήσω	ἐκέρδησα (these are the N.T. forms)				
φαίνω	φανοῦμαι				ἐφάνην	show forth
χαίρω	χαρήσομαι				ἐχάρην	rejoice

Division 3, presents in ευνω, ειρω, ῑνω, ῡρω, υνω, νρω, from stems in εν, ερ, ῑν, ῡρ, υν, νρ.

ἀποκτείνω	ἀποκτενῶ	ἀπέκτεινα			ἀπεκτάνθην	kill
γίνομαι γίγνομαι	γενήσομαι	ἐγενόμην	γέγονα	γεγένημαι	ἐγενήθην	become

Present	Future	Aorist	Perf. Act.	Perf. Pass.	Aorist Pass.	Meaning
ἐγείρω	ἐγερῶ	ἤγειρα	ἐγήγερκα	ἐγήγερμαι	ἠγέρθην	arouse
κρίνω	κρινῶ	ἔκρινα	κέκρικα	κέκριμαι	ἐκρίθην	judge
σπείρω	σπερῶ	ἔσπειρα		ἔσπαρμαι	ἐσπάρην	sow
φθείρω	φθερῶ	ἔφθειρα			ἐφθάρην	destroy

Class 7. Verbs which add ν or αν to the verbal stem to form the present stem.

ἁμαρτάνω	ἁμαρτήσω	ἡμάρτησα / ἥμαρτον	ἡμάρτηκα			sin
αὐξάνω	αὐξήσω	ηὔξησα			ηὐξήθην	increase
βαίνω	βήσομαι	ἔβην	βέβηκα			go
πίνω	πίομαι	ἔπιον	πέπωκα			drink

If the last vowel of the stem is short another ν which changes to μ or γ before a labial or guttural is added after the vowel.

λαμβάνω	λήψομαι	ἔλαβον	εἴληφα	εἴλημμαι	ἐλήφθην	take

Verbal stem λαβ, double augment instead of reduplication in the perfect.

μανθάνω	μαθήσομαι	ἔμαθον	μεμάθηκα			learn
τυγχάνω	τεύξομαι	ἔτυχον				happen

Class 8. Verbs which add σκ or ισκ to the verbal stem to form the present stem.

ἀποθνήσκω	ἀποθανοῦμαι	ἀπέθανον				die
ἀρέσκω	ἀρέσω	ἤρεσα				please
γιγνώσκω	γνώσομαι	ἔγνων	ἔγνωκα	ἔγνωσμαι	ἐγνώσθην	know
εὑρίσκω	εὑρήσω	εὗρον	εὕρηκα		εὑρέθην	find

Class 9. Verbs in μι.

Present	Future	Aorist	Perf. Act.	Perf. Pass.	Aorist Pass.	Meaning
ἀπόλλυμι ἀπολλύω	ἀπολέσω -λέσω ἀπολῶ	ἀπόλεσα ἀπωλόμην 2nd Aor. Mid.	ἀπόλωλα			destroy
ἀφίημι	ἀφήσω	ἀφῆκα	ἀφῆκα	ἀφέωνται (Doric 3rd pl.)	ἀφέθην	forgive
δείκνυμι δεικνύω	δείξω	ἔδειξα				show
δίδωμι	δώσω	ἔδωκα	δέδωκα	δέδομαι	ἐδόθην	give
ἵστημι	στήσω	ἔστησα ἔστην	ἕστηκα	ἕσταμαι	ἐστάθην	cause to stand
τίθημι	θήσω	ἔθηκα	τέθεικα	τέθειμαι	ἐτέθην	place
εἰμί	ἔσομαι	Imperfect ἦν				be
φημί		Imperfect ἔφην				say

Class 10. Defective verbs whose parts are formed by putting together tenses formed from several distinct verbal stems of the same meaning.

Present	Future	Aorist	Perf. Act.	Perf. Pass.	Aorist Pass.	Meaning
αἱρέω	αἱρήσω -ελῶ	-εἷλον			-ῃρέθην	take
ἔρχομαι	ἐλεύσομαι	ἦλθον	ἐλήλυθα			come or go
ἐσθίω	φάγομαι	ἔφαγον				eat
ἔχω	ἕξω	ἔσχον	ἔσχηκα Imperfect εἶχον			have
λέγω	λέξω ἐρῶ	ἔλεξα εἶπον	εἴρηκα	λέλεγμαι εἴρημαι	ἐλέχθην ἐρρέθην ἐρρήθην	say
ὁράω	ὄψομαι	εἶδον	ἑώρακα ἑόρακα		ὤφθην	see
πάσχω		ἔπαθον	πέπονθα			suffer
φέρω	οἴσω	ἤνεγκον ἤνεγκα	ἐνήνοχα		ἠνέχθην	bear

APPENDIX I

ILLUSTRATIVE PASSAGE FROM THE NEW TESTAMENT.

The numbers in the foot-notes refer to paragraphs in the Syntax.

Ἀνὴρ δέ τις ἐν Καισαρίᾳ [1]ὀνόματι Κορνήλιος, ἑκατοντάρχης ἐκ σπείρης τῆς καλουμένης Ἰταλικῆς, εὐσεβὴς καὶ [2]φοβούμενος τὸν Θεὸν σὺν παντὶ τῷ οἴκῳ αὐτοῦ, ποιῶν ἐλεημοσύνας πολλὰς τῷ λαῷ καὶ δεόμενος [3]τοῦ Θεοῦ διὰ παντός, εἶδεν ἐν ὁράματι φανερῶς, ὡσεὶ περὶ ὥραν ἐνάτην τῆς ἡμέρας, ἄγγελον τοῦ Θεοῦ [4]εἰσελθόντα πρὸς αὐτὸν καὶ εἰπόντα αὐτῷ Κορνήλιε. ὁ δὲ ἀτενίσας αὐτῷ καὶ ἔμφοβος γενόμενος εἶπεν Τί ἐστιν, Κύριε; εἶπεν δὲ αὐτῷ Αἱ προσευχαί σου καὶ αἱ ἐλεημοσύναι σου [5]ἀνέβησαν εἰς μνημόσυνον ἔμπροσθεν τοῦ Θεοῦ. καὶ νῦν [6]πέμψον ἄνδρας εἰς Ἰόππην καὶ [6]μετάπεμψαι Σίμωνά τινα ὃς ἐπικαλεῖται Πέτρος· οὗτος ξενίζεται παρά τινι Σίμωνι βυρσεῖ, [7]ᾧ ἐστιν οἰκία παρὰ θάλασσαν. ὡς δὲ ἀπῆλθεν ὁ ἄγγελος [8]ὁ λαλῶν αὐτῷ, φωνήσας δύο τῶν οἰκετῶν καὶ στρατιώτην εὐσεβῆ τῶν προσκαρτερούντων αὐτῷ, καὶ ἐξηγησάμενος ἅπαντα αὐτοῖς ἀπέστειλεν αὐτοὺς εἰς τὴν Ἰόππην. Τῇ δὲ ἐπαύριον [9]ὁδοιπορούντων ἐκείνων καὶ τῇ πόλει ἐγγιζόντων ἀνέβη Πέτρος ἐπὶ τὸ δῶμα [10]προσεύξασθαι περὶ ὥραν ἕκτην. ἐγένετο δὲ πρόσπεινος καὶ ἤθελεν γεύσασθαι· παρασκευαζόντων δὲ αὐτῶν ἐγένετο ἐπ' αὐτὸν ἔκστασις, καὶ [11]θεωρεῖ τὸν οὐρανὸν [12]ἀνεῳγμένον καὶ καταβαῖνον σκεῦός τι ὡς ὀθόνην μεγάλην, τέσσαρσιν ἀρχαῖς καθιέμενον ἐπὶ τῆς γῆς, ἐν ᾧ [13]ὑπῆρχεν πάντα τὰ τετράποδα καὶ ἑρπετὰ τῆς γῆς καὶ πετεινὰ τοῦ οὐρανοῦ. καὶ ἐγένετο φωνὴ πρὸς αὐτόν [14]Ἀναστάς, Πέτρε,

---

[1] ὀνόματι 41.　　[2] φοβούμενος 260.　　[3] τοῦ Θεοῦ 34 (5).　　[4] εἰσελθόντα...καὶ εἰπόντα 262, 150; these aorist participles have a present sense with reference to the main verb: contrast with ἀτενίσας καὶ ἔμφοβος γενόμενος below, see 263.　　[5] ἀνέβησαν 105.　　[6] πέμψον, μετάπεμψαι 125, 81.　[7] ᾧ 39.　　[8] ὁ λαλῶν 260.　　[9] ὁδοιπορούντων ἐκείνων 35.　　[10] προσεύξασθαι 138.　　[11] θεωρεῖ 88.　　[12] ἀνεῳγμένον 266, 150.　　[13] ὑπῆρχεν 10.　[14] ἀναστὰς θῦσον καὶ φάγε, participle of attendant circumstances 258.

θῦσον καὶ φάγε. ὁ δὲ Πέτρος εἶπεν Μηδαμῶς, Κύριε, ὅτι οὐδέποτε [15]ἔφαγον
πᾶν κοινὸν καὶ ἀκάθαρτον. καὶ φωνὴ πάλιν ἐκ δευτέρου πρὸς αὐτόν˙Α ὁ
Θεὸς [16]ἐκαθάρισεν σὺ μὴ [17]κοίνου. τοῦτο δὲ ἐγένετο ἐπὶ τρίς, καὶ εὐθὺς
ἀνελήμφθη τὸ σκεῦος εἰς τὸν οὐρανόν. Ὡς δὲ ἐν ἑαυτῷ διηπόρει ὁ Πέτρος
[18]τί ἂν εἴη τὸ ὅραμα ὃ [19]εἶδεν, ἰδοὺ οἱ ἄνδρες οἱ [20]ἀπεσταλμένοι ὑπὸ τοῦ
Κορνηλίου [21]διερωτήσαντες τὴν οἰκίαν τοῦ Σίμωνος ἐπέστησαν ἐπὶ τὸν
πυλῶνα, καὶ φωνήσαντες ἐπυνθάνοντο εἰ Σίμων ὁ ἐπικαλούμενος Πέτρος
ἐνθάδε [22]ξενίζεται. Τοῦ δὲ Πέτρου διενθυμουμένου περὶ τοῦ ὁράματος εἶπεν
τὸ Πνεῦμα Ἰδοὺ ἄνδρες δύο ζητοῦντές σε˙ ἀλλὰ ἀναστὰς κατάβηθι, καὶ
πορεύου σὺν αὐτοῖς μηδὲν διακρινόμενος, ὅτι ἐγὼ ἀπέσταλκα αὐτούς.
καταβὰς δὲ Πέτρος πρὸς τοὺς ἄνδρας εἶπεν Ἰδοὺ ἐγώ εἰμι ὃν ζητεῖτε˙ τίς ἡ
αἰτία δι᾽ ἣν πάρεστε; οἱ δὲ εἶπαν Κορνήλιος ἑκατοντάρχης, ἀνὴρ δίκαιος καὶ
φοβούμενος τὸν Θεόν, μαρτυρούμενός τε ὑπὸ ὅλου τοῦ ἔθνους τῶν Ἰουδαίων,
ἐχρηματίσθη ὑπὸ ἀγγέλου ἁγίου [23]μεταπέμψασθαί σε εἰς τὸν οἶκον αὐτοῦ
καὶ ἀκοῦσαι ῥήματα παρὰ σοῦ. εἰσκαλεσάμενος οὖν αὐτοὺς ἐξένισεν. Τῇ
δὲ ἐπαύριον ἀναστὰς ἐξῆλθεν σὺν αὐτοῖς, καί τινες τῶν ἀδελφῶν τῶν ἀπὸ
Ἰόππης συνῆλθον αὐτῷ. τῇ δὲ ἐπαύριον εἰσῆλθεν εἰς τὴν Καισαρίαν· ὁ δὲ
Κορνήλιος [24]ἦν προσδοκῶν αὐτούς, συνκαλεσάμενος τοὺς συγγενεῖς αὐτοῦ
καὶ τοὺς ἀναγκαίους φίλους. Ὡς δὲ ἐγένετο [25]τοῦ εἰσελθεῖν τὸν Πέτρον,
συναντήσας αὐτῷ ὁ Κορνήλιος πεσὼν ἐπὶ τοὺς πόδας προσεκύνησεν. ὁ δὲ
Πέτρος ἤγειρεν αὐτὸν [26]λέγων Ἀνάστηθι· καὶ ἐγὼ αὐτὸς ἄνθρωπός εἰμι.
καὶ συνομιλῶν αὐτῷ εἰσῆλθεν, καὶ εὑρίσκει συνεληλυθότας πολλούς, ἔφη τε
πρὸς αὐτοὺς Ὑμεῖς ἐπίστασθε ὡς ἀθέμιτόν ἐστιν ἀνδρὶ Ἰουδαίῳ κολλᾶσθαι
ἢ προσέρχεσθαι ἀλλοφύλῳ· κἀμοὶ ὁ Θεὸς ἔδειξεν [27]μηδένα κοινὸν ἢ
ἀκάθαρτον λέγειν ἄνθρωπον· διὸ καὶ ἀναντιρρήτως ἦλθον μεταπεμφθείς.
πυνθάνομαι οὖν τίνι λόγῳ μετεπέμψασθέ με; καὶ ὁ Κορνήλιος ἔφη Ἀπὸ
τετάρτης ἡμέρας μέχρι ταύτης τῆς ὥρας ἤμην [28]τὴν ἐνάτην προσευχόμενος
ἐν τῷ οἴκῳ μου, καὶ ἰδοὺ ἀνὴρ ἔστη ἐνώπιόν μου ἐν ἐσθῆτι λαμπρᾷ, καὶ
φησίν Κορνήλιε, [29]εἰσηκούσθη σου ἡ προσευχὴ καὶ αἱ ἐλεημοσύναι σου
ἐμνήσθησαν ἐνώπιον τοῦ Θεοῦ. πέμψον οὖν εἰς Ἰόππην καὶ μετακάλεσαι
Σίμωνα ὃς ἐπικαλεῖται Πέτρος· οὗτος ξενίζεται ἐν οἰκίᾳ Σίμωνος βυρσέως
παρὰ θάλασσαν. ἐξαυτῆς οὖν ἔπεμψα πρὸς σέ, σύ τε καλῶς [30]ἐποίησας
[31]παραγενόμενος. νῦν οὖν πάντες ἡμεῖς ἐνώπιον τοῦ Θεοῦ πάρεσμεν

[15] ἔφαγον 105.   [16] ἐκαθάρισεν 105.   [17] κοίνου 127.   [18] τί ἂν εἴη
161.   [19] εἶδεν 100.   [20] ἀπεσταλμένοι 266.   [21] διερωτήσαντες 263.
[22] ξενίζεται 160.   [23] μεταπέμψασθαι 159.   [24] ἦν προσδοκῶν 114.
[25] τοῦ εἰσελθεῖν τὸν Πέτρον 177.   [26] λέγων 259.   [27] μηδένα κοινὸν λέγειν
ἄνθρωπον 267, 145–148.   [28] τὴν ἐνάτην (understand ὥραν) 18.   [29] εἰσ-
ηκούσθη...ἐμνήσθησαν 106.   [30] ἐποίησας 105.   [31] παραγενόμενος 264.

ἀκοῦσαι πάντα τὰ προστεταγμένα σοι ὑπὸ τοῦ Κυρίου. Ἀνοίξας δὲ Πέτρος τὸ στόμα εἶπεν Ἐπ' ἀληθείας καταλαμβάνομαι ὅτι οὐκ ἔστιν προσωπολήμπτης ὁ Θεός, ἀλλ' ἐν παντὶ ἔθνει ὁ φοβούμενος αὐτὸν καὶ ἐργαζόμενος δικαιοσύνην δεκτὸς αὐτῷ ἐστιν· τὸν λόγον ὃν ἀπέστειλεν τοῖς υἱοῖς Ἰσραὴλ εὐαγγελιζόμενος εἰρήνην διὰ Ἰησοῦ Χριστοῦ· οὗτός ἐστιν πάντων Κύριος. ὑμεῖς οἴδατε τὸ γενόμενον ῥῆμα καθ' ὅλης τῆς Ἰουδαίας, ἀρξάμενος ἀπὸ τῆς Γαλιλαίας μετὰ τὸ βάπτισμα ὃ ἐκήρυξεν Ἰωάνης, Ἰησοῦν τὸν ἀπὸ Ναζαρέθ, ὡς ἔχρισεν αὐτὸν ὁ Θεὸς Πνεύματι Ἁγίῳ καὶ δυνάμει, ὃς διῆλθεν εὐεργετῶν καὶ ἰώμενος πάντας τοὺς καταδυναστευομένους ὑπὸ τοῦ διαβόλου, ὅτι ὁ Θεὸς ἦν μετ' αὐτοῦ· καὶ ἡμεῖς μάρτυρες πάντων [32]ὧν ἐποίησεν ἔν τε τῇ χώρᾳ τῶν Ἰουδαίων καὶ Ἱερουσαλήμ· ὃν καὶ ἀνεῖλαν κρεμάσαντες ἐπὶ ξύλου. τοῦτον ὁ Θεὸς ἤγειρεν ἐν τῇ τρίτῃ ἡμέρᾳ καὶ ἔδωκεν αὐτὸν ἐμφανῆ γενέσθαι, οὐ παντὶ τῷ λαῷ, ἀλλὰ μάρτυσιν τοῖς [33]προκεχειροτονημένοις ὑπὸ τοῦ Θεοῦ, ἡμῖν, οἵτινες συνεφάγομεν καὶ συνεπίομεν αὐτῷ [34]μετὰ τὸ ἀναστῆναι αὐτὸν ἐκ νεκρῶν· καὶ παρήγγειλεν ἡμῖν κηρύξαι τῷ λαῷ καὶ διαμαρτύρασθαι ὅτι οὗτός ἐστιν ὁ [35]ὡρισμένος ὑπὸ τοῦ Θεοῦ Κριτὴς ζώντων καὶ νεκρῶν. τούτῳ πάντες οἱ προφῆται μαρτυροῦσιν, ἄφεσιν ἁμαρτιῶν [36]λαβεῖν διὰ τοῦ ὀνόματος αὐτοῦ πάντα τὸν πιστεύοντα εἰς αὐτόν. Ἔτι λαλοῦντος τοῦ Πέτρου τὰ ῥήματα ταῦτα ἐπέπεσεν τὸ Πνεῦμα τὸ Ἅγιον ἐπὶ πάντας τοὺς ἀκούοντας τὸν λόγον. καὶ ἐξέστησαν οἱ ἐκ περιτομῆς πιστοὶ ὅσοι συνῆλθαν τῷ Πέτρῳ, ὅτι καὶ ἐπὶ τὰ ἔθνη ἡ δωρεὰ τοῦ Ἁγίου Πνεύματος ἐκκέχυται· ἤκουον γὰρ [37]αὐτῶν λαλούντων γλώσσαις καὶ μεγαλυνόντων τὸν Θεόν. τότε ἀπεκρίθη Πέτρος [38]Μήτι τὸ ὕδωρ δύναται κωλῦσαί τις [39]τοῦ μὴ βαπτισθῆναι τούτους, οἵτινες τὸ Πνεῦμα τὸ Ἅγιον [40]ἔλαβον ὡς καὶ ἡμεῖς; προσέταξεν δὲ αὐτοὺς ἐν τῷ ὀνόματι Ἰησοῦ Χριστοῦ βαπτισθῆναι. τότε ἠρώτησαν αὐτὸν ἐπιμεῖναι ἡμέρας τινάς. Acts x.

---

[32] ὧν 63.   [33] προκεχειροτονημένοις 266.   [34] μετὰ τὸ ἀναστῆναι αὐτόν 219. [35] ὡρισμένος 266.   [36] λαβεῖν 145–148; the infinitive seems to represent a timeless aorist in direct speech 151, 152, 91, 105.   [37] αὐτῶν λαλούντων 34 (3).   [38] μήτι 270.   [39] τοῦ μὴ βαπτισθῆναι 175, 34 (5), 178; the two ideas of purpose and prevention seem to be combined here.   [40] ἔλαβον 105.

APPENDIX II

The following selection of passages from Christian authors of the first two centuries has been added to this book in the hope that it may be useful to those who wish for some further knowledge of Greek than that which can be obtained from the study of a book whose contents are so familiar to them in an English version as are the contents of the Greek Testament.

In language and construction these passages very closely resemble the Greek Testament, but their subject-matter is unfamiliar, and this makes the study of them far more valuable as an exercise than the study of passages, the general meaning of which is well known.

References have been given in the footnotes to the paragraphs of the Syntax which explain the constructions which occur in these passages so far as they seem to stand in need of explanation.

A translation of the more uncommon words is also given.

It is hoped that these selections may prove interesting and valuable as affording first hand information about the beliefs and practices of the Christians of the first two centuries.

AN EARLY ACCOUNT OF THE ADMINISTRATION OF THE SACRAMENTS, FROM THE "TEACHING OF THE TWELVE APOSTLES." DATE ABOUT 100 A.D.

Περὶ δὲ τοῦ βαπτίσματος, οὕτω βαπτίσατε· ταῦτα πάντα προειπόντες βαπτίσατε [1] εἰς τὸ ὄνομα τοῦ Πατρὸς καὶ τοῦ Υἱοῦ καὶ τοῦ ἁγίου Πνεύματος ἐν ὕδατι ζῶντι. [2] ἐὰν δὲ μὴ ἔχῃς ὕδωρ ζῶν, εἰς ἄλλο ὕδωρ βάπτισον· [3] εἰ δ'

---

[1] Cf. Matt. xxviii. 19.   [2] ἐὰν δὲ μὴ ἔχῃς 241.   [3] εἰ δ' οὐ δύνασαι. This sentence if fully expressed would run εἰ δ' οὐ δύνασαι ἐν ψυχρῷ βαπτίζειν, ἐν θερμῷ βάπτισον. The Present indicative with εἰ is used here in exactly the same sense as the Subjunctive with ἐὰν above. For οὐ in the Protasis of a Conditional sentence see 267.

οὐ δύνασαι ἐν ψυχρῷ, ἐν θερμῷ. ἐὰν δὲ ἀμφότερα μὴ ἔχῃς, ἔκχεον εἰς τὴν κεφαλὴν τρὶς ὕδωρ εἰς ὄνομα Πατρὸς καὶ Υἱοῦ καὶ ἁγίου Πνεύματος. πρὸ δὲ τοῦ βαπτίσματος προνηστευσάτω [4]ὁ βαπτίζων καὶ [5]ὁ βαπτιζόμενος καὶ εἴ τινες ἄλλοι δύνανται. κελεύεις δὲ νηστεῦσαι τὸν βαπτιζόμενον [6]πρὸ μιᾶς ἢ δύο.

[4] ὁ βαπτίζων, for the meaning of a Present participle preceded by an article see 260.   [5] ὁ βαπτιζόμενος, τὸν βαπτιζόμενον, for the use of the Present to denote an action desired see 86.   [6] πρὸ μιᾶς ἢ δύο, understand ἡμέρας, and translate one or two days before.

Περὶ δὲ τῆς εὐχαριστίας, οὕτω εὐχαριστήσατε· πρῶτον περὶ τοῦ ποτηρίου· Εὐχαριστοῦμέν σοι, Πάτερ ἡμῶν, ὑπὲρ τῆς ἁγίας ἀμπέλου Δαυεὶδ τοῦ παιδός σου, [1]ἧς ἐγνώρισας ἡμῖν διὰ Ἰησοῦ τοῦ παιδός σου· σοὶ ἡ δόξα εἰς τοὺς αἰῶνας. περὶ δὲ τοῦ [2]κλάσματος· Εὐχαριστοῦμέν σοι, Πάτερ ἡμῶν, ὑπὲρ τῆς ζωῆς καὶ γνώσεως, [1]ἧς ἐγνώρισας ἡμῖν διὰ Ἰησοῦ τοῦ παιδός σου· [3]σοὶ ἡ δόξα εἰς τοὺς αἰῶνας. ὥσπερ ἦν τοῦτο [4]τὸ κλάσμα [5]διεσκορπισμένον ἐπάνω τῶν ὀρέων καὶ [6]συναχθὲν ἐγένετο ἕν, οὕτω συναχθήτω σου ἡ ἐκκλησία ἀπὸ τῶν περάτων τῆς γῆς εἰς τὴν σὴν βασιλείαν· ὅτι σοῦ ἐστιν ἡ δόξα καὶ ἡ δύναμις διὰ Ἰησοῦ Χριστοῦ εἰς τοὺς αἰῶνας. [7]μηδεὶς δὲ φαγέτω μηδὲ πιέτω ἀπὸ τῆς εὐχαριστίας ὑμῶν, ἀλλ' οἱ βαπτισθέντες εἰς ὄνομα Κυρίου. καὶ γὰρ περὶ τούτου εἴρηκεν ὁ Κύριος· [8]Μὴ δῶτε τὸ ἅγιον τοῖς κυσί.

μετὰ δὲ τὸ [9]ἐμπλησθῆναι οὕτως εὐχαριστήσατε· Εὐχαριστοῦμέν σοι, Πάτερ ἅγιε, ὑπὲρ τοῦ ἁγίου ὀνόματός σου, [1]οὗ κατεσκήνωσας ἐν ταῖς καρδίαις ἡμῶν, καὶ ὑπὲρ τῆς γνώσεως καὶ πίστεως καὶ ἀθανασίας, [1]ἧς ἐγνώρισας ἡμῖν διὰ Ἰησοῦ τοῦ παιδός σου· σοὶ ἡ δόξα εἰς τοὺς αἰῶνας. σύ, δέσποτα παντοκράτορ, ἔκτισας τὰ πάντα ἕνεκεν τοῦ ὀνόματός σου, τροφήν τε καὶ ποτὸν ἔδωκας τοῖς ἀνθρώποις εἰς ἀπόλαυσιν [10]ἵνα σοι εὐχαριστήσωσιν, ἡμῖν δὲ [11]ἐχαρίσω πνευματικὴν τροφὴν καὶ ποτὸν καὶ ζωὴν αἰώνιον διὰ τοῦ παιδός σου. πρὸ πάντων εὐχαριστοῦμέν σοι ὅτι δυνατὸς εἶ σύ· σοὶ ἡ δόξα εἰς τοὺς αἰῶνας. μνήσθητι, Κύριε, [12]τῆς ἐκκλησίας σου [13]τοῦ ῥύσασθαι αὐτὴν ἀπὸ παντὸς πονηροῦ καὶ τελειῶσαι αὐτὴν ἐν τῇ ἀγάπῃ σου, καὶ σύναξον αὐτὴν ἀπὸ τῶν τεσσάρων ἀνέμων,

[1] ἧς, for assimilation of Relative see 63.   [2] κλάσματος, cf. 1 Cor. x. 16.
[3] Understand ἐστί.   [4] κλάσμα, Broken bread.   [5] ἦν διεσκορπισμένον, Periphrastic Pluperfect 114, translate was scattered, see 99.   [6] συναχθέν 263, 218.   [7] μηδεὶς δὲ φαγέτω, for the use of the Present imperative to forbid the habitual doing of an action see 128, let no one ever eat or drink....
[8] μὴ δῶτε, for the use of the Aorist subjunctive to forbid the beginning of an action see 129.   [9] ἐμπλησθῆναι 1st Aor. Inf. Pass. from ἐμπίμπλημι: for const. see 219.   [10] ἵνα 189.   [11] ἐχαρίσω 2nd sing. 1st Aor. mid. from χαρίζομαι.   [12] τῆς ἐκκλησίας 34.   [13] τοῦ ῥύσασθαι 174, 175.

[14]τὴν ἁγιασθεῖσαν εἰς τὴν σὴν βασιλείαν, ἣν ἡτοίμασας αὐτῇ· ὅτι σοῦ ἐστιν
ἡ δύναμις καὶ ἡ δόξα εἰς τοὺς αἰῶνας. ἐλθέτω χάρις καὶ παρελθέτω ὁ κόσμος
οὗτος. ὡσαννὰ τῷ θεῷ Δαυείδ. εἴ τις ἅγιός ἐστιν, [15]ἐρχέσθω· εἴ τις [16]οὐκ
ἐστί, μετανοείτω. [17]μαρὰν ἀθά. ἀμήν. τοῖς δὲ προφήταις ἐπιτρέπετε
εὐχαριστεῖν ὅσα θέλουσιν.

[14] τὴν ἁγιασθεῖσαν with αὐτήν, *her that has been sanctified* 71, 262.
[15] ἐρχέσθω, for the force of the Present imperative see 125.   [16] οὐκ 267.
[17] μαρὰν ἀθά, Chaldee words meaning *Our Lord cometh*, cf. 1 Cor. xvi. 22.

Κατὰ κυριακὴν δὲ Κυρίου συναχθέντες κλάσατε ἄρτον καὶ εὐχαριστήσατε
προεξομολογησάμενοι τὰ παραπτώματα ὑμῶν, [1]ὅπως καθαρὰ ἡ θυσία ὑμῶν
ᾖ. πᾶς δὲ ἔχων τὴν [2]ἀμφιβολίαν μετὰ τοῦ ἑταίρου αὐτοῦ μὴ συνελθέτω ὑμῖν,
[3]ἕως οὗ διαλλαγῶσιν, ἵνα μὴ κοινωθῇ ἡ θυσία ὑμῶν. αὕτη γάρ ἐστιν ἡ
ῥηθεῖσα ὑπὸ Κυρίου· Ἐν παντὶ τόπῳ καὶ χρόνῳ [4]προσφέρειν μοι θυσίαν
καθαράν· ὅτι βασιλεὺς μέγας εἰμί, λέγει Κύριος, καὶ τὸ ὄνομά μου θαυμαστὸν
ἐν τοῖς ἔθνεσι.

χειροτονήσατε οὖν ἑαυτοῖς ἐπισκόπους καὶ διακόνους ἀξίους τοῦ Κυρίου,
ἄνδρας πραεῖς καὶ ἀφιλαργύρους καὶ ἀληθεῖς καὶ δεδοκιμασμένους· ὑμῖν
γὰρ [5]λειτουργοῦσι καὶ αὐτοὶ τὴν λειτουργίαν τῶν προφητῶν καὶ διδασκάλων.
μὴ οὖν [6]ὑπερίδητε αὐτούς· αὐτοὶ γάρ εἰσιν οἱ τετιμημένοι ὑμῶν μετὰ τῶν
προφητῶν καὶ διδασκάλων. ἐλέγχετε δὲ ἀλλήλους μὴ ἐν ὀργῇ, ἀλλ᾽ ἐν
εἰρήνῃ, ὡς ἔχετε ἐν τῷ εὐαγγελίῳ· καὶ παντὶ ἀστοχοῦντι κατὰ τοῦ ἑτέρου
μηδεὶς λαλείτω μηδὲ παρ᾽ ὑμῶν ἀκουέτω, ἕως οὗ μετανοήσῃ. τὰς δὲ εὐχὰς
ὑμῶν καὶ τὰς ἐλεημοσύνας καὶ πάσας τὰς πράξεις οὕτως ποιήσατε, ὡς ἔχετε
ἐν τῷ εὐαγγελίῳ τοῦ Κυρίου ἡμῶν.

[1] ὅπως 198.   [2] ἀμφιβολίαν *a dispute.*   [3] ἕως οὗ 213, 215.   [4] προσφέρειν Infinitive used as Imperative 137, cf. Malachi i. 11, 14.   [5] λειτουρ-
γοῦσι τὴν λειτουργίαν cognate accusative 17.   [6] ὑπερίδητε, see ὑπεροράω.

APOSTLES AND PROPHETS IN THE EARLY CHURCH.

Περὶ δὲ τῶν ἀποστόλων καὶ προφητῶν κατὰ τὸ δόγμα τοῦ εὐαγγελίου
οὕτως ποιήσατε. πᾶς δὲ ἀπόστολος [1]ἐρχόμενος πρὸς ὑμᾶς δεχθήτω ὡς
Κύριος· οὐ μενεῖ δὲ εἰ μὴ [2]ἡμέραν μίαν· ἐὰν δὲ ᾖ χρεία, καὶ τὴν ἄλλην·
τρεῖς δὲ ἐὰν μείνῃ, ψευδοπροφήτης ἐστίν· ἐξερχόμενος δὲ ὁ ἀπόστολος
μηδὲν λαμβανέτω εἰ μὴ ἄρτον, [3]ἕως οὗ [4]αὐλισθῇ· ἐὰν δὲ ἀργύριον αἰτῇ,
ψευδοπροφήτης ἐστί. καὶ πάντα προφήτην λαλοῦντα ἐν πνεύματι οὐ

[1] ἐρχόμενος *when he comes* 259, 218.   [2] ἡμέραν μίαν 18.   [3] ἕως οὗ
213, 215.   [4] αὐλισθῇ *he find shelter.*

πειράσετε οὐδὲ διακρινεῖτε· πᾶσα γὰρ ἁμαρτία ἀφεθήσεται, αὕτη δὲ ἡ ἁμαρτία οὐκ ἀφεθήσεται. [5]οὐ πᾶς δὲ ὁ λαλῶν ἐν πνεύματι προφήτης ἐστίν, ἀλλ' ἐὰν ἔχῃ τοὺς τρόπους Κυρίου. Ἀπὸ οὖν τῶν τρόπων γνωσθήσεται ὁ ψευδοπροφήτης καὶ ὁ προφήτης. καὶ πᾶς προφήτης ὁρίζων τράπεζαν ἐν πνεύματι οὐ φάγεται ἀπ' αὐτῆς· εἰ δὲ μήγε, ψευδοπροφήτης ἐστίν. πᾶς δὲ προφήτης διδάσκων τὴν ἀλήθειαν εἰ ἃ διδάσκει [6]οὐ ποιεῖ, ψευδοπροφήτης ἐστίν. πᾶς δὲ προφήτης [7]δεδοκιμασμένος ἀληθινὸς [8]ποιῶν εἰς μυστήριον κοσμικὸν ἐκκλησίας, μὴ διδάσκων δὲ ποιεῖν ὅσα αὐτὸς ποιεῖ, οὐ κριθήσεται ἐφ' ὑμῶν· μετὰ Θεοῦ γὰρ ἔχει τὴν κρίσιν· ὡσαύτως γὰρ ἐποίησαν καὶ οἱ ἀρχαῖοι προφῆται. [9]ὃς δ' ἂν εἴπῃ ἐν πνεύματι· Δός μοι ἀργύρια ἢ ἕτερά τινα, οὐκ ἀκούσεσθε [10]αὐτοῦ· ἐὰν δὲ περὶ ἄλλων [11]ὑστερούντων εἴπῃ δοῦναι, μηδεὶς αὐτὸν κρινέτω.

[5] οὐ πᾶς δὲ ὁ λαλῶν but not every one that speaketh 260.   [6] οὐ 267.
[7] δεδοκιμασμένος 266.   [8] ποιῶν etc. if he does aught as an outward mystery typical of the Church; for the Conditional participle see 245.   [9] ὃς δ' ἂν εἴπῃ 252.   [10] αὐτοῦ 34 (3).   [11] ὑστερούντων that are in want 260.

EXTRACTS FROM THE EPISTLE OF CLEMENT, BISHOP OF ROME, TO THE CORINTHIANS, WRITTEN ABOUT 95 A.D.

The Martyrdom of Peter and Paul.

Ἀλλ' [1]ἵνα τῶν ἀρχαίων ὑποδειγμάτων παυσώμεθα, [2]ἔλθωμεν ἐπὶ τοὺς ἔγγιστα γενομένους ἀθλητάς· λάβωμεν τῆς γενεᾶς ἡμῶν τὰ γενναῖα ὑποδείγματα. Διὰ ζῆλον καὶ φθόνον οἱ μέγιστοι καὶ δικαιότατοι στύλοι ἐδιώχθησαν καὶ ἕως θανάτου ἤθλησαν. Λάβωμεν πρὸ ὀφθαλμῶν ἡμῶν τοὺς ἀγαθοὺς ἀποστόλους· Πέτρον, ὃς διὰ ζῆλον ἄδικον οὐχ ἕνα οὐδὲ δύο ἀλλὰ πλείονας [3]ὑπήνεγκεν πόνους, καὶ οὕτω μαρτυρήσας ἐπορεύθη εἰς τὸν ὀφειλόμενον τόπον τῆς δόξης. Διὰ ζῆλον καὶ ἔριν Παῦλος ὑπομονῆς βραβεῖον [4]ὑπέδειξεν, ἑπτάκις δεσμὰ φορέσας, φυγαδευθείς, λιθασθείς, κήρυξ γενόμενος ἔν τε τῇ ἀνατολῇ καὶ ἐν τῇ δύσει, τὸ γενναῖον τῆς πίστεως αὐτοῦ κλέος ἔλαβεν, [5]δικαιοσύνην διδάξας ὅλον τὸν κόσμον καὶ ἐπὶ τὸ τέρμα τῆς δύσεως ἐλθών· καὶ μαρτυρήσας [6]ἐπὶ τῶν ἡγουμένων, [7]οὕτως ἀπηλλάγη τοῦ κόσμου καὶ εἰς τὸν ἅγιον τόπον ἐπορεύθη, ὑπομονῆς γενόμενος μέγιστος [8]ὑπογραμμός.

[1] ἵνα παυσώμεθα 198 but to pass from.... .   [2] ἔλθωμεν 119.   [3] ὑπήνεγκεν, see ὑποφέρω.   [4] ὑπέδειξεν from ὑποδείκνυμι pointed out.   [5] δικαιοσύνην διδάξας ὅλον τὸν κόσμον 19; for the participles see 263.   [6] ἐπὶ τῶν ἡγουμένων before the rulers.   [7] οὕτως ἀπηλλάγη τοῦ κόσμου so he departed from the world 34 (5), see ἀπαλλάσσω.   [8] ὑπογραμμός pattern.

The Resurrection.

[1]Κατανοήσωμεν, ἀγαπητοί, πῶς ὁ δεσπότης ἐπιδείκνυται [2]διηνεκῶς ἡμῖν [3]τὴν μέλλουσαν ἀνάστασιν ἔσεσθαι, ἧς τὴν ἀπαρχὴν ἐποιήσατο τὸν Κύριον Ἰησοῦν Χριστὸν ἐκ νεκρῶν [4]ἀναστήσας. ἴδωμεν, ἀγαπητοί, τὴν κατὰ καιρὸν γινομένην ἀνάστασιν. ἡμέρα καὶ νὺξ ἀνάστασιν ἡμῖν δηλοῦσιν· κοιμᾶται ἡ νύξ, ἀνίσταται ἡμέρα· ἡ ἡμέρα ἄπεισιν, νὺξ ἐπέρχεται. λάβωμεν τοὺς καρπούς· ὁ σπόρος πῶς καὶ [5]τίνα τρόπον γίνεται; [6]ἐξῆλθεν ὁ σπείρων καὶ ἔβαλεν εἰς τὴν γῆν ἕκαστον τῶν σπερμάτων, ἅτινα πεσόντα εἰς τὴν γῆν ξηρὰ καὶ γυμνὰ διαλύεται. εἶτ᾽ ἐκ τῆς διαλύσεως ἡ μεγαλειότης τῆς προνοίας τοῦ δεσπότου ἀνίστησιν αὐτά, καὶ ἐκ τοῦ ἑνὸς πλείονα αὔξει καὶ ἐκφέρει καρπόν.

ἴδωμεν τὸ παράδοξον σημεῖον, τὸ γινόμενον ἐν τοῖς [7]ἀνατολικοῖς τόποις, τουτέστιν τοῖς περὶ τὴν Ἀραβίαν. ὄρνεον γάρ ἐστιν ὃ προσονομάζεται [8]φοῖνιξ· τοῦτο μονογενὲς ὑπάρχον ζῇ ἔτη πεντακόσια· γενόμενόν τε ἤδη πρὸς ἀπόλυσιν [9]τοῦ ἀποθανεῖν αὐτό, [10]σηκὸν ἑαυτῷ ποιεῖ ἐκ λιβάνου καὶ σμύρνης καὶ τῶν λοιπῶν ἀρωμάτων, εἰς ὃν [11]πληρωθέντος τοῦ χρόνου εἰσέρχεται καὶ τελευτᾷ. σηπομένης δὲ τῆς σαρκὸς σκώληξ τις γεννᾶται, ὃς ἐκ τῆς [12]ἰκμάδος τοῦ [13]τετελευτηκότος ζώου ἀνατρεφόμενος [14]πτεροφυεῖ· εἶτα [15]γενναῖος γενόμενος αἴρει τὸν σηκὸν ἐκεῖνον ὅπου τὰ ὀστᾶ τοῦ προγεγονότος ἐστίν, καὶ ταῦτα βαστάζων [16]διανύει ἀπὸ τῆς Ἀραβικῆς χώρας ἕως τῆς Αἰγύπτου εἰς τὴν λεγομένην Ἡλιούπολιν· καὶ [17]ἡμέρας, βλεπόντων πάντων, [18]ἐπιπτὰς ἐπὶ τὸν τοῦ ἡλίου βωμὸν τίθησιν αὐτά, καὶ οὕτως εἰς [19]τοὐπίσω ἀφορμᾷ. οἱ οὖν ἱερεῖς ἐπισκέπτονται τὰς ἀναγραφὰς τῶν χρόνων καὶ εὑρίσκουσιν αὐτὸν πεντακοσιοστοῦ ἔτους πεπληρωμένου ἐληλυθέναι.

---

[1] κατανοήσωμεν 119.   [2] διηνεκῶς *continually*.   [3] τὴν μέλλουσαν ἀνάστασιν ἔσεσθαι 144–148, 112.   [4] 258.   [5] τίνα τρόπον 22.   [6] ἐξῆλθεν...ἔβαλεν Gnomic Aorists 95 note.   [7] ἀνατολικοῖς *Eastern*.   [8] φοῖνιξ *the Phoenix*.   [9] τοῦ ἀποθανεῖν 176.   [10] σηκόν *a coffin*.   [11] πληρωθέντος τοῦ χρόνου 35.   [12] ἰκμάδος gen. of ἰκμάς *moisture*.   [13] τετελευτηκότος 266.   [14] πτεροφυεῖ *puts forth wings*.   [15] γενναῖος *lusty*.   [16] διανύει *takes its journey*.   [17] ἡμέρας 29.   [18] ἐπιπτάς Aor. part. from ἐπιπέτομαι *I fly to*.   [19] τοὐπίσω *back again*.

The Praise of Love.

Ὁ ἔχων ἀγάπην ἐν Χριστῷ ποιησάτω τὰ τοῦ Χριστοῦ παραγγέλματα. τὸν δεσμὸν τῆς ἀγάπης τοῦ Θεοῦ τίς δύναται ἐξηγήσασθαι; τὸ μεγαλεῖον τῆς καλλονῆς αὐτοῦ τίς ἀρκετὸς ἐξειπεῖν; τὸ ὕψος εἰς ὃ ἀνάγει ἡ ἀγάπη [1]ἀνεκδιήγητόν ἐστιν. ἀγάπη κολλᾷ ἡμᾶς τῷ Θεῷ· [2]ἀγάπη καλύπτει πλῆθος ἁμαρτιῶν· ἀγάπη πάντα ἀνέχεται, πάντα μακροθυμεῖ· οὐδὲν [3]βάναυσον ἐν ἀγάπῃ, οὐδὲν ὑπερήφανον· ἀγάπη σχίσμα οὐκ ἔχει, ἀγάπη οὐ στασιάζει, ἀγάπη πάντα ποιεῖ ἐν ὁμονοίᾳ· ἐν τῇ ἀγάπῃ ἐτελειώθησαν πάντες οἱ ἐκλεκτοὶ τοῦ Θεοῦ· δίχα ἀγάπης οὐδὲν εὐάρεστόν ἐστιν τῷ Θεῷ· ἐν ἀγάπῃ [4]προσελάβετο ἡμᾶς ὁ δεσπότης· διὰ τὴν ἀγάπην, ἣν ἔσχεν πρὸς ἡμᾶς, τὸ αἷμα αὐτοῦ ἔδωκεν ὑπὲρ ἡμῶν Ἰησοῦς Χριστὸς ὁ Κύριος ἡμῶν ἐν θελήματι Θεοῦ, καὶ τὴν σάρκα ὑπὲρ τῆς σαρκὸς ἡμῶν καὶ τὴν ψυχὴν ὑπὲρ τῶν ψυχῶν ἡμῶν.

ὁρᾶτε, ἀγαπητοί, πῶς μέγα καὶ θαυμαστόν ἐστιν ἡ ἀγάπη, καὶ τῆς τελειότητος αὐτῆς οὐκ ἐστὶν ἐξήγησις· τίς ἱκανὸς ἐν αὐτῇ εὑρεθῆναι, εἰ μὴ [5]οὓς ἂν καταξιώσῃ ὁ Θεός; δεώμεθα οὖν καὶ αἰτώμεθα ἀπὸ τοῦ ἐλέους αὐτοῦ, [6]ἵνα ἐν ἀγάπῃ εὑρεθῶμεν δίχα [7]προσκλίσεως ἀνθρωπίνης ἄμωμοι.

[1] ἀνεκδιήγητον unspeakable.   [2] ἀγάπη καλύπτει 1 Pet. iv. 8. [3] βάναυσον coarse or vulgar.   [4] προσελάβετο took us to Himself.   [5] οὓς ἂν καταξιώσῃ 252.   [6] ἵνα ἐν ἀγάπῃ εὑρεθῶμεν 189.   [7] προσκλίσεως ἀνθρωπίνης the factiousness of men.

The Apostolic Succession.

[1]Οἱ ἀπόστολοι ἡμῖν εὐηγγελίσθησαν ἀπὸ τοῦ Κυρίου Ἰησοῦ Χριστοῦ, Ἰησοῦς ὁ Χριστὸς ἀπὸ τοῦ Θεοῦ ἐξεπέμφθη. ὁ Χριστὸς οὖν ἀπὸ τοῦ Θεοῦ, καὶ οἱ ἀπόστολοι ἀπὸ τοῦ Χριστοῦ· ἐγένοντο οὖν ἀμφότερα εὐτάκτως ἐκ θελήματος Θεοῦ. παραγγελίας οὖν λαβόντες καὶ πληροφορηθέντες διὰ τῆς ἀναστάσεως τοῦ Κυρίου ἡμῶν Ἰησοῦ Χριστοῦ καὶ [2]πιστωθέντες ἐν τῷ λόγῳ τοῦ Θεοῦ μετὰ πληροφορίας πνεύματος ἁγίου ἐξῆλθον, εὐαγγελιζόμενοι [3]τὴν βασιλείαν τοῦ Θεοῦ μέλλειν ἔρχεσθαι. κατὰ χώρας οὖν καὶ πόλεις κηρύσσοντες [4]καθίστανον τὰς ἀπαρχὰς αὐτῶν, δοκιμάσαντες τῷ πνεύματι, εἰς ἐπισκόπους καὶ διακόνους τῶν μελλόντων πιστεύειν. καὶ τοῦτο οὐ καινῶς, ἐκ γὰρ δὴ πολλῶν χρόνων ἐγέγραπτο περὶ ἐπισκόπων καὶ διακόνων·

[1] οἱ ἀπόστολοι ἡμῖν εὐηγγελίσθησαν ἀπό... The Apostles received the Gospel for us from....   [2] πιστωθέντες being fully persuaded.   [3] τὴν βασιλείαν μέλλειν ἔρχεσθαι 145—148.   [4] καθίστανον τὰς ἀπαρχάς they appointed their firstfruits (i.e. their first converts)...to be bishops and deacons.

οὕτως γάρ που λέγει ἡ γραφή· [5]Καταστήσω τοὺς ἐπισκόπους αὐτῶν ἐν δικαιοσύνῃ καὶ τοὺς διακόνους αὐτῶν ἐν πίστει.

καὶ οἱ ἀπόστολοι ἡμῶν ἔγνωσαν διὰ τοῦ Κυρίου ἡμῶν Ἰησοῦ Χριστοῦ ὅτι ἔρις ἔσται ἐπὶ τοῦ ὀνόματος τῆς ἐπισκοπῆς. Διὰ ταύτην οὖν τὴν αἰτίαν πρόγνωσιν [6]εἰληφότες τελείαν κατέστησαν τοὺς [7]προειρημένους, καὶ [8]μεταξὺ ἐπιμονὴν δεδώκασιν [9]ὅπως, ἐὰν κοιμηθῶσιν, διαδέξωνται ἕτεροι δεδοκιμασμένοι ἄνδρες τὴν λειτουργίαν αὐτῶν. Τοὺς οὖν κατασταθέντας ὑπ' ἐκείνων ἢ μεταξὺ ὑφ' ἑτέρων ἐλλογίμων ἀνδρῶν, συνευδοκησάσης τῆς ἐκκλησίας πάσης, καὶ λειτουργήσαντας ἀμέμπτως τῷ ποιμνίῳ τοῦ Χριστοῦ μετὰ ταπεινοφροσύνης ἡσύχως καὶ [10]ἀβαναύσως, μεμαρτυρημένους τε πολλοῖς χρόνοις ὑπὸ πάντων, τούτους [11]οὐ δικαίως νομίζομεν ἀποβάλλεσθαι τῆς λειτουργίας. ἁμαρτία γὰρ οὐ μικρὰ ἡμῖν ἔσται, ἐὰν τοὺς ἀμέμπτως καὶ ὁσίως προσενεγκόντας τὰ δῶρα τῆς ἐπισκοπῆς ἀποβάλωμεν. μακάριοι οἱ [12]προοδοιπορήσαντες πρεσβύτεροι, οἵτινες [13]ἔγκαρπον καὶ τελείαν ἔσχον τὴν ἀνάλυσιν· οὐ γὰρ [14]εὐλαβοῦνται μή τις αὐτοὺς μεταστήσῃ ἀπὸ τοῦ ἱδρυμένου αὐτοῖς τόπου.

[5] καταστήσω Is. lx. 17.　　　　[6] εἰληφότες Perf. part. act. from λαμβάνω.
[7] προειρημένους Perf. part. pass. from προλέγω.　　[8] μεταξὺ ἐπιμονὴν δεδώκασιν
afterwards they provided a continuance.　　[9] ὅπως, ἐὰν κοιμηθῶσιν 198, 241 ;
the subject of κοιμηθῶσιν is the bishops and deacons.　　[10] ἀβαναύσως
without vulgar ostentation, modestly.　　[11] οὐ δικαίως to be taken together,
unjustly.　　[12] προοδοιπορήσαντες who have gone before.　　[13] ἔγκαρπον
fruitful.　　[14] εὐλαβοῦνται for they have no fear lest... 192.

CLEMENT REBUKES THE CORINTHIANS.

Ἀναλάβετε τὴν ἐπιστολὴν τοῦ μακαρίου Παύλου τοῦ ἀποστόλου. τί πρῶτον ὑμῖν ἐν ἀρχῇ τοῦ εὐαγγελίου ἔγραψεν; ἐπ' ἀληθείας πνευματικῶς [1]ἐπέστειλεν ὑμῖν περὶ αὐτοῦ τε καὶ Κηφᾶ τε καὶ Ἀπολλώ, [2]διὰ τὸ καὶ τότε [3]προσκλίσεις ὑμᾶς πεποιῆσθαι· ἀλλ' ἡ πρόσκλισις ἐκείνη ἥττονα ἁμαρτίαν ὑμῖν προσήνεγκεν· [4]προσεκλίθητε γὰρ ἀποστόλοις μεμαρτυρημένοις καὶ ἀνδρὶ δεδοκιμασμένῳ παρ' αὐτοῖς. [5]νυνὶ δὲ κατανοήσατε τίνες ὑμᾶς [6]διέστρεψαν καὶ [7]τὸ σεμνὸν τῆς περιβοήτου φιλαδελφίας ὑμῶν [6]ἐμείωσαν. αἰσχρά, ἀγαπητοί, καὶ λίαν αἰσχρά, καὶ ἀνάξια τῆς ἐν Χριστῷ [8]ἀγωγῆς, ἀκούεσθαι τὴν βεβαιοτάτην καὶ ἀρχαίαν Κορινθίων ἐκκλησίαν δι' ἐν ᾗ δύο πρόσωπα στασιάζειν πρὸς τοὺς πρεσβυτέρους. καὶ αὕτη ἡ ἀκοὴ οὐ μόνον

[1] ἐπέστειλεν he charged you.　　[2] διὰ τὸ πεποιῆσθαι 228, 96, 97, 111.
[3] προσκλίσεις parties.　　[4] προσεκλίθητε ye were partizans of.　　[5] νυνὶ δὲ
κατανοήσατε... but now mark you who they are that have perverted you...
[6] διέστρεψαν 105.　　[7] τὸ σεμνόν the glory 71.　　[8] ἀγωγῆς conduct.

εἰς ἡμᾶς ἐχώρησεν ἀλλὰ καὶ εἰς τοὺς [9]ἑτεροκλινεῖς ὑπάρχοντας ἀφ' ἡμῶν, [10]ὥστε καὶ βλασφημίας ἐπιφέρεσθαι τῷ ὀνόματι Κυρίου διὰ τὴν ὑμετέραν ἀφροσύνην, ἑαυτοῖς δὲ κίνδυνον ἐπεξεργάζεσθαι.

[11]ἐξάρωμεν οὖν τοῦτο ἐν τάχει καὶ προσπέσωμεν τῷ δεσπότῃ καὶ κλαύσωμεν ἱκετεύοντες αὐτόν, ὅπως ἵλεως γενόμενος [12]ἐπικαταλλαγῇ ἡμῖν καὶ ἐπὶ τὴν σεμνὴν τῆς φιλαδελφίας ἡμῶν ἁγνὴν ἀγωγὴν [13]ἀποκαταστήσῃ ἡμᾶς. πύλη γὰρ δικαιοσύνης [14]ἀνεῳγυῖα εἰς ζωὴν αὕτη, καθὼς γέγραπται· Ἀνοίξατέ μοι πύλας δικαιοσύνης, ἵνα εἰσελθὼν ἐν αὐταῖς ἐξομολογήσωμαι τῷ Κυρίῳ· αὕτη ἡ πύλη τοῦ Κυρίου, δίκαιοι [15]εἰσελεύσονται ἐν αὐτῇ. Πολλῶν οὖν πυλῶν ἀνεῳγυιῶν, ἡ ἐν δικαιοσύνῃ αὕτη ἐστὶν ἡ ἐν Χριστῷ, ἐν ᾗ μακάριοι πάντες οἱ εἰσελθόντες καὶ κατευθύνοντες τὴν πορείαν αὐτῶν ἐν ὁσιότητι καὶ δικαιοσύνῃ, ἀταράχως πάντα ἐπιτελοῦντες. ἤτω τις πιστός, ἤτω δυνατὸς γνῶσιν ἐξειπεῖν, ἤτω σοφὸς ἐν διακρίσει λόγων, ἤτω [16]γοργὸς ἐν ἔργοις, ἤτω ἁγνός. τοσούτῳ γὰρ μᾶλλον ταπεινοφρονεῖν ὀφείλει, ὅσῳ δοκεῖ μᾶλλον μείζων εἶναι, καὶ ζητεῖν τὸ [17]κοινωφελὲς πᾶσιν καὶ μὴ τὸ ἑαυτοῦ.

[9] ἑτεροκλινεῖς opposed. [10] ὥστε 231. [11] ἐξάρωμεν from ἐξαίρω. [12] ἐπικαταλλαγῇ 2 Aor. pass. subj. ἐπικαταλλάσσω that He may be reconciled to us. [13] ἀποκαταστήσῃ 1st Aor. subj. act. from ἀποκαθίστημι that He may restore us to (ἐπί) the seemly and pure conduct... . [14] ἀνεῳγυῖα 2nd Perf. part. act. from ἀνοίγνυμι. [15] εἰσελεύσονται, see εἰσέρχομαι. [16] γοργός strenuous. [17] κοινωφελές the common advantage.

A VISION OF HERMAS CONCERNING THE CHURCH.

Hermas was a Roman Christian, the brother of Pius, Bishop of Rome (142–157), according to the Muratorian Fragment.

He imagined himself to be favoured with a series of revelations which were made to him by an ancient lady who declared herself to be the personification of the Church.

In the introduction to the Vision given below he describes how he was commanded to meet this lady in the country and how she made him sit beside her on a couch, and then revealed the Vision to him, that he might report it for the edification of his brethren.

Καὶ [1]ἐπάρασα ῥάβδον τινὰ λαμπρὰν λέγει μοι· Βλέπεις μέγα πρᾶγμα; λέγω αὐτῇ· Κυρία, οὐδὲν βλέπω. λέγει μοι· Ἰδοὺ οὐχ ὁρᾷς κατέναντί σου πύργον μέγαν οἰκοδομούμενον ἐπὶ ὑδάτων λίθοις τετραγώνοις λαμπροῖς;

[1] ἐπάρασα Aor. part. from ἐπαίρω.

ἐν τετραγώνῳ δὲ ᾠκοδομεῖτο ὁ πύργος ὑπὸ τῶν ἓξ νεανίσκων τῶν ἐληλυθό-
των μετ᾽ αὐτῆς· ἄλλαι δὲ μυριάδες ἀνδρῶν παρέφερον λίθους, οἱ μὲν ἐκ
[2]τοῦ βυθοῦ, οἱ δὲ ἐκ τῆς γῆς, καὶ ἐπεδίδουν τοῖς ἓξ νεανίσκοις. ἐκεῖνοι δὲ
ἐλάμβανον καὶ ᾠκοδόμουν· τοὺς μὲν ἐκ τοῦ βυθοῦ λίθους ἑλκομένους πάντας
οὕτως ἐτίθεσαν εἰς τὴν οἰκοδομήν· ἡρμοσμένοι γὰρ ἦσαν καὶ συνεφώνουν
[3]τῇ ἁρμογῇ μετὰ τῶν ἑτέρων λίθων· καὶ οὕτως [4]ἐκολλῶντο ἀλλήλοις, [5]ὥστε
τὴν ἁρμογὴν αὐτῶν μὴ φαίνεσθαι. ἐφαίνετο δὲ ἡ οἰκοδομὴ τοῦ πύργου ὡς
ἐξ ἑνὸς λίθου ᾠκοδομημένη. τοὺς δὲ ἑτέρους λίθους τοὺς φερομένους ἀπὸ
τῆς ξηρᾶς τοὺς μὲν ἀπέβαλλον, τοὺς δὲ ἐτίθουν εἰς τὴν οἰκοδομήν· ἄλλους
δὲ κατέκοπτον καὶ ἔρριπτον μακρὰν ἀπὸ τοῦ πύργου. ἄλλοι δὲ λίθοι
πολλοὶ κύκλῳ τοῦ πύργου ἔκειντο, καὶ οὐκ ἐχρῶντο αὐτοῖς εἰς τὴν οἰκο-
δομήν· ἦσαν γάρ τινες ἐξ αὐτῶν [6]ἐψωριακότες, ἕτεροι δὲ [7]σχισμὰς ἔχοντες,
ἄλλοι δὲ [8]κεκολοβωμένοι, ἄλλοι δὲ λευκοὶ καὶ [9]στρογγύλοι, μὴ ἁρμόζοντες
εἰς τὴν οἰκοδομήν. ἔβλεπον δὲ ἑτέρους λίθους ῥιπτομένους μακρὰν ἀπὸ
τοῦ πύργου καὶ ἐρχομένους εἰς τὴν ὁδὸν καὶ μὴ μένοντας ἐν τῇ ὁδῷ, ἀλλὰ
[10]κυλιομένους εἰς τὴν ἀνοδίαν· ἑτέρους δὲ ἐπὶ πῦρ ἐμπίπτοντας καὶ καιο-
μένους· ἑτέρους δὲ πίπτοντας ἐγγὺς ὑδάτων καὶ μὴ δυναμένους κυλισθῆναι
εἰς τὸ ὕδωρ, [11]καίπερ [12]θελόντων κυλισθῆναι καὶ ἐλθεῖν εἰς τὸ ὕδωρ.

δείξασά μοι ταῦτα ἤθελεν [13]ἀποτρέχειν. λέγω αὐτῇ· Κυρία, τί μοι
ὄφελος ταῦτα [14]ἑωρακότι καὶ μὴ γινώσκοντι τί ἐστιν τὰ πράγματα;
ἀποκριθεῖσά μοι λέγει· [15]Πανοῦργος εἶ ἄνθρωπος, θέλων γινώσκειν τὰ
περὶ τὸν πύργον. Ναί, φημί, κυρία, ἵνα τοῖς ἀδελφοῖς ἀναγγείλω, [16]καὶ
ἀκούσαντες γινώσκωσιν τὸν Κύριον ἐν πολλῇ δόξῃ. ἡ δὲ ἔφη· Ἀκούσονται
μὲν πολλοί· ἀκούσαντες δέ τινες ἐξ αὐτῶν χαρήσονται, τινὲς δὲ [17]κλαύ-
σονται· ἀλλὰ καὶ οὗτοι, ἐὰν ἀκούσωσιν καὶ μετανοήσωσιν, καὶ αὐτοὶ
χαρήσονται. ἄκουε οὖν τὰς παραβολὰς τοῦ πύργου· ἀποκαλύψω γάρ σοι
πάντα. καὶ μηκέτι μοι κόπους πάρεχε περὶ ἀποκαλύψεως· αἱ γὰρ ἀποκα-
λύψεις αὗται τέλος ἔχουσιν· πεπληρωμέναι γάρ εἰσιν. ἀλλ᾽ οὐ παύσῃ
αἰτούμενος ἀποκαλύψεις· ἀναιδὴς γὰρ εἶ. ὁ μὲν πύργος ὃν βλέπεις
οἰκοδομούμενον, ἐγώ εἰμι ἡ Ἐκκλησία, ἡ ὀφθεῖσά σοι καὶ νῦν καὶ τὸ
πρότερον· ὃ ἂν οὖν θελήσῃς ἐπερώτα περὶ τοῦ πύργου, καὶ ἀποκαλύψω

[2] βυθός the deep. [3] τῇ ἁρμογῇ in their joining. [4] ἐκολλῶντο they
adhered. [5] ὥστε 231. [6] ἐψωριακότες mildewed; for the tense see 266.
[7] σχισμάς cracks. [8] κεκολοβωμένοι too short 266. [9] στρογγύλοι rounded.
[10] κυλιομένους εἰς τὴν ἀνοδίαν rolling to where there was no way; for the force
of the present tense in these participles see 259 (1). [11] καίπερ 246.
[12] θελόντων a genitive absolute irregularly introduced, see 35; the proper
case would be accusative agreeing with λίθους. [13] ἀποτρέχειν to hurry
away. [14] ἑωρακότι καὶ μὴ γινώσκοντι, observe the force of the tenses.
[15] πανοῦργος insatiable. [16] καὶ ἀκούσαντες..., understand ἵνα. [17] κλαύ-
σονται Future from κλαίω.

σοι, ἵνα χαρῇς μετὰ τῶν ἁγίων. λέγω αὐτῇ· Κυρία, ἐπεὶ ἅπαξ ἄξιόν με
[18]ἡγήσω τοῦ πάντα μοι ἀποκαλύψαι, ἀποκάλυψον. ἡ δὲ λέγει μοι· [19]Ὃ
ἐὰν ἐνδέχηταί σοι ἀποκαλυφθῆναι, ἀποκαλυφθήσεται. μόνον ἡ καρδία σου
πρὸς τὸν Θεὸν ἤτω καὶ μὴ [20]διψυχήσεις ὃ ἂν ἴδῃς. ἐπηρώτησα αὐτήν·
Διατί ὁ πύργος ἐπὶ ὑδάτων ᾠκοδόμηται, κυρία; Εἶπά σοι, φησίν, καὶ τὸ
πρότερον, καὶ ἐκζητεῖς ἐπιμελῶς· ἐκζητῶν οὖν εὑρίσκεις τὴν ἀλήθειαν.
διατί οὖν ἐπὶ ὑδάτων ᾠκοδόμηται ὁ πύργος, ἄκουε· ὅτι ἡ ζωὴ ὑμῶν [21]διὰ
ὕδατος ἐσώθη καὶ σωθήσεται. [22]τεθεμελίωται δὲ ὁ πύργος τῷ ῥήματι τοῦ
παντοκράτορος καὶ ἐνδόξου ὀνόματος, [23]κρατεῖται δὲ ὑπὸ τῆς ἀοράτου
δυνάμεως τοῦ δεσπότου.

ἀποκριθεὶς λέγω αὐτῇ· Κυρία, μεγάλως καὶ θαυμαστῶς ἔχει τὸ πρᾶγμα
τοῦτο. οἱ δὲ νεανίσκοι οἱ ἓξ οἱ οἰκοδομοῦντες τίνες εἰσίν, κυρία; Οὗτοί
εἰσιν οἱ ἅγιοι ἄγγελοι τοῦ Θεοῦ οἱ πρῶτοι κτισθέντες, οἷς παρέδωκεν ὁ
Κύριος πᾶσαν τὴν κτίσιν αὐτοῦ, αὔξειν καὶ οἰκοδομεῖν καὶ δεσπόζειν τῆς
κτίσεως πάσης. διὰ τούτων οὖν τελεσθήσεται ἡ οἰκοδομὴ τοῦ πύργου.
Οἱ δὲ ἕτεροι οἱ παραφέροντες τοὺς λίθους τίνες εἰσίν; Καὶ αὐτοὶ ἅγιοι
ἄγγελοι τοῦ Θεοῦ· οὗτοι δὲ οἱ ἓξ [24]ὑπερέχοντες αὐτούς εἰσιν. συντελε-
σθήσεται οὖν ἡ οἰκοδομὴ τοῦ πύργου, καὶ πάντες ὁμοῦ εὐφρανθήσονται
κύκλῳ τοῦ πύργου καὶ δοξάσουσιν τὸν Θεόν, ὅτι ἐτελέσθη ἡ οἰκοδομὴ τοῦ
πύργου. ἐπηρώτησα αὐτὴν λέγων· Κυρία, ἤθελον γνῶναι τῶν λίθων [25]τὴν
ἔξοδον καὶ τὴν δύναμιν αὐτῶν, ποταπή ἐστιν. ἀποκριθεῖσά μοι λέγει·
Οὐχ ὅτι σὺ ἐκ πάντων ἀξιώτερος εἶ ἵνα σοι ἀποκαλυφθῇ· ἄλλοι γάρ σου
πρότεροί εἰσιν καὶ βελτίονές σου, οἷς ἔδει ἀποκαλυφθῆναι τὰ ὁράματα
ταῦτα· ἀλλ' ἵνα δοξασθῇ τὸ ὄνομα τοῦ Θεοῦ, σοὶ ἀπεκαλύφθη καὶ ἀποκαλυφθήσεται διὰ τοὺς διψύχους, τοὺς διαλογιζομένους ἐν ταῖς καρδίαις αὐτῶν
εἰ ἄρα ἔστιν ταῦτα ἢ οὐκ ἔστιν. λέγε αὐτοῖς ὅτι ταῦτα πάντα ἐστὶν ἀληθῆ,
καὶ οὐθὲν ἔξωθέν ἐστιν τῆς ἀληθείας, ἀλλὰ πάντα ἰσχυρὰ καὶ βέβαια καὶ
[26]τεθεμελιωμένα ἐστίν.

ἄκουε νῦν περὶ [27]τῶν λίθων τῶν ὑπαγόντων εἰς τὴν οἰκοδομήν. οἱ μὲν
οὖν λίθοι οἱ τετράγωνοι καὶ λευκοὶ καὶ συμφωνοῦντες ταῖς ἁρμογαῖς αὐτῶν,
οὗτοί εἰσιν [28]οἱ ἀπόστολοι καὶ ἐπίσκοποι καὶ διδάσκαλοι καὶ διάκονοι οἱ
πορευθέντες κατὰ τὴν σεμνότητα τοῦ Θεοῦ καὶ ἐπισκοπήσαντες καὶ διδά-

---

[18] ἡγήσω 2nd sing. 1st Aor. mid. ἡγέομαι. [19] ὃ ἐὰν ἐνδέχηται...
whatever is possible to be revealed to thee shall be revealed. [20] διψυχήσεις,
the Future used in a prohibition instead of the Aorist subj. 129, *doubt not,*
James i. 8. [21] διὰ ὕδατος 1 Pet. iii. 20. [22] τεθεμελίωται 97, cf. 1 Cor.
iii. 11. [23] κρατεῖται *it is sustained.* [24] ὑπερέχοντες αὐτούς εἰσιν *are
superior to them.* [25] τὴν ἔξοδον *the end.* [26] τεθεμελιωμένα 266. [27] τῶν
λίθων τῶν ὑπαγόντων... *the stones that go to the building.* [28] οἱ ἀπόστολοι,
cf. Revelation xxi. 14.

ξαντες καὶ διακονήσαντες ἁγνῶς καὶ σεμνῶς τοῖς ἐκλεκτοῖς τοῦ Θεοῦ, οἱ μὲν
[26]κεκοιμημένοι, οἱ δὲ ἔτι ὄντες· καὶ πάντοτε ἑαυτοῖς συμφωνήσαντες καὶ ἐν
ἑαυτοῖς εἰρήνην ἔσχον καὶ ἀλλήλων ἤκουον· διὰ τοῦτο ἐν τῇ οἰκοδομῇ τοῦ
πύργου συμφωνοῦσιν αἱ ἁρμογαὶ αὐτῶν. Οἱ δὲ ἐκ τοῦ βυθοῦ ἑλκόμενοι καὶ
ἐπιτιθέμενοι εἰς τὴν οἰκοδομὴν καὶ συμφωνοῦντες ταῖς ἁρμογαῖς αὐτῶν μετὰ
τῶν ἑτέρων λίθων τῶν ἤδη ᾠκοδομημένων τίνες εἰσίν; Οὗτοί εἰσιν οἱ
παθόντες ἕνεκεν τοῦ ὀνόματος τοῦ Κυρίου. Τοὺς δὲ ἑτέρους λίθους τοὺς
φερομένους ἀπὸ τῆς ξηρᾶς θέλω γνῶναι τίνες εἰσίν, κυρία. ἔφη· Τοὺς
μὲν εἰς τὴν οἰκοδομὴν ὑπάγοντας καὶ [29]μὴ λατομουμένους, τούτους ὁ Κύριος
ἐδοκίμασεν, ὅτι ἐπορεύθησαν ἐν τῇ εὐθύτητι τοῦ Κυρίου καὶ κατωρθώσαντο
τὰς ἐντολὰς αὐτοῦ. Οἱ δὲ ἀγόμενοι καὶ τιθέμενοι εἰς τὴν οἰκοδομὴν τίνες
εἰσίν; Νέοι εἰσὶν ἐν τῇ πίστει καὶ πιστοί. νουθετοῦνται δὲ ὑπὸ τῶν
ἀγγέλων εἰς τὸ ἀγαθοποιεῖν, διότι εὑρέθη ἐν αὐτοῖς πονηρία. Οὓς δὲ [30]ἀπέ-
βαλλον καὶ ἐρίπτουν, τίνες εἰσίν; Οὗτοί εἰσιν [26]ἡμαρτηκότες καὶ θέλοντες
μετανοῆσαι· διὰ τοῦτο μακρὰν οὐκ ἀπερίφησαν ἔξω τοῦ πύργου, ὅτι
εὔχρηστοι ἔσονται εἰς τὴν οἰκοδομήν, ἐὰν μετανοήσωσιν. οἱ οὖν μέλλοντες
μετανοεῖν, ἐὰν μετανοήσωσιν, ἰσχυροὶ ἔσονται ἐν τῇ πίστει, ἐὰν νῦν μετανοήσωσιν ἐν ᾧ οἰκοδομεῖται ὁ πύργος. ἐὰν δὲ τελεσθῇ ἡ οἰκοδομή, οὐκέτι
ἔχουσιν τόπον, ἀλλ᾽ ἔσονται ἔκβολοι. μόνον δὲ τοῦτο ἔχουσιν, παρὰ τῷ
πύργῳ κεῖσθαι.

τοὺς δὲ [31]κατακοπτομένους καὶ μακρὰν ῥιπτομένους ἀπὸ τοῦ πύργου
θέλεις γνῶναι; οὗτοί εἰσιν οἱ υἱοὶ τῆς ἀνομίας· ἐπίστευσαν δὲ ἐν ὑποκρίσει,
καὶ πᾶσα πονηρία οὐκ ἀπέστη ἀπ᾽ αὐτῶν· διὰ τοῦτο οὐκ ἔχουσιν σωτηρίαν,
ὅτι οὐκ εἰσὶν εὔχρηστοι εἰς οἰκοδομὴν διὰ τὰς πονηρίας αὐτῶν. διὰ τοῦτο
συνεκόπησαν καὶ πόρρω ἀπερίφησαν διὰ τὴν ὀργὴν τοῦ Κυρίου, ὅτι παρώρ-
γισαν αὐτόν. τοὺς δὲ ἑτέρους οὓς ἑώρακας πολλοὺς κειμένους, μὴ ὑπάγοντας
εἰς τὴν οἰκοδομήν, οὗτοι οἱ μὲν ἐψωριακότες εἰσίν, οἱ [26]ἐγνωκότες τὴν
ἀλήθειαν, μὴ ἐπιμείναντες δὲ ἐν αὐτῇ μηδὲ [32]κολλώμενοι τοῖς ἁγίοις· διὰ
τοῦτο ἄχρηστοί εἰσιν. Οἱ δὲ τὰς σχισμὰς ἔχοντες τίνες εἰσίν; Οὗτοί εἰσιν
οἱ κατ᾽ ἀλλήλων ἐν ταῖς καρδίαις ἔχοντες καὶ μὴ εἰρηνεύοντες ἐν ἑαυτοῖς,
ἀλλὰ πρόσωπον εἰρήνης ἔχοντες, ὅταν δὲ ἀπ᾽ ἀλλήλων ἀποχωρήσωσιν, αἱ
πονηρίαι αὐτῶν ἐν ταῖς καρδίαις ἐμμένουσιν. αὗται οὖν αἱ σχισμαί εἰσιν ἃς
ἔχουσιν οἱ λίθοι. οἱ δὲ κεκολοβωμένοι, οὗτοί εἰσιν πεπιστευκότες μὲν καὶ
τὸ πλεῖον μέρος ἔχοντες ἐν τῇ δικαιοσύνῃ, τινὰ δὲ μέρη ἔχουσιν τῆς ἀνομίας·
διὰ τοῦτο [33]κολοβοὶ καὶ οὐχ ὁλοτελεῖς εἰσιν. Οἱ δὲ λευκοὶ καὶ στρογγύλοι
καὶ μὴ ἁρμόζοντες εἰς τὴν οἰκοδομὴν τίνες εἰσίν, κυρία; ἀποκριθεῖσά μοι

---

[29] μὴ λατομουμένους that are not cut.   [30] ἀπέβαλλον καὶ ἐρίπτουν 89.
[31] κατακοπτομένους broken in pieces, p. 36, note.   [32] κολλώμενοι τοῖς
ἁγίοις 43.   [33] κολοβοί too short.

λέγει· Ἔως πότε μωρὸς εἶ καὶ ἀσύνετος, καὶ πάντα ἐπερωτᾷς καὶ οὐδὲν
νοεῖς; οὗτοί εἰσιν ἔχοντες μὲν πίστιν, ἔχοντες δὲ καὶ πλοῦτον τοῦ αἰῶνος
τούτου. ὅταν γένηται θλῖψις, διὰ τὸν πλοῦτον αὐτῶν καὶ διὰ τὰς πραγ-
ματείας ἀπαρνοῦνται τὸν Κύριον αὐτῶν. καὶ ἀποκριθεὶς αὐτῇ λέγω· Κυρία,
πότε οὖν εὔχρηστοι ἔσονται εἰς τὴν οἰκοδομήν; Ὅταν, φησίν, [34] περικοπῇ
αὐτῶν ὁ πλοῦτος [35] ὁ ψυχαγωγῶν αὐτούς, τότε εὔχρηστοι ἔσονται τῷ Θεῷ.
ὥσπερ γὰρ ὁ λίθος ὁ στρογγύλος ἐὰν μὴ περικοπῇ καὶ ἀποβάλῃ ἐξ αὐτοῦ τι,
οὐ δύναται τετράγωνος γενέσθαι, οὕτω καὶ οἱ πλουτοῦντες ἐν τούτῳ τῷ
αἰῶνι, ἐὰν μὴ περικοπῇ αὐτῶν ὁ πλοῦτος, οὐ δύνανται τῷ Κυρίῳ εὔχρηστοι
γενέσθαι. ἀπὸ σεαυτοῦ πρῶτον γνῶθι· ὅτε ἐπλούτεις, ἄχρηστος ἦς· νῦν
δὲ εὔχρηστος εἶ καὶ ὠφέλιμος τῇ ζωῇ. εὔχρηστοι γίνεσθε τῷ Θεῷ· καὶ γὰρ
σὺ αὐτὸς [36] χρᾶσαι ἐκ τῶν αὐτῶν λίθων.

Τοὺς δὲ ἑτέρους λίθους, οὓς εἶδες μακρὰν ἀπὸ τοῦ πύργου ῥιπτομένους
καὶ πίπτοντας εἰς τὴν ὁδὸν καὶ κυλιομένους ἐκ τῆς ὁδοῦ εἰς τὰς ἀνοδίας·
οὗτοί εἰσιν οἱ πεπιστευκότες μέν, ἀπὸ δὲ τῆς διψυχίας αὐτῶν [37] ἀφίουσιν
τὴν ὁδὸν αὐτῶν τὴν ἀληθινήν· δοκοῦντες οὖν βελτίονα ὁδὸν δύνασθαι
εὑρεῖν, πλανῶνται καὶ ταλαιπωροῦσιν περιπατοῦντες ἐν ταῖς ἀνοδίαις. οἱ
δὲ πίπτοντες εἰς τὸ πῦρ καὶ καιόμενοι, οὗτοί εἰσιν οἱ εἰς τέλος ἀποστάντες
τοῦ Θεοῦ τοῦ ζῶντος, καὶ οὐκέτι αὐτοῖς ἀνέβη ἐπὶ τὴν καρδίαν τοῦ μετανοῆσαι
διὰ τὰς ἐπιθυμίας τῆς ἀσελγείας αὐτῶν καὶ τῶν πονηριῶν [38] ὧν εἰργάσαντο.
τοὺς δὲ ἑτέρους τοὺς πίπτοντας ἐγγὺς τῶν ὑδάτων καὶ μὴ δυναμένους
κυλισθῆναι εἰς τὸ ὕδωρ θέλεις γνῶναι τίνες εἰσίν; οὗτοί εἰσιν οἱ τὸν λόγον
ἀκούσαντες καὶ θέλοντες βαπτισθῆναι εἰς τὸ ὄνομα τοῦ Κυρίου· εἶτα ὅταν
αὐτοῖς ἔλθῃ εἰς μνείαν ἡ ἁγνότης τῆς ἀληθείας, μετανοοῦσιν, καὶ πορεύονται
πάλιν ὀπίσω τῶν ἐπιθυμιῶν αὐτῶν τῶν πονηρῶν. ἐτέλεσεν οὖν τὴν
ἐξήγησιν τοῦ πύργου. [39] ἀναιδευσάμενος ἔτι αὐτὴν ἐπηρώτησα, εἰ ἄρα
πάντες οἱ λίθοι οὗτοι οἱ ἀποβεβλημένοι καὶ μὴ ἁρμόζοντες εἰς τὴν οἰκοδομὴν
τοῦ πύργου, εἰ ἔστιν αὐτοῖς μετάνοια καὶ ἔχουσιν τόπον εἰς τὸν πύργον
τοῦτον. Ἔχουσιν, φησίν, μετάνοιαν, ἀλλὰ εἰς τοῦτον τὸν πύργον οὐ δύνανται ἁρμόσαι. ἑτέρῳ δὲ τόπῳ ἁρμόσουσιν πολὺ ἐλάττονι, καὶ τοῦτο ὅταν
βασανισθῶσιν καὶ ἐκπληρώσωσιν τὰς ἡμέρας τῶν ἁμαρτιῶν αὐτῶν. καὶ
διὰ τοῦτο [40] μετατεθήσονται, ὅτι μετέλαβον τοῦ ῥήματος τοῦ δικαίου. καὶ
τότε αὐτοῖς συμβήσεται μετατεθῆναι ἐκ τῶν βασάνων αὐτῶν, ἐὰν ἀναβῇ ἐπὶ
τὴν καρδίαν αὐτῶν τὰ ἔργα ἃ εἰργάσαντο πονηρά. ἐὰν δὲ μὴ ἀναβῇ ἐπὶ τὴν
καρδίαν αὐτῶν, οὐ σώζονται διὰ τὴν σκληροκαρδίαν αὐτῶν.

[34] περικοπῇ αὐτῶν ὁ πλοῦτος when their wealth shall be cut off, 209.
[35] ὁ ψυχαγωγῶν that leads away their souls. [36] χρᾶσαι thou art taken.
[37] ἀφίουσιν they abandon. [38] ὧν 63. [39] ἀναιδευσάμενος being still
importunate. [40] μετατεθήσονται they shall be changed.

A SELECTION FROM THE GOSPEL ACCORDING TO PETER.

This was discovered in a cemetery in Egypt in 1886. It is of a docetic character. The fragment begins with the account of Pilate washing his hands, and ends before the appearances after the resurrection. The text is reproduced here by kind permission of Dr Robinson, Dean of Wells, from his edition published in 1892.

οἱ δὲ λαβόντες τὸν Κύριον ὤθουν αὐτὸν τρέχοντες καὶ ἔλεγον [1]Σύρωμεν τὸν υἱὸν τοῦ θεοῦ ἐξουσίαν [2]αὐτοῦ ἔχοντες· καὶ πορφύραν [3]αὐτὸν περιέβαλλον, καὶ ἐκάθισαν αὐτὸν ἐπὶ καθέδραν κρίσεως λέγοντες Δικαίως κρῖνε, βασιλεῦ τοῦ Ἰσραήλ. καί τις αὐτῶν ἐνεγκὼν στέφανον ἀκάνθινον ἔθηκεν ἐπὶ τῆς κεφαλῆς τοῦ Κυρίου. καὶ ἕτεροι ἑστῶτες ἐνέπτυον αὐτοῦ ταῖς ὄψεσι καὶ ἄλλοι τὰς [4]σιαγόνας αὐτοῦ [5]ἐράπισαν· ἕτεροι καλάμῳ [6]ἔνυσσον αὐτόν· καί τινες αὐτὸν [7]ἐμάστιζον λέγοντες Ταύτῃ τῇ τιμῇ τιμήσωμεν τὸν υἱὸν τοῦ θεοῦ. καὶ ἤνεγκον δύο κακούργους καὶ ἐσταύρωσαν ἀνὰ μέσον αὐτῶν τὸν Κύριον. αὐτὸς δὲ ἐσιώπα ὡς μηδὲν πόνον ἔχων[8]. καὶ ὅτε ὄρθωσαν τὸν σταυρὸν ἐπέγραψαν ὅτι Οὗτός ἐστιν ὁ βασιλεὺς τοῦ Ἰσραήλ. εἷς δέ τις τῶν κακούργων ἐκείνων ὠνείδισεν αὐτοὺς λέγων Ἡμεῖς διὰ τὰ κακὰ ἃ ἐποιήσαμεν οὕτω πεπόνθαμεν· οὗτος δὲ σωτὴρ γενόμενος τῶν ἀνθρώπων τί ἠδίκησεν ὑμᾶς; καὶ ἀγανακτήσαντες ἐπ᾽ αὐτῷ ἐκέλευσαν [9]ἵνα [10]μὴ σκελοκοπηθῇ, [11]ὅπως βασανιζόμενος ἀποθάνοι. ἦν δὲ [12]μεσημβρία, καὶ σκότος κατέσχε πᾶσαν τὴν Ἰουδαίαν· καὶ ἐθορυβοῦντο [13]μήποτε ὁ ἥλιος ἔδυε, ἐπειδὴ ἔτι ἔζη· καί τις αὐτῶν εἶπεν Ποτίσατε αὐτὸν χολὴν μετὰ ὄξους· καὶ κεράσαντες ἐπότισαν. καὶ ὁ Κύριος ἀνεβόησε λέγων Ἡ δύναμίς μου, ἡ δύναμίς μου κατέλειψάς με. καὶ εἰπὼν ἀνελήφθη. καὶ τότε ἀπέσπασαν τοὺς [14]ἥλους ἀπὸ τῶν χειρῶν τοῦ Κυρίου, καὶ ἔθηκαν αὐτὸν ἐπὶ τῆς γῆς· καὶ ἡ γῆ πᾶσα ἐσείσθη, καὶ φόβος μέγας ἐγένετο. τότε ἥλιος ἔλαμψε καὶ εὑρέθη ὥρα ἐνάτη· ἐχάρησαν δὲ οἱ Ἰουδαῖοι, καὶ [15]δεδώκασι τῷ Ἰωσὴφ τὸ σῶμα αὐτοῦ ἵνα αὐτὸ θάψῃ, ἐπειδὴ [16]θεασάμενος ἦν ὅσα ἀγαθὰ ἐποίησεν.

[1] σύρωμεν 119. [2] αὐτοῦ 28. [3] αὐτόν 19. [4] σιαγόνας cheeks.
[5] ἐράπισαν struck. [6] ἔνυσσον pricked. [7] ἐμάστιζον beat. [8] αὐτὸς...
ἔχων: this passage shows that this Gospel was written in the interest of those Gnostics who taught that our Lord was a man only in appearance, and never really suffered anything. [9] ἵνα 189. [10] μὴ σκελοκοπηθῇ that his legs should not be broken. [11] ὅπως...ἀποθάνοι that he might die in torment, 184. [12] μεσημβρία noon. [13] μήποτε...ἔδυε lest the sun had set, 193. [14] ἥλους nails. [15] δεδώκασι 96. [16] θεασάμενος ἦν: this is a curious periphrastic tense made up of the aorist part. and the imperf. of εἶναι: translate had seen, 114.

λαβὼν δὲ τὸν Κύριον ἔλουσε καὶ [17]εἴλησε σινδόνι καὶ εἰσήγαγεν εἰς ἴδιον τάφον, καλούμενον κῆπον Ἰωσήφ.

συναχθέντες δὲ οἱ γραμματεῖς καὶ Φαρισαῖοι καὶ πρεσβύτεροι πρὸς ἀλλήλους, ἀκούσαντες ὅτι ὁ λαὸς ἅπας γογγύζει καὶ κόπτεται τὰ στήθη λέγοντες ὅτι Εἰ τῷ θανάτῳ αὐτοῦ ταῦτα τὰ μέγιστα σημεῖα γέγονεν, [18]ἴδετε ὅτι πόσον δίκαιός ἐστιν· ἐφοβήθησαν οἱ πρεσβύτεροι καὶ ἦλθον πρὸς τὸν Πειλᾶτον δεόμενοι αὐτοῦ καὶ λέγοντες Παράδος ἡμῖν στρατιώτας, ἵνα φυλάξωσι τὸ [19]μνῆμα αὐτοῦ ἐπὶ τρεῖς ἡμέρας, μήποτε ἐλθόντες οἱ μαθηταὶ αὐτοῦ κλέψωσιν αὐτόν, καὶ ὑπολάβῃ ὁ λαὸς ὅτι ἐκ νεκρῶν ἀνέστη, καὶ ποιήσωσιν ἡμῖν κακά.

ὁ δὲ Πειλᾶτος ἔδωκεν αὐτοῖς Πετρώνιον τὸν κεντυρίωνα μετὰ στρατιωτῶν [20]φυλάσσειν τὸν τάφον· καὶ σὺν αὐτοῖς ἦλθον πρεσβύτεροι καὶ γραμματεῖς ἐπὶ τὸ μνῆμα, καὶ [21]κυλίσαντες λίθον μέγαν μετὰ τοῦ κεντυρίωνος καὶ τῶν στρατιωτῶν ὁμοῖ πάντες οἱ ὄντες ἐκεῖ ἔθηκαν ἐπὶ τῇ θύρᾳ τοῦ μνήματος· καὶ [22]ἐπέχρισαν ἑπτὰ σφραγῖδας, καὶ [23]σκηνὴν ἐκεῖ πήξαντες ἐφύλαξαν.

πρωΐας δὲ ἐπιφώσκοντος τοῦ σαββάτου ἦλθεν ὄχλος ἀπὸ Ἱερουσαλὴμ καὶ τῆς περιχώρου, ἵνα ἴδωσι τὸ μνημεῖον ἐσφραγισμένον· τῇ δὲ νυκτὶ [24]ᾗ ἐπέφωσκεν ἡ κυριακή, φυλασσόντων τῶν στρατιωτῶν [25]ἀνὰ δύο δύο κατὰ φρουράν, μεγάλη φωνὴ ἐγένετο ἐν τῷ οὐρανῷ, καὶ εἶδον ἀνοιχθέντας τοὺς οὐρανοὺς καὶ δύο ἄνδρας κατελθόντας ἐκεῖθε, πολὺ φέγγος ἔχοντας, καὶ ἐπιστάντας τῷ τάφῳ· ὁ δὲ λίθος ἐκεῖνος ὁ βεβλημένος ἐπὶ τῇ θύρᾳ ἀφ' ἑαυτοῦ κυλισθεὶς ἐπεχώρησε [26]παρὰ μέρος· καὶ ὁ τάφος ἠνοίγη, καὶ ἀμφότεροι οἱ νεανίσκοι εἰσῆλθον.

ἰδόντες οὖν οἱ στρατιῶται ἐκεῖνοι ἐξύπνισαν τὸν κεντυρίωνα καὶ τοὺς πρεσβυτέρους· παρῆσαν γὰρ καὶ αὐτοὶ φυλάσσοντες.

καὶ ἐξηγουμένων αὐτῶν ἃ εἶδον, πάλιν ὁρῶσιν ἐξελθόντας ἀπὸ τοῦ τάφου τρεῖς ἄνδρας, καὶ τοὺς δύο τὸν ἕνα [27]ὑπορθοῦντας, καὶ σταυρὸν ἀκολουθοῦντα αὐτοῖς· καὶ τῶν μὲν δύο τὴν κεφαλὴν χωροῦσαν μέχρι τοῦ οὐρανοῦ, τοῦ δὲ [28]χειραγωγουμένου ὑπ' αὐτῶν ὑπερβαίνουσαν τοὺς οὐρανούς· καὶ φωνῆς ἤκουον ἐκ τῶν οὐρανῶν λεγούσης Ἐκήρυξας τοῖς κοιμωμένοις; καὶ [29]ὑπακοὴ ἠκούετο ἀπὸ τοῦ σταυροῦ [30]ὅτι Ναί. [31]συνεσκέπτοντο οὖν ἀλλήλοις ἐκεῖνοι

---

[17] εἴλησε σινδόνι *wrapped him in linen.*   [18] ἴδετε...δίκαιός ἐστιν *see how righteous he was.*   [19] μνῆμα *tomb.*   [20] φυλάσσειν 138.   [21] κυλίσαντες *rolling.*   [22] ἐπέχρισαν ἑπτὰ σφραγῖδας *they stamped seven seals.*   [23] σκηνὴν πήξαντες *pitching a tent.*   [24] ᾗ ἐπέφωσκεν ἡ κυριακή *on which the Lord's day was dawning.*   [25] ἀνὰ δύο δύο *two by two.*   [26] παρὰ μέρος *on one side.*   [27] ὑπορθοῦντας *supporting.* For the construction of the whole passage see 150.   [28] χειραγωγουμένου *of the one led by the hand.*   [29] This apparently means 'answer' here.   [30] ὅτι 158.   [31] συνεσκέπτοντο *they were consulting together.*

ἀπελθεῖν καὶ ἐμφανίσαι ταῦτα τῷ Πειλάτῳ. καὶ ἔτι ³¹διανοουμένων αὐτῶν φαίνονται πάλιν ἀνοιχθέντες οἱ οὐρανοί, καὶ ἄνθρωπός τις κατελθὼν εἰς τὸ μνῆμα.

ταῦτα ἰδόντες οἱ περὶ τὸν κεντυρίωνα νυκτὸς ἔσπευσαν πρὸς Πειλᾶτον, ἀφέντες τὸν τάφον ὃν ἐφύλασσον· καὶ ἐξηγήσαντο πάντα ἅπερ εἶδον, ³²ἀγωνιῶντες μεγάλως καὶ λέγοντες Ἀληθῶς υἱὸς ἦν θεοῦ. ἀποκριθεὶς ὁ Πειλᾶτος ἔφη Ἐγὼ καθαρεύω τοῦ αἵματος τοῦ υἱοῦ τοῦ θεοῦ· ὑμῖν δὲ ³³ταῦτα ἔδοξεν. εἶτα προσελθόντες πάντες ἐδέοντο αὐτοῦ καὶ παρεκάλουν κελεῦσαι τῷ κεντυρίωνι καὶ τοῖς στρατιώταις μηδὲν εἰπεῖν ἃ εἶδον. Συμφέρει γάρ, φασίν, ἡμῖν ³⁴ὀφλῆσαι μεγίστην ἁμαρτίαν ἔμπροσθεν τοῦ θεοῦ, καὶ μὴ ἐμπεσεῖν εἰς χεῖρας τοῦ λαοῦ τῶν Ἰουδαίων καὶ λιθασθῆναι. ἐκέλευσεν οὖν ὁ Πειλᾶτος τῷ κεντυρίωνι καὶ τοῖς στρατιωταῖς μηδὲν εἰπεῖν.

³¹ διανοουμένων *while they were thinking thereon.*   ³² ἀγωνιῶντες *being distressed.*   ³³ ταῦτα ἔδοξεν *this seemed good.*   ³⁴ ὀφλῆσαι *to incur.*

THE CHRISTIANS IN THE WORLD, BY AN UNKNOWN AUTHOR, PROBABLY OF THE SECOND CENTURY.

Χριστιανοὶ γὰρ οὔτε γῇ οὔτε φωνῇ οὔτε ἔθεσι [1]διακεκριμένοι τῶν λοιπῶν εἰσὶν ἀνθρώπων. οὔτε γάρ που πόλεις ἰδίας κατοικοῦσιν οὔτε [2]διαλέκτῳ τινὶ παρηλλαγμένῃ χρῶνται οὔτε βίον [3]παράσημον ἀσκοῦσιν. οὐ μὴν ἐπινοίᾳ τινὶ καὶ φροντίδι [4]πολυπραγμόνων ἀνθρώπων μάθημα τοιοῦτ' αὐτοῖς ἐστιν εὑρημένον, οὐδὲ δόγματος ἀνθρωπίνου [5]προεστᾶσιν ὥσπερ ἔνιοι. κατοικοῦντες δὲ πόλεις Ἑλληνίδας τε καὶ βαρβάρους ὡς ἕκαστος ἐκληρώθη, καὶ [6]τοῖς ἐγχωρίοις ἔθεσιν ἀκολουθοῦντες ἔν τε ἐσθῆτι καὶ διαίτῃ καὶ τῷ λοιπῷ βίῳ, θαυμαστὴν καὶ ὑμολογουμένως παράδοξον ἐνδείκνυνται τὴν κατάστασιν τῆς ἑαυτῶν πολιτείας. πατρίδας οἰκοῦσιν ἰδίας, ἀλλ' ὡς πάροικοι· μετέχουσι πάντων ὡς πολῖται, καὶ πάνθ' ὑπομένουσιν ὡς ξένοι· πᾶσα ξένη πατρίς ἐστιν αὐτῶν, καὶ πᾶσα πατρὶς ξένη. γαμοῦσιν ὡς πάντες, τεκνογονοῦσιν· ἀλλ' οὐ ῥίπτουσι τὰ γεννώμενα. τράπεζαν κοινὴν παρατίθενται, ἀλλ' οὐ κοίτην. ἐν σαρκὶ τυγχάνουσιν, ἀλλ' οὐ κατὰ σάρκα ζῶσιν. ἐπὶ γῆς διατρίβουσιν, ἀλλ' ἐν οὐρανῷ πολιτεύονται. πείθονται τοῖς ὡρισμένοις νόμοις, καὶ τοῖς ἰδίοις βίοις νικῶσι τοὺς νόμους. ἀγαπῶσι πάντας, καὶ ὑπὸ πάντων διώκονται. ἀγνοοῦνται, καὶ κατακρίνονται· θανατοῦνται, καὶ ζωοποιοῦνται. πτωχεύουσι, καὶ πλουτίζουσι πολλούς· πάντων ὑστεροῦνται, καὶ ἐν πᾶσι περισσεύουσιν. ἀτιμοῦνται, καὶ ἐν ταῖς ἀτιμίαις δοξάζονται· βλασφημοῦνται, καὶ δικαιοῦνται. λοιδοροῦνται, καὶ εὐλογοῦσιν· ὑβρίζονται, καὶ τιμῶσιν. ἀγαθοποιοῦντες ὡς κακοὶ κολάζονται· κολαζόμενοι χαίρουσιν ὡς ζωοποιούμενοι. ὑπὸ Ἰουδαίων ὡς ἀλλόφυλοι πολεμοῦνται καὶ ὑπὸ Ἑλλήνων διώκονται, καὶ τὴν αἰτίαν τῆς ἔχθρας εἰπεῖν οἱ μισοῦντες οὐκ ἔχουσιν.

ἁπλῶς δ' εἰπεῖν, ὅπερ ἐστὶν ἐν σώματι ψυχή, τοῦτ' εἰσὶν ἐν κόσμῳ Χριστιανοί. ἔσπαρται κατὰ πάντων τῶν τοῦ σώματος μελῶν ἡ ψυχή, καὶ Χριστιανοὶ κατὰ τὰς τοῦ κόσμου πόλεις. οἰκεῖ μὲν ἐν τῷ σώματι ψυχή, οὐκ ἔστι δὲ ἐκ τοῦ σώματος· καὶ Χριστιανοὶ ἐν κόσμῳ οἰκοῦσιν, οὐκ εἰσὶ δὲ ἐκ τοῦ κόσμου. ἀόρατος ἡ ψυχὴ ἐν ὁρατῷ φρουρεῖται τῷ σώματι· καὶ Χριστιανοὶ γινώσκονται μὲν ὄντες ἐν τῷ κόσμῳ, ἀόρατος δὲ αὐτῶν ἡ θεοσέβεια μένει. μισεῖ τὴν ψυχὴν ἡ σὰρξ καὶ πολεμεῖ μηδὲν ἀδικουμένη, διότι [2]ταῖς ἡδοναῖς κωλύεται χρῆσθαι· μισεῖ καὶ Χριστιανοὺς ὁ κόσμος μηδὲν

---

[1] διακεκριμένοι εἰσίν are distinguished.   [2] διαλέκτῳ παρηλλαγμένῃ a different dialect; this is the object of χρῶνται which is followed by a dative case.   [3] παράσημον extraordinary.   [4] πολυπραγμόνων ingenious.
[5] προεστᾶσιν 2nd Perf. from προΐστημι are they masters of.   [6] τοῖς ἐγχωρίοις ἔθεσι, for case see 43.

ἀδικούμενος, ὅτι ταῖς ἡδοναῖς ἀντιτάσσονται. ἡ ψυχὴ τὴν μισοῦσαν ἀγαπᾷ σάρκα καὶ τὰ μέλη· καὶ Χριστιανοὶ τοὺς μισοῦντας ἀγαπῶσιν. [7]ἐγκέκλεισται μὲν ἡ ψυχὴ τῷ σώματι, συνέχει δὲ αὐτὴ τὸ σῶμα· καὶ Χριστιανοὶ κατέχονται μὲν ὡς ἐν φρουρᾷ τῷ κόσμῳ, αὐτοὶ δὲ συνέχουσι τὸν κόσμον. ἀθάνατος ἡ ψυχὴ ἐν θνητῷ σκηνώματι κατοικεῖ· καὶ Χριστιανοὶ παροικοῦσιν ἐν φθαρτοῖς, τὴν ἐν οὐρανοῖς ἀφθαρσίαν προσδεχόμενοι. κακουργουμένη σιτίοις καὶ ποτοῖς ἡ ψυχὴ βελτιοῦται· καὶ Χριστιανοὶ κολαζόμενοι καθ᾽ ἡμέραν πλεονάζουσι μᾶλλον. εἰς τοσαύτην αὐτοὺς τάξιν ἔθετο ὁ Θεός, ἣν οὐ θεμιτὸν αὐτοῖς παραιτήσασθαι.

οὐ γὰρ ἐπίγειον, ὡς ἔφην, εὕρημα τοῦτ᾽ αὐτοῖς παρεδόθη, οὐδὲ θνητὴν ἐπίνοιαν φυλάσσειν οὕτως ἀξιοῦσιν ἐπιμελῶς, οὐδὲ ἀνθρωπίνων [8]οἰκονομίαν μυστηρίων πεπίστευνται. ἀλλ᾽ αὐτὸς ἀληθῶς ὁ παντοκράτωρ καὶ παντοκτίστης καὶ ἀόρατος Θεός, αὐτὸς ἀπ᾽ οὐρανῶν τὴν ἀλήθειαν καὶ τὸν λόγον τὸν ἅγιον καὶ [9]ἀπερινόητον ἀνθρώποις ἐνίδρυσε καὶ ἐγκατεστήριξε ταῖς καρδίαις αὐτῶν, οὐ καθάπερ ἄν τις εἰκάσειεν ἄνθρωπος, ὑπηρέτην τινὰ πέμψας ἢ ἄγγελον ἢ ἄρχοντα ἤ τινα [10]τῶν διεπόντων τὰ ἐπίγεια ἤ τινα τῶν [11]πεπιστευμένων τὰς ἐν οὐρανοῖς διοικήσεις, ἀλλ᾽ αὐτὸν τὸν τεχνίτην καὶ δημιουργὸν τῶν ὅλων, ᾧ τοὺς οὐρανοὺς ἔκτισεν, ᾧ τὴν θάλασσαν ἰδίοις ὅροις ἐνέκλεισεν, [12]οὗ τὰ μυστήρια πιστῶς πάντα φυλάσσει τὰ στοιχεῖα, παρ᾽ οὗ τὰ μέτρα τῶν τῆς ἡμέρας δρόμων ἥλιος εἴληφε φυλάσσειν, ᾧ πειθαρχεῖ σελήνη νυκτὶ φαίνειν κελεύοντι, ᾧ πειθαρχεῖ τὰ ἄστρα τῷ τῆς σελήνης ἀκολουθοῦντα δρόμῳ, ᾧ πάντα διατέτακται καὶ διώρισται καὶ ὑποτέτακται, οὐρανοὶ καὶ τὰ ἐν οὐρανοῖς, γῆ καὶ τὰ ἐν τῇ γῇ, θάλασσα καὶ τὰ ἐν τῇ θαλάσσῃ, πῦρ, ἀήρ, ἄβυσσος, τὰ ἐν ὕψεσι, τὰ ἐν βάθεσι, τὰ ἐν τῷ μεταξύ· τοῦτον πρὸς αὐτοὺς ἀπέστειλεν. ἆρά γε, ὡς ἀνθρώπων ἄν τις λογίσαιτο, ἐπὶ τυραννίδι καὶ φόβῳ καὶ καταπλήξει; οὐμενοῦν· ἀλλ᾽ ἐν ἐπιεικείᾳ πραΰτητι ὡς βασιλεὺς πέμπων υἱὸν βασιλέα ἔπεμψεν, ὡς Θεὸν ἔπεμψεν, ὡς πρὸς ἀνθρώπους ἔπεμψεν, ὡς σῴζων ἔπεμψεν, ὡς πείθων, οὐ βιαζόμενος· [13]βία γὰρ οὐ πρόσεστι τῷ Θεῷ. ἔπεμψεν ὡς καλῶν, οὐ διώκων· ἔπεμψεν ὡς ἀγαπῶν, οὐ κρίνων. πέμψει γὰρ αὐτὸν κρίνοντα, καὶ τίς αὐτοῦ τὴν παρουσίαν ὑποστήσεται;

---

[7] ἐγκέκλεισται Perf. pass. from ἐγκλείω. [8] οἰκονομίαν πεπίστευνται 20.
[9] ἀπερινόητον that surpasses the wit of man. [10] τῶν διεπόντων of those
that direct.... [11] πεπιστευμένων...διοικήσεις 20. [12] οὗ τὰ μυστήρια
whose mysteries all the elements faithfully observe. [13] βία γάρ for force
is no attribute of God.

THE MARTYRDOM OF IGNATIUS BISHOP OF ANTIOCH.

The Acts from which this selection is adapted are not strictly historical, but are probably based on a sound tradition.

Trajan was apparently not in Antioch at the time at which the trial of Ignatius before him is placed by the writer, and, if Ignatius had been tried by him, it is not likely that he would have written to the Romans asking them not to intercede for him that his sentence might be commuted, because there would have been no appeal from the sentence of the Emperor.

The tendency to bring together celebrated persons living at the same era is common to all writers of historical romances.

What is certain in the story is that Ignatius was Bishop of Antioch and that he suffered martyrdom in Rome by being thrown to the beasts about 107 A.D.

Ἄρτι δεξαμένου τὴν Ῥωμαίων ἀρχὴν Τραιανοῦ, Ἰγνάτιος, ὁ τοῦ ἀποστόλου Ἰωάννου μαθητής, ἀνὴρ ἀποστολικός, [1]ἐκυβέρνα τὴν ἐκκλησίαν Ἀντιοχέων ἐπιμελῶς. [2]λωφήσαντος οὖν πρὸς ὀλίγον τοῦ διωγμοῦ, ηὐφραίνετο μὲν [3]ἐπὶ τῷ τῆς ἐκκλησίας ἀσαλεύτῳ, [4]ἤσχαλλεν δὲ καθ᾽ ἑαυτὸν ὡς μήπω τῆς [5]ὄντως εἰς Χριστὸν ἀγάπης ἐφαψάμενος, μηδὲ τῆς τελείας τοῦ μαθητοῦ τάξεως. ἐνενόει γὰρ τὴν διὰ μαρτυρίου γενομένην ὁμολογίαν [6]πλεῖον αὐτὸν προσοικειοῦσαν τῷ Κυρίῳ. ὅθεν [7]ἔτεσιν ὀλίγοις ἔτι παραμένων τῇ ἐκκλησίᾳ καὶ [8]λύχνου δίκην θείκου τὴν ἑκάστου φωτίζων διάνοιαν διὰ τῆς τῶν θείων γραφῶν ἐξηγήσεως, ἐτύγχανεν [9]τῶν κατ᾽ εὐχήν. ὁ μὲν οὖν Τραιανὸς ἐννάτῳ ἔτει τῆς αὐτοῦ βασιλείας, ἐπαρθεὶς ἐπὶ τῇ νίκῃ τῇ κατὰ Σκυθῶν καὶ Δακῶν, κατηνάγκαζεν πάντας τοὺς εὐσεβῶς ζῶντας ἢ θύειν ἢ τελευτᾶν, ὁ δὲ Ἰγνάτιος τότε, φοβηθεὶς ὑπὲρ τῆς Ἀντιοχέων ἐκκλησίας, ἑκουσίως ἤγετο πρὸς Τραιανὸν διάγοντα μὲν κατ᾽ ἐκεῖνον τὸν καιρὸν κατὰ τὴν Ἀντιόχειαν. ὡς δὲ κατὰ πρόσωπον αὐτοῦ ἔστη, εἶπεν αὐτῷ ὁ βασιλεὺς Τίς εἶ, [10]κακοδαῖμον, τὰς ἡμετέρας σπουδάζων ὑπερβαίνειν, καὶ ἑτέρους ἀναπείθειν ἵνα κακῶς ἀπολοῦνται;

---

[1] ἐκυβέρνα *was guiding.*   [2] λωφήσαντος *growing milder.*   [3] ἐπὶ τῷ τῆς ἐκκλησίας ἀσαλεύτῳ *at the tranquillity of the church.*   [4] ἤσχαλλεν *he was grieved.*   [5] ὄντως *real.*   [6] πλεῖον αὐτὸν προσοικειοῦσαν *would rather consummate his union with....*   [7] ἔτεσιν ὀλίγοις *dat. of duration of time,* cf. Jn. ii. 20.   [8] λύχνου δίκην θείκου *like a divine light.*   [9] τῶν κατ᾽ εὐχήν *his desire.*   [10] κακοδαῖμον, this is difficult to translate so as to keep up the play on the word in the reply of Ignatius. It properly means *possessed with an evil genius, poor wretch.* Ignatius uses it as if it meant first *possessed by an evil spirit,* and secondly *grievous to,* or *potent against evil spirits.*

ὁ δὲ Ἰγνάτιος εἶπεν Οὐδεὶς [11]Θεοφόρον ἀποκαλεῖ κακοδαίμονα, ἀφεστή-
κασι γὰρ ἀπὸ τῶν δούλων τοῦ θεοῦ τὰ δαιμόνια. εἰ δὲ ὅτι τούτοις [20]ἐπαχθής
εἰμι, καὶ κακόν με πρὸς τοὺς δαίμονας ἀποκαλεῖς, συνομολογῶ. Χριστὸν
γὰρ ἔχων ἐπουράνιον βασιλέα, τὰς τούτων καταλύω ἐπιβουλάς.

Τραιανὸς εἶπεν· Καὶ τίς ἐστι θεοφόρος; Ἰγνάτιος ἀπεκρίνατο· Ὁ Χριστὸν
ἔχων ἐν στέρνοις. Τραιανὸς εἶπεν· Ἡμεῖς οὖν σοι δοκοῦμεν κατὰ νοῦν μὴ
ἔχειν θεούς, οἷς καὶ χρώμεθα συμμάχοις πρὸς τοὺς πολεμίους; Ἰγνάτιος
εἶπεν· Τὰ δαιμόνια τῶν ἐθνῶν θεοὺς προσαγορεύεις [12]πλανώμενος. εἷς γάρ
ἐστι θεὸς ὁ ποιήσας τὸν οὐρανὸν καὶ γῆν καὶ τὴν θάλασσαν, καὶ πάντα τὰ
ἐν αὐτοῖς, καὶ εἷς Χριστὸς Ἰησοῦς ὁ υἱὸς τοῦ θεοῦ ὁ μονογενής, οὗ τῆς
βασιλείας [13]ὀναίμην. Τραιανὸς εἶπεν· Τὸν σταυρωθέντα λέγεις ἐπὶ Ποντίου
Πιλάτου; Ἰγνάτιος εἶπεν· Τὸν ἀνασταυρώσαντα τὴν ἐμὴν ἁμαρτίαν μετὰ τοῦ
ταύτης εὑρετοῦ, καὶ πᾶσαν [14]καταδικάσαντα δαιμονικὴν πλάνην καὶ κακίαν
ὑπὸ τοὺς πόδας τῶν αὐτὸν ἐν καρδίᾳ φορούντων. Τραιανὸς εἶπεν· Σὺ οὖν
ἐν ἑαυτῷ φέρεις τὸν σταυρωθέντα; Ἰγνάτιος εἶπεν· Ναί· γέγραπται γάρ·
ἐνοικήσω ἐν αὐτοῖς καὶ ἐμπεριπατήσω. Τραιανὸς [15]ἀπεφήνατο· Ἰγνάτιον
προσετάξαμεν τὸν ἐν ἑαυτῷ λέγοντα περιφέρειν τὸν ἐσταυρωμένον, δέσμιον
ὑπὸ στρατιωτῶν γενόμενον, ἄγεσθαι παρὰ τὴν μεγάλην Ῥώμην βρῶμα
γενησόμενον θηρίων εἰς τέρψιν τοῦ δήμου. ταύτης ὁ ἅγιος μάρτυς ἐπα-
κούσας τῆς ἀποφάσεως μετὰ χαρᾶς ἐβόησεν· Εὐχαριστῶ σοι, δέσποτα, ὅτι
με τελείᾳ τῇ πρός σε ἀγάπῃ τιμῆσαι κατηξίωσας, τῷ ἀποστόλῳ σου Παύλῳ
δέσμοις συνδήσας σιδηροῖς. ταῦτα εἰπών, καὶ μετ᾽ εὐφροσύνης περιθέμενος
τὰ δέσμα, προσευξάμενος πρότερον ὑπὲρ τῆς ἐκκλησίας, καὶ ταύτην [16]παρα-
θέμενος μετὰ δακρύων τῷ Κυρίῳ, ὥσπερ [17]κριὸς ἐπίσημος ἀγέλης καλῆς
ἡγούμενος, [18]ὑπὸ θηριώδους στρατιωτικῆς δεινότητος συνηρπάζετο, θηρίοις
αἱμοβόροις ἐπὶ τὴν Ῥώμην ἀπαχθησόμενος [19]πρὸς βοράν. οὕτως πρὸς τὴν
Ῥώμην ἀφικόμενος ὤμοις παρὰ τῷ ναῷ παρεβλήθη, ὥστε τοῦ ἁγίου μάρτυρος
Ἰγνατίου πληροῦσθαι τὴν ἐπιθυμίαν κατὰ τὸ γεγραμμένον· ἐπιθυμία δικαίου
δεκτή· ἵνα μηδενὶ τῶν ἀδελφῶν [20]ἐπαχθὴς διὰ τῆς συλλογῆς τοῦ [21]λειψάνου
γένηται, καθὼς ἐν τῇ ἐπιστολῇ τὴν ἰδίαν ἐπεθύμει γενέσθαι τελείωσιν. μόνα
γὰρ τὰ [22]τραχύτερα τῶν ἁγίων αὐτοῦ λειψάνων περιελείφθη, ἅτινα εἰς τὴν
Ἀντιόχειαν ἀπεκομίσθη, καὶ ἐν λίνῳ κατέθη, θησαυρὸς ἄτιμος ὑπὸ τῆς ἐν

---

[11] Θεοφόρον the God-bearer, this was a name given to Ignatius in the
Church.   [12] πλανώμενος in error.   [13] ὀναίμην may I be partaker.   [14] κατα-
δικάσαντα condemn.   [15] ἀπεφήνατο pronounced sentence.   [16] παραθέμενος
...τῷ Κυρίῳ committing it to the Lord.   [17] κριὸς ἐπίσημος a distinguished
ram.   [18] ὑπὸ θηριώδους στρατιωτικῆς δεινότητος by the ferocious violence of
the soldiers.   [19] πρὸς βοράν to feed blood-devouring beasts.   [20] ἐπαχθής
burdensome.   [21] λειψάνου of his remains.   [22] τραχύτερα the harder parts.

τῷ μάρτυρι χάριτος τῇ ἁγίᾳ ἐκκλησίᾳ καταλείφθεντα. τούτων αὐτόπται
γενόμενοι, μετὰ δακρύων κατ᾽ οἶκόν τε παννυχίσαντες, καὶ πολλὰ μετὰ
[22]γονυκλισίας καὶ δεήσεως παρακαλέσαντες τὸν Κύριον [23]πληροφόρησαι
τοὺς ἀσθενεῖς ἡμᾶς ἐπὶ τοῖς προγεγόνοσιν, μικρὸν ἀφυπνώσαντες, οἱ μὲν
ἐξαίφνης ἐπίσταντα καὶ [24]περιπτυσσόμενον ἡμᾶς ἐβλέπομεν, οἱ δὲ πάλιν
προσευχόμενον ὑπὲρ ἡμῶν τὸν μακάριον Ἰγνάτιον, ἄλλοι δὲ [25]σταζόμενον
ὑφ᾽ ἱδρῶτος ὡς ἐκ καμάτου πολλοῦ παραγενόμενον, καὶ παρεστῶτα τῷ
Κυρίῳ. μετὰ πολλῆς τοίνυν χαρᾶς ταῦτα ἰδόντες καὶ συμβαλόντες τὰς
ὄψεις τῶν ὀνειράτων, ὑμνήσαντες τὸν θεὸν τὸν δοτῆρα τῶν ἀγαθῶν, καὶ
μακαρίσαντες τὸν ἅγιον, ἐφανερώσαμεν ὑμῖν καὶ τὴν ἡμέραν καὶ τὸν χρόνον,
ἵνα κατὰ καιρον τοῦ μαρτυρίου συναγόμενοι κοινωνῶμεν τῷ ἀθλητῇ καὶ
γενναίῳ μάρτυρι Χριστοῦ, καταπατήσαντι τὸν διάβολον, καὶ τὸν τῆς φιλο-
χρίστου ἐπιθυμίας τελειώσαντι δρόμον ἐν Χριστῷ Ἰησοῦ τῷ Κυρίῳ ἡμῶν,
δι᾽ οὗ καὶ μεθ᾽ οὗ τῷ πατρὶ ἡ δόξα καὶ τὸ κράτος σὺν τῷ ἁγίῳ πνεύματι εἰς
αἰῶνας.

[22] γονυκλισίας with bending of the knee.　　　[23] πληροφόρησαι, Lk. i. 1.
[24] περιπτυσσόμενον embracing.　　　[25] σταζόμενον ὑφ᾽ ἱδρῶτος dripping with
sweat.

THE MARTYRDOM OF CARPUS.

This passage is adapted from the Proconsular Acts of the martyrdom of Carpus, Papylus and Agathonice who were put to death in
Asia either in the persecution of Marcus Aurelius or in that of Decius.

ἐνδημοῦντος τοῦ ἀνθυπάτου ἐν Περγάμῳ προσήχθη αὐτῷ ὁ μακάριος
Κάρπος, μάρτυς τοῦ Χριστοῦ. ὁ δὲ ἀνθύπατος [1]προκαθίσας ἔφη Τίς καλῇ;
ὁ δὲ μάκαριος ἔφη· Τὸ πρῶτον καὶ ἐξαίτερον ὄνομα Χριστιανός, εἰ δὲ τὸ ἐν
τῷ κόσμῳ ζητεῖς, Κάρπος. ὁ ἀνθύπατος εἶπεν· [2]Ἔγνωσταί σοι πάντως
τὰ προστάγματα τῶν Αὐγούστων [3]περὶ τοῦ δεῖν ὑμᾶς σέβειν τοὺς θεοὺς
τοὺς τὰ πάντα διοικοῦντας· ὅθεν συμβουλεύω σοι προσελθεῖν καὶ θῦσαι.

Κάρπος εἶπεν· Ἐγὼ Χριστιανός εἰμι, Χριστὸν τὸν υἱὸν τοῦ θεοῦ σέβομαι,
τὸν ἐλθόντα ἐν ὑστέροις καιροῖς ἐπὶ σωτηρίᾳ ἡμῶν καὶ ῥυσάμενον ἡμᾶς [4]τῆς

[1] προκαθίσας having taken his seat.　　　[2] ἔγνωσται 10.　　　[3] περὶ τοῦ
δεῖν 173.　　　[4] τῆς πλάνης 34 (5).

πλάνης τοῦ διαβόλου, τοιούτοις δὲ εἰδώλοις οὐ θύω. ποίει ὃ θέλεις· ἐμὲ γὰρ ἀδύνατον θῦσαι ⁵κιβδήλοις φάσμασιν δαιμόνων· οἱ γὰρ τούτοις θύοντες ὅμοιοι αὐτοῖς εἰσιν. ὁ δὲ ἀνθύπατος θυμωθεὶς ἔφη· Θύσατε τοῖς θεοῖς καὶ μὴ μωραίνετε. ὁ Κάρπος εἶπεν· Οἱ ζῶντες τοῖς νεκροῖς οὐ θύουσιν. ὁ ἀνθύπατος εἶπεν· Οἱ θεοὶ δοκοῦσίν σοι νεκροὶ εἶναι; Κάρπος εἶπεν· Θέλεις ἀκοῦσαι; οὗτοι οὔτε ἄνθρωποι ὄντες ποτὲ ἔζησαν ⁶ἵνα καὶ ἀποθάνωσι θέλεις δὲ μαθεῖν ὅτι ἀληθές ἐστι τοῦτο; ἆρον τὴν τιμήν σου ἀπ᾽ αὐτῶν ἣν δοκεῖς προσφέρειν αὐτοῖς, καὶ γνώσῃ ὅτι οὐδέν εἰσιν· ὕλη γῆς ὑπάρχοντα καὶ τῷ χρόνῳ φθειρόμενα, ὁ γὰρ θεὸς ἡμῶν ἄχρονος ὢν καὶ τοὺς αἰῶνας ποιήσας, αὐτὸς ἄφθαρτος καὶ αἰώνιος διαμένει, ὁ αὐτὸς ἀεὶ ὤν, μήτε αὔξησιν μήτε μείωσιν ἐπιδεχόμενος· οὗτοι δὲ καὶ γίγνονται ὑπὸ ἀνθρώπων καὶ φθείρονται, ὡς ἔφην, ὑπὸ τοῦ χρόνου.

τὸ δὲ ⁷χρησμεύειν καὶ ἀπατᾶν αὐτοὺς μὴ θαυμάσῃς· ὁ γὰρ διάβολος ἀπ᾽ ἀρχῆς πεσὼν ἐκ τῆς ἐνδόξου αὐτοῦ τάξεως, οἰκείᾳ μοχθηρίᾳ τὴν πρὸς τὸν ἄνθρωπον θεοῦ ⁸στοργὴν πολέμει καὶ καταπιεζόμενος ὑπὸ τῶν ἁγίων, τούτοις ἀνταγωνίζεται καὶ προκατασκευάζει πολέμους καὶ ⁹προλαμβάνων ἀπαγγέλλει τοῖς ἰδίοις. ὁμοίως καὶ ἐκ τῶν καθ᾽ ἡμέραν ἡμῖν συμβαινόντων, ἀρχαιότερος ὢν τῷ χρόνῳ, ¹⁰ἀποπειράσας τὰ συμβησόμενα προλέγει, ἅπερ αὐτὸς μέλλει κακοποιεῖν.

ἔχει γὰρ ἐκ τῆς ¹¹ἀποφάσεως τοῦ θεοῦ τὴν ἀδικίαν καὶ ¹²τὸ εἰδέναι, καὶ ¹³κατὰ συγχώρησιν θεοῦ πειράζει τὸν ἄνθρωπον, ζητῶν πλανῆσαι ¹⁴τῆς εὐσεβείας. πείσθητι οὖν μοι ὅτι ἐν ματαιότητί ἐστε οὐ μικρᾷ.

ὁ ἀνθύπατος εἶπεν· Πολλὰ ἐάσας σε ¹⁵φλυαρῆσαι εἰς βλασφημίαν ἤγαγόν σε τῶν θεῶν καὶ τῶν Σεβαστῶν· ἵνα οὖν μὴ ἐπὶ πλεῖόν σοι προχωρήσῃ, θύεις, ἢ τί λέγεις; Κάρπος εἶπεν· Ἀδύνατον ὅτι θύω, οὐ γὰρ πώποτε ἔθυσα εἰδώλοις. εὐθὺς οὖν ἐκέλευσεν αὐτὸν κρεμασθέντα ¹⁶ξέεσθαι. ὁ δὲ ἔκραζεν· Χριστιανός εἰμι. ἐπὶ πολὺ δὲ ξεόμενος ἔκαμνεν καὶ οὐκέτι ἴσχυσεν λαλῆσαι. ἰδὼν δὲ ὁ ἀνθύπατος τὴν ὑπερβάλλουσαν αὐτοῦ ὑπομονὴν κελεύει αὐτὸν ζῶντα ¹⁷καῆναι. καὶ κατερχόμενος ἔσπευδε ἐπὶ τὸ ἀμφιθέατρον, ὅπως ταχέως ἀπαλλάγῃ τοῦ κόσμου.

⁵ κιβδήλοις φάσμασιν δαιμόνων to false phantoms of demons. ⁶ ἵνα καὶ ἀποθάνωσι 185. ⁷ χρησμεύειν to give oracles. ⁸ στοργήν love. ⁹ προλαμβάνων being ready beforehand. ¹⁰ ἀποπειράσας having experience of the things that happen to us day by day through being the most ancient of creatures foretells what is to come to pass. ¹¹ ἀποφάσεως τοῦ θεοῦ the sentence of God. ¹² τὸ εἰδέναι knowledge 172. ¹³ κατὰ συγχώρησιν θεοῦ by the permission of God. ¹⁴ τῆς εὐσεβείας 34 (5). ¹⁵ φλυαρῆσαι to talk nonsense. ¹⁶ ξέεσθαι to be torn with hooks. ¹⁷ καῆναι Aor. pass. inf. from καίω.

Καὶ [18] προσηλωθεὶς εἰς τὸ ξύλον ὁ Κάρπος [19] προσεμειδίασεν· οἱ δὲ παρεστῶτες ἐκπλησσόμενοι ἔλεγον αὐτῷ· Τί ἐστιν ὅτι ἐγέλασας; ὁ δὲ μακάριος εἶπεν· [20] Εἶδον τὴν δόξαν Κυρίου καὶ ἐχάρην, ἅμα δὲ καὶ ὑμῶν ἀπαλλαγὴν καὶ οὔκ εἰμι μέτοχος τῶν ὑμετέρων κακῶν. ταῦτα εἰπὼν καὶ προσφερομένου τοῦ πυρὸς προσηύξατο λέγων· Εὐλογητὸς εἶ, Κύριε Ἰησοῦ Χριστέ, υἱὲ τοῦ θεοῦ, ὅτι κατηξίωσας καὶ ἐμὲ τὸν ἁμαρτωλὸν ταύτης σου τῆς μερίδος, καὶ τοῦτο εἰπὼν ἀπέδωκεν τὴν ψυχήν.

[18] προσηλωθεὶς *being nailed.*   [19] προσεμειδίασεν *smiled.*   [20] Εἶδον...ἐχάρην 95.

THE MARTYRDOM OF POLYCARP, BISHOP OF SMYRNA, A.D. 155.

Ὁ δὲ θαυμασιώτατος Πολύκαρπος [1]τὸ μὲν πρῶτον ἀκούσας οὐκ ἐταράχθη, ἀλλ᾽ ἐβούλετο [2]κατὰ πόλιν μένειν· οἱ δὲ πλείους ἔπειθον αὐτὸν ὑπεξελθεῖν. καὶ ὑπεξῆλθεν εἰς ἀγρίδιον οὐ [3]μακρὰν ἀπέχον ἀπὸ τῆς πόλεως, καὶ διέτριβε μετ᾽ ὀλίγων, [4]νύκτα καὶ ἡμέραν οὐδὲν ἕτερον [5]ποιῶν ἢ προσευχόμενος περὶ πάντων καὶ τῶν κατὰ τὴν οἰκουμένην ἐκκλησιῶν· ὅπερ ἦν σύνηθες αὐτῷ. καὶ προσευχόμενος ἐν ὀπτασίᾳ γέγονεν [6]πρὸ τριῶν ἡμερῶν τοῦ συλληφθῆναι αὐτόν, καὶ εἶδεν τὸ [7]προσκεφάλαιον αὐτοῦ ὑπὸ πυρὸς κατακαιόμενον· καὶ στραφεὶς εἶπεν πρὸς τοὺς σὺν αὐτῷ, [8]Δεῖ με ζῶντα [9]καῆναι.

καὶ [10]ἐπιμενόντων τῶν ζητούντων αὐτόν, μετέβη εἰς ἕτερον ἀγρίδιον· καὶ εὐθέως ἐπέστησαν οἱ ζητοῦντες αὐτόν. καὶ [11]μὴ εὑρόντες συνελάβοντο παιδάρια δύο, ὧν τὸ ἕτερον βασανιζόμενον ὡμολόγησεν· [12]ἦν γὰρ καὶ ἀδύνατον λαθεῖν αὐτόν, ἐπεὶ καὶ οἱ προδιδόντες αὐτὸν οἰκεῖοι ὑπῆρχον. καὶ [13]ὁ εἰρήναρχος, [14]ὁ κεκληρωμένος [15]τὸ αὐτὸ ὄνομα, Ἡρώδης ἐπιλεγόμενος, ἔσπευδεν εἰς τὸ στάδιον αὐτὸν εἰσαγαγεῖν, ἵνα ἐκεῖνος μὲν τὸν ἴδιον κλῆρον [16]ἀπαρτίσῃ, Χριστοῦ κοινωνὸς γενόμενος, οἱ δὲ προδόντες αὐτὸν τὴν [17]αὐτοῦ τοῦ Ἰούδα ὑπόσχοιεν τιμωρίαν.

ἔχοντες οὖν τὸ παιδάριον, τῇ παρασκευῇ περὶ δείπνου ὥραν ἐξῆλθον [18]διωγμῖται καὶ ἱππεῖς μετὰ τῶν συνήθων αὐτοῖς ὅπλων, ὡς ἐπὶ λῃστὴν τρέχοντες. καὶ ὀψὲ τῆς ὥρας συνεπελθόντες, ἐκεῖνον μὲν εὗρον ἔν τινι δωματίῳ κατακείμενον ὑπερῴῳ· κἀκεῖθεν δὲ ἠδύνατο εἰς ἕτερον χωρίον ἀπελθεῖν, ἀλλ᾽ οὐκ ἠβουλήθη, εἰπών· Τὸ θέλημα τοῦ θεοῦ γενέσθω. [19]ἀκούσας οὖν παρόντας, καταβὰς διελέχθη αὐτοῖς, θαυμαζόντων τῶν παρόντων τὴν ἡλικίαν αὐτοῦ καὶ [20]τὸ εὐσταθές, [21]εἰ τοσαύτη σπουδὴ ἦν τοῦ συλληφθῆναι τοιοῦτον πρεσβύτην ἄνδρα. εὐθέως οὖν αὐτοῖς ἐκέλευσε

---

[1] τὸ μὲν πρῶτον at the first, adverbial acc. 22. [2] κατὰ πόλιν in the city. [3] μακράν, understand ὁδόν 18. [4] νύκτα καὶ ἡμέραν 18. [5] ποιῶν 259 (1). [6] πρὸ τριῶν ἡμερῶν three days before he was taken; the second genitive has an ablative force, starting from, or reckoning from the day when he was taken. See J. H. Moulton, Prolegomena, p. 101. [7] προσκεφάλαιον a pillow. [8] δεῖ με ζῶντα καῆναι 142. [9] καῆναι 2 Aor. inf. pass. from καίω. [10] ἐπιμενόντων persisted 35. [11] μὴ εὑρόντες 267. [12] ἦν γὰρ ἀδύνατον λαθεῖν αὐτόν 142. [13] εἰρήναρχος the captain of the police. [14] κεκληρωμένος Perf. part. mid. from κληρόω who had allotted to him the very same name. [15] τὸ αὐτό 53. [16] ἀπαρτίσῃ fulfil. [17] αὐτοῦ τοῦ Ἰούδα 51. [18] διωγμῖται police. [19] ἀκούσας οὖν παρόντας 150. [20] εὐσταθές constancy. [21] εἰ τοσαύτη σπουδὴ ἦν 167.

παρατεθῆναι [22]φαγεῖν καὶ πιεῖν ἐν ἐκείνῃ τῇ ὥρᾳ, [23]ὅσον ἂν βούλωνται· ἐξῃτήσατο δὲ αὐτούς, [24]ἵνα δῶσιν αὐτῷ ὥραν [25]πρὸς τὸ προσεύξασθαι ἀδεῶς. τῶν δὲ ἐπιτρεψάντων, σταθεὶς προσηύξατο πλήρης ὢν τῆς χάριτος τοῦ Θεοῦ οὕτως, [26]ὡς ἐπὶ δύο ὥρας μὴ δύνασθαι σιγῆσαι, καὶ ἐκπλήττεσθαι τοὺς ἀκούοντας, πολλούς τε μετανοεῖν ἐπὶ τῷ ἐληλυθέναι ἐπὶ τοιοῦτον [27]θεοπρεπῆ πρεσβύτην.

ἐπεὶ δέ ποτε κατέπαυσε τὴν προσευχήν, μνημονεύσας [28]ἁπάντων καὶ τῶν πώποτε συμβεβληκότων αὐτῷ, μικρῶν τε καὶ μεγάλων, ἐνδόξων τε καὶ ἀδόξων, καὶ πάσης τῆς κατὰ τὴν οἰκουμένην καθολικῆς ἐκκλησίας, τῆς ὥρας ἐλθούσης τοῦ ἐξιέναι, ὄνῳ καθίσαντες αὐτὸν ἤγαγον εἰς τὴν πόλιν, ὄντος σαββάτου μεγάλου. καὶ ὑπήντα αὐτῷ ὁ εἰρήναρχος Ἡρώδης καὶ ὁ πατὴρ αὐτοῦ Νικήτης, οἳ καὶ μεταθέντες αὐτὸν ἐπὶ [29]τὴν καροῦχαν [30]ἔπειθον παρακαθεζόμενοι καὶ λέγοντες· Τί γὰρ κακόν ἐστιν εἰπεῖν, [31]Κύριος Καῖσαρ, καὶ ἐπιθῦσαι, [32]καὶ τὰ τούτοις ἀκόλουθα, καὶ [33]διασώζεσθαι; ὁ δὲ τὰ μὲν πρῶτα οὐκ ἀπεκρίνατο αὐτοῖς, ἐπιμενόντων δὲ αὐτῶν ἔφη· Οὐ μέλλω ποιεῖν ὃ συμβουλεύετέ μοι. οἱ δέ, [34]ἀποτυχόντες τοῦ πεῖσαι αὐτόν, δεινὰ ῥήματα ἔλεγον καὶ μετὰ σπουδῆς [35]καθῄρουν αὐτόν, [36]ὡς κατιόντα ἀπὸ τῆς καροῦχας ἀποσῦραι [37]τὸ ἀντικνήμιον. καὶ μὴ ἐπιστραφείς, [38]ὡς οὐδὲν πεπονθώς, προθύμως μετὰ σπουδῆς ἐπορεύετο, ἀγόμενος εἰς τὸ στάδιον, θορύβου τηλικούτου ὄντος ἐν τῷ σταδίῳ ὡς μηδὲ ἀκουσθῆναί τινα δύνασθαι.

Τῷ δὲ Πολυκάρπῳ εἰσιόντι εἰς τὸ στάδιον φωνὴ ἐξ οὐρανοῦ ἐγένετο· Ἴσχυε Πολύκαρπε καὶ ἀνδρίζου. καὶ τὸν μὲν εἰπόντα οὐδεὶς εἶδεν, τὴν δὲ φωνὴν τῶν ἡμετέρων οἱ παρόντες ἤκουσαν. καὶ λοιπὸν προσαχθέντος αὐτοῦ θόρυβος ἦν μέγας ἀκουσάντων [39]ὅτι Πολύκαρπος συνείληπται. προσαχθέντα οὖν αὐτὸν ἀνηρώτα [40]ὁ ἀνθύπατος, [41]εἰ αὐτὸς εἴη· τοῦ δὲ ὁμολογοῦντος, ἔπειθεν ἀρνεῖσθαι λέγων, Αἰδέσθητί σου τὴν ἡλικίαν, καὶ ἕτερα τούτοις ἀκόλουθα, ὡς ἔθος αὐτοῖς λέγειν· [42]Ὄμοσον τὴν Καίσαρος τύχην, μετανόησον, εἶπον, Αἶρε τοὺς ἀθέους. ὁ δὲ Πολύκαρπος [43]ἐμβριθεῖ

[22] φαγεῖν καὶ πιεῖν, examples of the dative sense of the infinitive 133, 171. [23] ὅσον ἂν βούλωνται 252.   [24] ἵνα δῶσιν 189.   [25] πρὸς τὸ προσεύξασθαι 202.   [26] ὡς equivalent to ὥστε so that 230.   [27] θεοπρεπῆ venerable. [28] ἁπάντων 34 (7).   [29] καροῦχαν carriage.   [30] ἔπειθον tried to persuade him 90.   [31] Κύριος Καῖσαρ, cf. 1 Cor. xii. 3.   [32] καὶ τὰ τούτοις ἀκόλουθα and more to this effect.   [33] διασώζεσθαι middle voice 81.   [34] ἀποτυχόντες failing to persuade him 34 (5).   [35] καθῄρουν from καθαιρέω made him dismount.   [36] ὡς for ὥστε 230.   [37] ἀντικνήμιον shin.   [38] ὡς οὐδὲν πεπονθώς, ὡς comparative as if he had not suffered anything.   [39] ὅτι Πολύκαρπος συνείληπται from συλλαμβάνω 96, 97, 153.   [40] ἀνθύπατος the proconsul.   [41] εἰ αὐτὸς εἴη 51, 161.   [42] ὄμοσον 1st Aor. imper. act. from ὄμνυμι.   [43] ἐμβριθεῖ τῷ προσώπῳ with a solemn countenance; ἐμβριθεῖ is a predicative adjective 76.

τῷ προσώπῳ εἰς πάντα τὸν ὄχλον τὸν ἐν τῷ σταδίῳ ἀνόμων ἐθνῶν ἐμβλέψας καὶ ἐπισείσας αὐτοῖς τὴν χεῖρα, στενάξας τε καὶ ἀναβλέψας εἰς τὸν οὐρανόν, εἶπεν· Αἶρε τοὺς ἀθέους. ἐγκειμένου δὲ τοῦ ἀνθυπάτου καὶ λέγοντος· Ὄμοσον, καὶ ἀπολύω σε· λοιδόρησον τὸν Χριστόν· ἔφη ὁ Πολύκαρπος· Ὀγδοήκοντα καὶ ἓξ ἔτη δουλεύω αὐτῷ, καὶ οὐδέν με ἠδίκησεν· καὶ πῶς δύναμαι βλασφημῆσαι τὸν βασιλέα μου, τὸν σώσαντά με;

ἐπιμένοντος δὲ πάλιν αὐτοῦ καὶ λέγοντος, Ὄμοσον τὴν Καίσαρος τύχην, ἀπεκρίνατο· Εἰ [44]κενοδοξεῖς [45]ἵνα ὀμόσω τὴν Καίσαρος τύχην, ὡς σὺ λέγεις, προσποιεῖ δὲ ἀγνοεῖν με τίς εἰμι, μετὰ παρρησίας ἄκουε, Χριστιανός εἰμι. εἰ δὲ θέλεις τὸν τοῦ χριστιανισμοῦ μαθεῖν λόγον, δὸς ἡμέραν καὶ ἄκουσον. ἔφη ὁ ἀνθύπατος· Πεῖσον τὸν δῆμον. ὁ δὲ Πολύκαρπος εἶπεν· [46]Σὲ μὲν κἂν λόγου ἠξίωσα· [47]δεδιδάγμεθα γὰρ ἀρχαῖς καὶ ἐξουσίαις ὑπὸ Θεοῦ [47]τεταγμέναις τιμὴν κατὰ τὸ προσῆκον τὴν μὴ βλάπτουσαν ἡμᾶς, ἀπονέμειν· ἐκείνους δὲ οὐκ ἀξίους ἡγοῦμαι τοῦ ἀπολογεῖσθαι αὐτοῖς.

ὁ δὲ ἀνθύπατος εἶπεν· Θηρία ἔχω, τούτοις σε παραβαλῶ, ἐὰν μὴ μετανοήσῃς. ὁ δὲ εἶπεν· Κάλει· [48]ἀμετάθετος γὰρ ἡμῖν ἡ ἀπὸ τῶν κρειττόνων ἐπὶ τὰ χείρω μετάνοια· καλὸν δὲ μετατίθεσθαι ἀπὸ τῶν χαλεπῶν ἐπὶ τὰ δίκαια. ὁ δὲ πάλιν πρὸς αὐτόν· Πυρί σε ποιῶ δαπανηθῆναι, εἰ [49]τῶν θηρίων καταφρονεῖς, ἐὰν μὴ μετανοήσῃς. ὁ δὲ Πολύκαρπος· Πῦρ ἀπειλεῖς τὸ πρὸς ὥραν καιόμενον καὶ μετ᾽ ὀλίγον σβεννύμενον· ἀγνοεῖς γὰρ τὸ τῆς μελλούσης κρίσεως καὶ αἰωνίου κολάσεως τοῖς ἀσεβέσι τηρούμενον πῦρ. ἀλλὰ τί βραδύνεις; φέρε ὃ βούλει.

ταῦτα δὲ καὶ ἕτερα πλείονα λέγων, [50]θάρσους καὶ χαρᾶς ἐνεπίμπλατο, καὶ τὸ πρόσωπον αὐτοῦ χάριτος ἐπληροῦτο, [51]ὥστε οὐ μόνον μὴ συμπεσεῖν ταραχθέντα ὑπὸ τῶν λεγομένων πρὸς αὐτόν, ἀλλὰ τοὐναντίον τὸν ἀνθύπατον ἐκστῆναι πέμψαι τε τὸν ἑαυτοῦ κήρυκα, ἐν μέσῳ τῷ σταδίῳ κηρῦξαι τρίς· Πολύκαρπος ὡμολόγησεν ἑαυτὸν Χριστιανὸν εἶναι. τούτου λεχθέντος ὑπὸ τοῦ κήρυκος, ἅπαν τὸ πλῆθος ἐθνῶν τε καὶ Ἰουδαίων τῶν τὴν Σμύρναν κατοικούντων [52]ἀκατασχέτῳ θυμῷ καὶ μεγάλῃ φωνῇ ἐπεβόα· Οὗτός ἐστιν ὁ τῆς Ἀσίας διδάσκαλος, ὁ πατὴρ τῶν Χριστιανῶν, ὁ τῶν ἡμετέρων θεῶν καθαιρέτης, ὁ πολλοὺς διδάσκων μὴ θύειν μηδὲ προσκυνεῖν. ταῦτα λέγοντες ἐπεβόων καὶ ἠρώτων τὸν Ἀσιάρχην Φίλιππον, [53]ἵνα ἐπαφῇ τῷ Πολυκάρπῳ

---

[44] κενοδοξεῖς *thou thinkest vainly.*
use mentioned in 180 and 189 etc.
thee worthy of discourse: the apodosis of an unfulfilled conditional sentence
with the protasis suppressed 239.
tense see 96, 266.   [48] ἀμετάθετος *inadmissible.*   [49] τῶν θηρίων 34 (8).
[50] θάρσους καὶ χαρᾶς 34 (2).   [51] ὥστε 230.   [52] ἀκατασχέτῳ *ungovernable.*
[53] ἵνα...ἐπαφῇ 189, ἐπαφῇ 2 Aor. subj. from ἐπαφίημι.
[45] ἵνα ὀμόσω, an extension of the
[46] κἂν = καὶ ἂν *I should have thought*
[47] δεδιδάγμεθα, τεταγμέναις, for the

λέοντα. ὁ δὲ ἔφη [54]μὴ εἶναι ἐξὸν αὐτῷ, ἐπειδὴ πεπληρώκει τὰ κυνηγέσια.
τότε ἔδοξεν αὐτοῖς ὁμοθυμαδὸν ἐπιβοῆσαι, ὥστε τὸν Πολύκαρπον ζῶντα
κατακαῦσαι. ἔδει γὰρ [55]τὸ τῆς φανερωθείσης ἐπὶ τοῦ προσκεφαλαίου
ὀπτασίας πληρωθῆναι, ὅτε ἰδὼν αὐτὸ καιόμενον προσευχόμενος εἶπεν
ἐπιστραφεὶς τοῖς σὺν αὐτῷ πιστοῖς προφητικῶς· Δεῖ με ζῶντα καῆναι.

ταῦτα οὖν μετὰ τοσούτου τάχους ἐγένετο, [56]θᾶττον ἢ ἐλέγετο, τῶν
ὄχλων παραχρῆμα συναγόντων ἔκ τε τῶν [57]ἐργαστηρίων καὶ βαλανείων
ξύλα καὶ [58]φρύγανα, μάλιστα Ἰουδαίων προθύμως, ὡς ἔθος αὐτοῖς, εἰς ταῦτα
ὑπουργούντων. ὅτε δὲ ἡ [59]πυρκαϊὰ ἡτοιμάσθη, ἀποθέμενος [60]ἑαυτῷ πάντα
τὰ ἱμάτια καὶ λύσας τὴν ζώνην, ἐπειρᾶτο καὶ [61]ὑπολύειν ἑαυτόν, μὴ πρότερον
τοῦτο ποιῶν [62]διὰ τὸ ἀεὶ ἕκαστον τῶν πιστῶν σπουδάζειν [63]ὅστις τάχιον
τοῦ χρωτὸς αὐτοῦ ἅψηται· παντὶ γὰρ ἀγαθῆς ἕνεκεν πολιτείας καὶ [64]πρὸ
τῆς πολιᾶς ἐκεκόσμητο. εὐθέως οὖν αὐτῷ περιετίθετο τὰ πρὸς τὴν πυρὰν
ἡρμοσμένα ὄργανα. μελλόντων δὲ αὐτῶν καὶ [65]προσηλοῦν εἶπεν· Ἄφετέ
με οὕτως· ὁ γὰρ δοὺς ὑπομεῖναι τὸ πῦρ δώσει καὶ χωρὶς τῆς ὑμετέρας ἐκ
τῶν ἥλων ἀσφαλείας [66]ἄσκυλτον ἐπιμεῖναι τῇ πυρᾷ.

οἱ δὲ οὐ καθήλωσαν μέν, προσέδησαν δὲ αὐτόν. ὁ δὲ ὀπίσω τὰς χεῖρας
ποιήσας καὶ προσδεθείς, ὥσπερ κριὸς ἐπίσημος ἐκ μεγάλου ποιμνίου εἰς
προσφοράν, ὁλοκαύτωμα δεκτὸν τῷ Θεῷ ἡτοιμασμένον, ἀναβλέψας εἰς τὸν
οὐρανὸν εἶπεν· Κύριε ὁ Θεὸς ὁ παντοκράτωρ, ὁ τοῦ ἀγαπητοῦ καὶ εὐλογητοῦ
παιδός σου Ἰησοῦ Χριστοῦ πατήρ, δι᾽ οὗ τὴν περὶ σοῦ ἐπίγνωσιν εἰλήφαμεν,
[67]ὁ Θεὸς ἀγγέλων καὶ δυνάμεων καὶ πάσης κτίσεως παντός τε τοῦ γένους
τῶν δικαίων οἳ ζῶσιν ἐνώπιόν σου· εὐλογῶ σε, ὅτι κατηξίωσάς με τῆς
ἡμέρας καὶ ὥρας ταύτης, [68]τοῦ λαβεῖν με μέρος ἐν ἀριθμῷ τῶν μαρτύρων ἐν
τῷ ποτηρίῳ τοῦ Χριστοῦ εἰς ἀνάστασιν ζωῆς αἰωνίου ψυχῆς τε καὶ σώματος
ἐν ἀφθαρσίᾳ πνεύματος ἁγίου· ἐν οἷς [69]προσδεχθείην ἐνώπιόν σου σήμερον
ἐν θυσίᾳ πίονι καὶ προσδεκτῇ, καθὼς προητοίμασας καὶ προεφανέρωσας καὶ
ἐπλήρωσας, ὁ ἀψευδὴς καὶ ἀληθινὸς Θεός. διὰ τοῦτο καὶ περὶ πάντων σε
αἰνῶ, σὲ εὐλογῶ, σὲ δοξάζω διὰ τοῦ αἰωνίου καὶ ἐπουρανίου ἀρχιερέως Ἰησοῦ
Χριστοῦ, ἀγαπητοῦ σου παιδός, δι᾽ οὗ σοι σὺν αὐτῷ καὶ πνεύματι ἁγίῳ δόξα
καὶ νῦν καὶ εἰς τοὺς μέλλοντας αἰῶνας. ἀμήν.

ἀναπέμψαντος δὲ αὐτοῦ τὸ ἀμὴν καὶ πληρώσαντος τὴν εὐχήν, οἱ τοῦ

---

[54] μὴ εἶναι ἐξὸν αὐτῷ... 145, 156.   [55] τὸ τῆς...ὀπτασίας the matter of his
vision.   [56] θᾶττον ἢ ἐλέγετο quicker than words could tell.   [57] ἐργαστηρίων
καὶ βαλανείων workshops and baths.   [58] φρύγανα faggots.   [59] πυρκαϊὰ
the pile.   [60] ἑαυτῷ 38.   [61] ὑπολύειν to take off his shoes.   [62] διὰ
τὸ ἀεὶ... 228.   [63] ὅστις...ἅψηται, a dependent deliberative question 121,
162; τοῦ χρωτὸς 34 (1).   [64] πρὸ τῆς πολιᾶς even before his hair became
white.   [65] προσηλοῦν to nail.   [66] ἄσκυλτον unmoved.   [67] ὁ Θεός 13.
[68] τοῦ λαβεῖν 177.   [69] προσδεχθείην 131.

πυρὸς ἄνθρωποι ἐξῆψαν τὸ πῦρ. μεγάλης δὲ ἐκλαμψάσης φλογός, θαῦμα
εἴδομεν, οἷς ἰδεῖν ἐδόθη· οἳ καὶ ἐτηρήθημεν εἰς τὸ ἀναγγεῖλαι τοῖς λοιποῖς τὰ
γενόμενα. τὸ γὰρ πῦρ [70]καμάρας εἶδος [71]ποιῆσαν, ὥσπερ [72]ὀθόνη πλοίου
ὑπὸ πνεύματος πληρουμένη, κύκλῳ περιετείχισεν τὸ σῶμα τοῦ μάρτυρος·
καὶ ἦν μέσον, οὐχ ὡς σὰρξ καιομένη, ἀλλ᾽ ὡς χρυσὸς καὶ ἄργυρος ἐν καμίνῳ
πυρούμενος. καὶ γὰρ εὐωδίας τοσαύτης ἀντελαβόμεθα, ὡς [73]λιβανωτοῦ
πνέοντος ἢ ἄλλου τινὸς τῶν τιμίων ἀρωμάτων.

πέρας οὖν ἰδόντες οἱ ἄνομοι [74]μὴ δυνάμενον αὐτοῦ τὸ σῶμα ὑπὸ τοῦ
πυρὸς [75]δαπανηθῆναι, ἐκέλευσαν προσελθόντα αὐτῷ [76]κομφέκτορα [77]παρα-
βῦσαι ξιφίδιον. καὶ τοῦτο ποιήσαντος, ἐξῆλθε πλῆθος αἵματος, ὥστε
[78]κατασβέσαι τὸ πῦρ καὶ [79]θαυμάσαι πάντα τὸν ὄχλον, εἰ τοσαύτη τις
διαφορὰ μεταξὺ τῶν τε ἀπίστων καὶ τῶν ἐκλεκτῶν· ὧν εἷς καὶ οὗτος
γεγόνει ὁ θαυμασιώτατος, ἐν τοῖς καθ᾽ ἡμᾶς χρόνοις διδάσκαλος ἀποστολικὸς
καὶ προφητικὸς γενόμενος, ἐπίσκοπος τῆς ἐν Σμύρνῃ ἁγίας ἐκκλησίας· πᾶν
γὰρ ῥῆμα, ὃ ἀφῆκεν ἐκ τοῦ στόματος αὐτοῦ, ἐτελειώθη καὶ τελειωθήσεται.

ὁ δὲ ἀντίζηλος καὶ [80]βάσκανος καὶ πονηρός, ὁ ἀντικείμενος τῷ γένει
τῶν δικαίων, ἰδὼν τό τε μέγεθος αὐτοῦ τῆς μαρτυρίας καὶ τὴν ἀπ᾽ ἀρχῆς
ἀνεπίληπτον πολιτείαν, [81]ἐστεφανωμένον τε τὸν τῆς ἀφθαρσίας στέφανον
καὶ βραβεῖον [82]ἀναντίρρητον [83]ἀπενηνεγμένον, ἐπετήδευσεν ὡς μηδὲ τὸ
σωμάτιον αὐτοῦ ὑφ᾽ ἡμῶν ληφθῆναι, [84]καίπερ πολλῶν ἐπιθυμούντων τοῦτο
ποιῆσαι καὶ κοινωνῆσαι τῷ ἁγίῳ αὐτοῦ σαρκίῳ. [85]ὑπέβαλεν γοῦν Νικήτην
τὸν τοῦ Ἡρώδου πατέρα, ἀδελφὸν δὲ Ἄλκης, ἐντυχεῖν τῷ ἄρχοντι ὥστε μὴ
δοῦναι αὐτοῦ τὸ σῶμα, [86]μή, φησίν, ἀφέντες τὸν ἐσταυρωμένον, τοῦτον
ἄρξωνται σέβεσθαι· [87]καὶ ταῦτα ὑποβαλλόντων καὶ ἐνισχυόντων τῶν
Ἰουδαίων, οἳ καὶ ἐτήρησαν, μελλόντων ἡμῶν ἐκ τοῦ πυρὸς αὐτὸν
λαμβάνειν, ἀγνοοῦντες ὅτι οὔτε τὸν Χριστόν ποτε καταλιπεῖν δυνησόμεθα,
τὸν ὑπὲρ τῆς τοῦ παντὸς κόσμου τῶν σωζομένων σωτηρίας παθόντα,
ἄμωμον ὑπὲρ ἁμαρτωλῶν, οὔτε ἕτερόν τινα σέβεσθαι. τοῦτον μὲν γὰρ

[70] καμάρας of a vault. [71] ποιῆσαν neut. sing. 1st Aor. part. act. ποιέω.
[72] ὀθόνη the sail. [73] λιβανωτοῦ frankincense. [74] μὴ δυνάμενον 150.
[75] δαπανηθῆναι to be consumed. [76] κομφέκτορα an executioner (Latin
confector). [77] παραβῦσαι ξιφίδιον to stab him with a dagger. [78] κατα-
σβέσαι from κατασβέννυμι. [79] θαυμάσαι εἰ... wondered that... 167.
[80] βάσκανος envious. [81] ἐστεφανωμένον τὸν τῆς ἀφθαρσίας στέφανον and
that he was crowned with the crown of immortality 19, 20. [82] ἀναντίρρητον
which none could gainsay. [83] ἀπενηνεγμένον Perf. pass. part. ἀποφέρω.
[84] καίπερ πολλῶν ἐπιθυμούντων... 246. [85] ὑπέβαλεν γοῦν Therefore he (the
Evil One) put forward...to plead with the magistrate.... [86] μή, φησίν,...
τοῦτον ἄρξωνται σέβεσθαι lest, as he said, ... they should begin to worship this
man 184. [87] καὶ ταῦτα ὑποβαλλόντων... this being done at the instigation
and earnest entreaty of the Jews.

υἱὸν ὄντα τοῦ Θεοῦ προσκυνοῦμεν, τοὺς δὲ μάρτυρας ὡς μαθητὰς καὶ μιμητὰς τοῦ Κυρίου ἀγαπῶμεν ἀξίως ἕνεκεν [88]εὐνοίας ἀνυπερβλήτου τῆς εἰς τὸν ἴδιον βασιλέα καὶ διδάσκαλον· ὧν γένοιτο καὶ ἡμᾶς συγκοινωνούς τε καὶ συμμαθητὰς γενέσθαι.

ἰδὼν οὖν ὁ κεντυρίων τὴν τῶν Ἰουδαίων γενομένην φιλονεικίαν, θεὶς αὐτὸν ἐν μέσῳ, ὡς ἔθος αὐτοῖς, ἔκαυσεν. οὕτως τε ἡμεῖς ὕστερον ἀνελόμενοι τὰ τιμιώτερα λίθων πολυτελῶν καὶ δοκιμώτερα ὑπὲρ χρυσίον ὀστᾶ αὐτοῦ, ἀπεθέμεθα [89]ὅπου καὶ ἀκόλουθον ἦν. ἔνθα ὡς δυνατὸν ἡμῖν συναγομένοις ἐν ἀγαλλιάσει καὶ χαρᾷ παρέξει ὁ Κύριος ἐπιτελεῖν τὴν τοῦ μαρτυρίου αὐτοῦ ἡμέραν γενέθλιον, εἴς τε τὴν τῶν [90]προηθληκότων μνήμην καὶ τῶν μελλόντων ἄσκησίν τε καὶ ἑτοιμασίαν.

[88] εὐνοίας affection. [89] ὅπου καὶ ἀκόλουθον ἦν in a suitable place. [90] προηθληκότων gen. pl. Perf. part. act. προαθλέω of those that have already fought the contest.

A DESCRIPTION OF THE EUCHARIST IN THE SECOND CENTURY FROM THE APOLOGY OF JUSTIN MARTYR.

[1]Ἡμεῖς δέ, μετὰ τὸ οὕτως λοῦσαι τὸν πεπεισμένον καὶ συγκατατεθειμένον, ἐπὶ τοὺς λεγομένους ἀδελφοὺς ἄγομεν, ἔνθα συνηγμένοι εἰσί, κοινὰς εὐχὰς [2]ποιησόμενοι ὑπέρ τε ἑαυτῶν καὶ τοῦ [3]φωτισθέντος, καὶ ἄλλων πανταχοῦ πάντων εὐτόνως, [4]ὅπως καταξιωθῶμεν, τὰ ἀληθῆ μαθόντες, καὶ δι' ἔργων ἀγαθοὶ [5]πολιτευταί, καὶ φύλακες τῶν [6]ἐντεταλμένων εὑρεθῆναι, ὅπως τὴν αἰώνιον [7]σωτηρίαν σωθῶμεν. ἀλλήλους φιλήματι ἀσπαζόμεθα παυσάμενοι [8]τῶν εὐχῶν. ἔπειτα προσφέρεται τῷ [9]προεστῶτι τῶν ἀδελφῶν ἄρτος, καὶ ποτήριον ὕδατος καὶ [10]κράματος· καὶ οὗτος, λαβών, αἶνον καὶ δόξαν τῷ Πατρὶ τῶν ὅλων διὰ τοῦ ὀνόματος τοῦ Υἱοῦ καὶ τοῦ Πνεύματος τοῦ Ἁγίου ἀναπέμπει· καὶ εὐχαριστίαν [11]ὑπὲρ τοῦ κατηξιῶσθαι [12]τούτων παρ' αὐτοῦ ἐπὶ πολὺ ποιεῖται· οὗ συντελέσαντος τὰς εὐχὰς καὶ τὴν εὐχαριστίαν,

[1] ἡμεῖς δέ But we, after having baptized in this way the man who has believed and gives his assent to our doctrine, bring him to those whom we call "Brethren." [2] ποιησόμενοι 265. [3] φωτισθέντος the man who has been enlightened, a common name in the Early Church for a baptised person. [4] ὅπως καταξιωθῶμεν 188. [5] πολιτευταί citizens. [6] ἐντεταλμένων from ἐντέλλω. [7] σωτηρίαν 17. [8] τῶν εὐχῶν 34 (5). [9] προεστῶτι dat. of προεστώς the president. [10] κράματος gen. of κράμα mixed wine. [11] ὑπὲρ τοῦ κατηξιῶσθαι 173; for the tense see 111. [12] τούτων 34 (8).

πᾶς ὁ παρὼν λαὸς [13]ἐπευφημεῖ λέγων Ἀμήν. τὸ δὲ Ἀμὴν τῇ Ἑβραΐδι φωνῇ τὸ Γένοιτο σημαίνει. εὐχαριστήσαντος δὲ τοῦ προεστῶτος, καὶ ἐπευφημήσαντος παντὸς τοῦ λαοῦ, οἱ καλούμενοι παρ' ἡμῖν διάκονοι διδόασιν ἑκάστῳ τῶν παρόντων μεταλαβεῖν ἀπὸ τοῦ εὐχαριστηθέντος ἄρτου καὶ οἴνου καὶ ὕδατος, καὶ τοῖς οὐ παροῦσιν ἀποφέρουσιν.

καὶ ἡ τροφὴ αὕτη καλεῖται παρ' ἡμῖν εὐχαριστία· ἧς οὐδενὶ ἄλλῳ μετασχεῖν ἐξόν ἐστιν ἢ τῷ πιστεύοντι ἀληθῆ εἶναι τὰ δεδιδαγμένα ὑφ' ἡμῶν, καὶ [14]λουσαμένῳ τὸ ὑπὲρ ἀφέσεως ἁμαρτιῶν καὶ εἰς ἀναγέννησιν [15]λουτρόν, καὶ οὕτως βιοῦντι ὡς ὁ Χριστὸς παρέδωκεν. οὐ γὰρ ὡς κοινὸν ἄρτον οὐδὲ κοινὸν πόμα ταῦτα λαμβάνομεν· ἀλλ' [16]ὃν τρόπον [17]διὰ Λόγου Θεοῦ σαρκοποιηθεὶς Ἰησοῦς Χριστὸς ὁ Σωτὴρ ἡμῶν, καὶ σάρκα καὶ αἷμα ὑπὲρ σωτηρίας ἡμῶν ἔσχεν, οὕτως καὶ τὴν δι' εὐχῆς λόγου τοῦ παρ' αὐτοῦ εὐχαριστηθεῖσαν τροφήν, ἐξ ἧς αἷμα καὶ σάρκες κατὰ μεταβολὴν τρέφονται ἡμῶν, ἐκείνου τοῦ σαρκοποιηθέντος Ἰησοῦ καὶ σάρκα καὶ αἷμα ἐδιδάχθημεν εἶναι. οἱ γὰρ ἀπόστολοι ἐν τοῖς γενομένοις ὑπ' αὐτῶν [18]ἀπομνημονεύμασιν, ἃ καλεῖται Εὐαγγέλια, οὕτως παρέδωκαν [6]ἐντετάλθαι αὐτοῖς τὸν Ἰησοῦν· [19]λαβόντα ἄρτον, εὐχαριστήσαντα εἰπεῖν· "τοῦτο ποιεῖτε εἰς τὴν ἀνάμνησίν μου· τοῦτό ἐστι τὸ σῶμά μου·" καὶ τὸ ποτήριον ὁμοίως λαβόντα καὶ εὐχαριστήσαντα εἰπεῖν· "τοῦτό ἐστι τὸ αἷμά μου." καὶ μόνοις αὐτοῖς [20]μεταδοῦναι. ὅπερ καὶ ἐν τοῖς τοῦ Μίθρα μυστηρίοις παρέδωκαν γίνεσθαι μιμησάμενοι οἱ πονηροὶ δαίμονες. ὅτι γὰρ ἄρτος καὶ ποτήριον ὕδατος τίθεται [21]ἐν ταῖς τοῦ μυουμένου τελεταῖς μετ' ἐπιλόγων τινῶν, ἢ ἐπίστασθε, ἢ μαθεῖν δύνασθε.

ἡμεῖς δὲ μετὰ ταῦτα λοιπὸν ἀεὶ τούτων ἀλλήλους ἀναμιμνήσκομεν· καὶ οἱ ἔχοντες [22]τοῖς λειπομένοις πᾶσιν ἐπικουροῦμεν, καὶ σύνεσμεν ἀλλήλοις ἀεί. [23]ἐπὶ πᾶσί τε οἷς προσφερόμεθα, εὐλογοῦμεν τὸν Ποιητὴν τῶν πάντων διὰ τοῦ Υἱοῦ αὐτοῦ Ἰησοῦ Χριστοῦ καὶ διὰ Πνεύματος τοῦ Ἁγίου.

---

[13] ἐπευφημεῖ assents thereto.   [14] λουσαμένῳ Middle voice, that has allowed himself to be baptized 81.   [15] λουτρόν 17.   [16] ὃν τρόπον 22 For even as Jesus Christ our Saviour, having been made flesh by the Word of God, took flesh and blood for our salvation, so we have been taught that the food, for which we return thanks in a prayer containing His very words and from which our flesh and blood are nourished by its transformation, is the flesh and blood of that incarnate Jesus.   [17] διὰ Λόγου, for the omission of the article see end of 68.   [18] ἀπομνημονεύμασιν memoirs.   [19] λαβόντα ἄρτον namely that He took bread, and, when He had given thanks, He said... 146, for the participles see 258, 218.   [20] μεταδοῦναι, this infinitive is dependent on the idea of saying implied in παρέδωκαν, as are the other infinitives above, 146.   [21] ἐν ταῖς τοῦ μυουμένου τελεταῖς in the rites of initiation.   [22] τοῖς λειπομένοις to those that are in want.   [23] ἐπὶ πᾶσί τε οἷς προσφερόμεθα in all our prayers 63.

καὶ τῇ τοῦ Ἡλίου λεγομένῃ ἡμέρᾳ πάντων κατὰ πόλεις ἢ ἀγροὺς μενόντων ἐπὶ τὸ αὐτὸ συνέλευσις γίνεται, καὶ τὰ ἀπομνημονεύματα τῶν ἀποστόλων, ἢ τὰ συγγράμματα τῶν προφητῶν ἀναγινώσκεται [24]μέχρις ἐγχωρεῖ. εἶτα παυσαμένου τοῦ ἀναγινώσκοντος, ὁ προεστὼς διὰ λόγου τὴν νουθεσίαν καὶ πρόκλησιν τῆς τῶν καλῶν τούτων μιμήσεως ποιεῖται. ἔπειτα ἀνιστάμεθα κοινῇ πάντες, καὶ εὐχὰς πέμπομεν· καὶ ὡς προέφημεν, παυσαμένων ἡμῶν τῆς εὐχῆς, ἄρτος προσφέρεται καὶ οἶνος καὶ ὕδωρ· καὶ ὁ προεστὼς εὐχὰς ὁμοίως καὶ εὐχαριστίας, ὅση δύναμις αὐτῷ, ἀναπέμπει, καὶ ὁ λαὸς ἐπευφημεῖ λέγων τὸ Ἀμήν· καὶ ἡ διάδοσις καὶ ἡ μετάληψις ἀπὸ τῶν εὐχαριστηθέντων ἑκάστῳ γίνεται, καὶ τοῖς οὐ παροῦσι διὰ τῶν διακόνων πέμπεται. οἱ εὐποροῦντες δὲ καὶ βουλόμενοι, κατὰ προαίρεσιν ἕκαστος τὴν ἑαυτοῦ, ὃ βούλεται δίδωσι· καὶ τὸ συλλεγόμενον παρὰ τῷ προεστῶτι ἀποτίθεται, καὶ αὐτὸς ἐπικουρεῖ ὀρφανοῖς τε καὶ χήραις, καὶ τοῖς διὰ νόσον ἢ δι᾽ ἄλλην αἰτίαν λειπομένοις, καὶ τοῖς ἐν δεσμοῖς οὖσι, καὶ τοῖς παρεπιδήμοις οὖσι ξένοις, καὶ ἁπλῶς πᾶσι τοῖς ἐν χρείᾳ οὖσι κηδεμὼν γίνεται. τὴν δὲ τοῦ Ἡλίου ἡμέραν κοινῇ πάντες τὴν συνέλευσιν ποιούμεθα· ἐπειδὴ πρώτη ἐστὶν ἡμέρα, ἐν ᾗ ὁ Θεός, τὸ σκότος καὶ τὴν ὕλην [25]τρέψας, κόσμον ἐποίησε, καὶ Ἰησοῦς Χριστὸς ὁ ἡμέτερος Σωτὴρ τῇ αὐτῇ ἡμέρᾳ ἐκ νεκρῶν ἀνέστη. τῇ γὰρ πρὸ τῆς Κρονικῆς ἐσταύρωσαν αὐτόν· καὶ τῇ μετὰ τὴν Κρονικήν, ἥτις ἐστὶν Ἡλίου ἡμέρα, φανεὶς τοῖς ἀποστόλοις αὐτοῦ καὶ μαθηταῖς, ἐδίδαξε ταῦτα, ἅπερ [26]εἰς ἐπίσκεψιν καὶ ὑμῖν ἀνεδώκαμεν.

[24] μέχρις ἐγχωρεῖ *as long as time permits.*   [25] τρέψας *having changed.*
[26] εἰς ἐπίσκεψιν *for your consideration.*

A HOSTILE OUTSIDER'S VIEW OF CHRISTIANITY.

Lucian, the writer of this piece, was a native of Samosata on the Euphrates, and lived in the second century A.D.

He was a cultivated man of the world who despised and ridiculed all religious and philosophic sects alike.

In the book from which this passage is taken he is describing the death of Proteus Peregrinus, a Cynic philosopher, who burnt himself alive at the Olympian Games to show his contempt for death.

Lucian says that after a disreputable youth Peregrinus joined the sect of the Christians, and gives the following account of his relationship with them. Peregrinus afterwards ceased to be a Christian, and, becoming a Cynic, ended his life in the manner described above.

Ὅτεπερ καὶ τὴν θαυμαστὴν σοφίαν τῶν Χριστιανῶν ἐξέμαθε περὶ τὴν Παλαιστίνην τοῖς ἱερεῦσι καὶ γραμματεῦσιν αὐτῶν συγγενόμενος. [1]καὶ τί γάρ; ἐν βραχεῖ παῖδας αὐτοὺς ἀπέφηνε, προφήτης, καὶ [2]θιασάρχης, καὶ [3]συναγωγεύς, καὶ πάντα μόνος αὐτὸς ὤν. καὶ τῶν [4]βίβλων τὰς μὲν [5]ἐξηγεῖτο, καὶ διεσάφει, πολλὰς δὲ αὐτὸς καὶ συνέγραφε, καὶ ὡς θεὸν αὐτὸν ἐκεῖνοι ἡγοῦντο, καὶ [6]νομοθέτῃ ἐχρῶντο, καὶ προστάτην ἐπέγραφον. τὸν μέγαν γοῦν ἐκεῖνον ἔτι σέβουσιν ἄνθρωπον, τὸν ἐν τῇ Παλαιστίνῃ [7]ἀνασκολοπισθέντα, ὅτι καινὴν ταύτην τελετὴν εἰσήγαγεν ἐς τὸν βίον.

τότε δὴ καὶ συλληφθεὶς ἐπὶ τούτῳ ὁ Πρωτεὺς ἐνέπεσεν εἰς τὸ δεσμωτήριον. ὅπερ καὶ αὐτὸ οὐ μικρὸν αὐτῷ ἀξίωμα περιεποίησε πρὸς τὸν [8]ἑξῆς βίον, καὶ τὴν [9]τερατείαν, καὶ [10]δοξοκοπίαν, [11]ὧν ἐρῶν ἐτύγχανεν. ἐπεὶ δ᾽ οὖν ἐδέδετο οἱ Χριστιανοί, συμφορὰν ποιούμενοι τὸ πρᾶγμα, πάντα ἐκίνουν, ἐξαρπάσαι πειρώμενοι αὐτόν. εἶτ᾽ ἐπεὶ τοῦτο ἦν ἀδύνατον, [12]ἦγε ἄλλη θεραπεία πᾶσα οὐ παρέργως ἀλλὰ σὺν σπουδῇ ἐγίγνετο· καὶ ἕωθεν μὲν εὐθὺς ἦν ὁρᾶν παρὰ τῷ δεσμωτηρίῳ περιμένοντα [13]γραΐδια, χήρας τινάς, καὶ παιδία ὀρφανά. οἱ δὲ ἐν τέλει αὐτῶν καὶ συνεκάθευδον ἔνδον μετ᾽ αὐτοῦ, διαφθείροντες τοὺς δεσμοφύλακας· εἶτα δεῖπνα ποικίλα εἰσεκομίζετο, καὶ λόγοι ἱεροὶ αὐτῶν ἐλέγοντο, καὶ ὁ βέλτιστος Περεγρῖνος (ἔτι γὰρ τοῦτο ἐκαλεῖτο) καινὸς Σωκράτης ὑπ᾽ αὐτῶν ὠνομάζετο.

[14]καὶ μὴν καὶ τῶν ἐν Ἀσίᾳ πόλεών ἐστιν ὧν ἧκόν τινες, τῶν Χριστιανῶν στελλόντων ἀπὸ τοῦ κοινοῦ, βοηθήσοντες, καὶ συναγορεύσοντες, καὶ παραμυθησόμενοι τὸν ἄνδρα. ἀμήχανον δέ τι τὸ τάχος ἐπιδείκνυται, [15]ἐπειδάν τι τοιοῦτον γένηται δημόσιον.

[16]ἐν βραχεῖ γάρ, ἀφειδοῦσι πάντων. καὶ δὴ καὶ τῷ Περεγρίνῳ πολλὰ τότε ἧκε χρήματα παρ᾽ αὐτῶν ἐπὶ προφάσει τῶν δεσμῶν, καὶ πρόσοδον οὐ μικρὰν ταύτην ἐποιήσατο.

[17]πεπείκασι γὰρ αὐτοὺς οἱ κακοδαίμονες [18]τὸ μὲν ὅλον ἀθάνατοι ἔσεσθαι, καὶ βιώσεσθαι [19]τὸν ἀεὶ χρόνον.

παρ᾽ ὃ καὶ καταφρονοῦσι [20]τοῦ θανάτου, καὶ ἑκόντες αὐτοὺς ἐπιδιδόασιν

---

[1] καὶ τί γάρ; why say more?   [2] θιασάρχης leader of the company.
[3] συναγωγεύς convener.   [4] βίβλος ἡ a book.   [5] for the force of these
Imperfects see 89, 101, 102.   [6] νομοθέτῃ 44.   [7] ἀνασκολοπισθέντα
crucified.   [8] τὸν ἑξῆς βίον the life to come.   [9] τερατεία jugglery.
[10] δοξοκοπίαν thirst for notoriety.   [11] ὧν ἐρῶν ἐτύγχανεν with which things
he was in love.   [12] ἦγε made up of ἦ and γε.   [13] γραΐδια wretched
old women.   [14] καὶ μὴν καὶ... And there were actually some of the cities
of Asia from which there came certain men sent by the Christians by common
consent (35) to help, and defend, and comfort the man (203).   [15] ἐπειδὰν
γένηται (209).   [16] ἐν βραχεῖ γάρ in a word they spare nothing.   [17] πεπείκασι 97.   [18] τὸ μὲν ὅλον 22.   [19] τὸν ἀεὶ χρόνον 18.   [20] τοῦ θανάτου 34 (8).

οἱ πολλοί. ἔπειτα δὲ ὁ νομοθέτης ὁ πρῶτος ἔπεισεν αὐτοὺς ὡς ἀδελφοὶ πάντες ²¹εἶεν ἀλλήλων, ἐπειδὰν ἅπαξ παραβάντες, θεοὺς μὲν τοὺς Ἑλληνικοὺς ἀπαρνήσωνται, τὸν δὲ ἀνεσκολοπισμένον ἐκεῖνον σοφιστὴν αὐτῶν προσκυνῶσι, καὶ κατὰ τοὺς ἐκείνου νόμους βιῶσι.

καταφρονοῦσιν οὖν ἁπάντων ἐξ ἴσης, καὶ κοινὰ ἡγοῦνται, ²²ἄνευ τινὸς ἀκριβοῦς πίστεως τὰ τοιαῦτα παραδεξάμενοι.

ἢν τοίνυν παρέλθῃ τις εἰς αὐτοὺς γόης καὶ τεχνίτης ἄνθρωπος καὶ πράγμασι χρῆσθαι δυνάμενος, αὐτίκα μάλα πλούσιος ἐν βραχεῖ ²³ἐγένετο, ²⁴ἰδιώταις ἀνθρώποις ἐγχανών.

πλὴν ἀλλ' ὁ Περεγρῖνος ²⁵ἀφείθη ὑπὸ τοῦ τότε τῆς Συρίας ἄρχοντος, ἀνδρὸς φιλοσοφίᾳ χαίροντος, ὃς ²⁶συνεὶς τὴν ἀπόνοιαν αὐτοῦ, καὶ ὅτι ²⁷δέξαιτ' ἂν ἀποθανεῖν, ὡς δόξαν ἐπὶ τούτῳ ²⁸ἀπολίποι, ἀφῆκεν αὐτόν, οὐδὲ τῆς κολάσεως ὑπολαβὼν ἄξιον.

²¹ εἶεν 154.   ²² ἄνευ τινὸς ἀκριβοῦς πίστεως *without any sufficient evidence.* ²³ ἐγένετο *he becomes,* Gnomic Aorist 95.   ²⁴ ἰδιώταις... *making a mock of simple men.*   ²⁵ ἀφείθη *was let go,* from ἀφίημι.   ²⁶ συνεὶς *knowing,* from συνίημι.   ²⁷ δέξαιτ' ἄν 132, 276.   ²⁸ ὡς ἀπολίποι 184.   ὡς = ἵνα.

THE LAST WORDS OF SOCRATES TO HIS JUDGES.

These selections may fitly close with one of the noblest and yet easiest passages in Classical literature. Socrates was condemned to death by the Athenians on the charge of corrupting the youth and of introducing the worship of strange gods. The passage below consists of part of his address to the judges who voted for his acquittal.

ἐννοήσωμεν δὲ καὶ τῇδε, ὡς πολλὴ ἐλπίς ἐστιν ἀγαθὸν ¹αὐτὸ εἶναι· ²δυοῖν γὰρ θάτερόν ἐστιν τὸ τεθνάναι· ἢ γὰρ ³μηδὲν εἶναι μηδ' αἴσθησιν μηδεμίαν μηδενὸς ἔχειν τὸν τεθνεῶτα, ἢ κατὰ τὰ λεγόμενα μεταβολή τις τυγχάνει οὖσα καὶ μετοίκησις τῇ ψυχῇ ἐνθένδε εἰς ἄλλον τόπον. καὶ εἴτε μηδεμία αἴσθησίς ἐστιν, ἀλλ' οἶον ὕπνος, ἐπειδάν τις καθεύδων μηδ' ὄναρ μηδὲν ὁρᾷ, θαυμάσιον κέρδος ⁴ἂν εἴη ὁ θάνατος. καὶ γὰρ οὐδὲν πλείων ὁ πᾶς χρόνος φαίνεται οὕτω δὴ εἶναι ἢ μία νύξ. εἰ δ' αὖ οἶον ἀποδημῆσαί ἐστιν ὁ θάνατος ἐνθένδε εἰς ἄλλον τόπον, καὶ ἀληθῆ ἐστιν τὰ λεγόμενα, ὡς ἄρα ἐκεῖ εἰσιν ἅπαντες οἱ τεθνεῶτες, τί μεῖζον ἀγαθὸν τούτου ⁴εἴη ἄν, ὦ ἄνδρες

¹ αὐτό i.e. *death.*   ² δυοῖν the gen. of the dual *of two things.* ³ μηδέν 267.   ⁴ ἂν εἴη 132, 276.

δικασταί; πάντως οὐ δήπου τούτου γε ἕνεκα οἱ ἐκεῖ ἀποκτείνουσι· τά τε γὰρ ἄλλα εὐδαιμονέστεροί εἰσιν οἱ ἐκεῖ τῶν ἐνθάδε, καὶ ἤδη τὸν λοιπὸν χρόνον ἀθάνατοί εἰσιν, εἴπερ γε τὰ λεγόμενα ἀληθῆ ἐστιν.

ἀλλὰ καὶ ὑμᾶς χρή, ὦ ἄνδρες δικασταί, εὐέλπιδας εἶναι πρὸς τὸν θάνατον, καὶ ἕν τι τοῦτο διανοεῖσθαι ἀληθές, ὅτι οὐκ ἔστιν ἀνδρὶ ἀγαθῷ κακὸν οὐδὲν οὔτε ζῶντι οὔτε τελευτήσαντι, οὐδὲ ἀμελεῖται ὑπὸ θεῶν τὰ τούτου πράγματα. οὐδὲ τὰ ἐμὰ νῦν ἀπὸ τοῦ αὐτομάτου γέγονεν, ἀλλά μοι δῆλόν ἐστι τοῦτο, ὅτι ἤδη τεθνάναι καὶ ἀπαλλαχθῆναι πραγμάτων βέλτιον ἦν μοι. ἀλλὰ γὰρ ἤδη ὥρα ἀπιέναι, ἐμοὶ μὲν ἀποθανουμένῳ, ὑμῖν δὲ βιωσομένοις· ὁπότεροι δὲ ἡμῶν ἔρχονται ἐπὶ ἄμεινον πρᾶγμα, ἄδηλον παντὶ πλὴν ἢ τῷ θεῷ.

Plato, Apology (abridged).

ENGLISH INDEX

The references are to sections in all cases

Ablative Case 23
Accusative Case 14–22
  adverbial 22
  cognate 17
  extent 18
  object 15
  two accusatives with one verb 19, 20
  predicate accusative 21
  subject of infinitive 9, 16
Active voice 79
Adjectives 45, 46
  used as nouns 47, 48
Adjectival clauses 250–254
Adverbial clauses 197–249
Antecedent 60
  assimilation of 67
  attraction of 66
  omission of 62, 65
Aorist tense 91–95
  dramatic 95
  epistolary 95
  gnomic 95
  inceptive 93
  resultative 94
  distinction between aorist and imperfect 101, 102
  distinction between aorist and perfect 101, 103
  used where English requires perfect 104–106
  used where English requires pluperfect 98–100
  aorist subjunctive in prohibitions 126, 129, 130
  imperative 125
  participle 262–264
Apodosis 235

Article, definite 68–76
  forming nouns of adjectives, phrases etc. 71–73
  attributive position 75
  predicative position 76
  with infinitive 172
  as a personal pronoun 54
Assimilation of relative pronoun 63–66
Attempted action, present of 86
  imperfect of 90

Cases, meanings of 12
Causal clauses 225–229
Clause, definition of 115
Clauses, subordinate classification of 118
Comparative clauses 249
Complement 11
Concessive clauses 246–248
Conditional clauses 235–245 a
  future conditions 240–243
  general conditions 244
  present and past conditions 238, 239
  participle 245
Consecutive clauses 139, 176, 185, 230–232, 234

Dative case 36–44
  of cause 42
  indirect object 37
  of instrument 42
  of interest 38
  of manner 42
  of possession 39
  of resemblance or union 43
  of sphere 41

Dative of place or time 40
    after verbs 44
Deliberative subjunctive 121
Dependent commands 159
Dependent questions 160
Dependent statements 145–157
Direct quotations introduced by ὅτι 158

Epexegetic or Explanatory clauses 170, 178, 195, 196

Final clauses 198–204
    introduced by ἵνα etc. 184, 198
    with infinitive 138, 175, 201, 202
    with participle 203
    final relative clauses 204
Final particles, clauses introduced by 180–196
  commands 183
  consecutive clauses 185
  explanatory clauses 195, 196
  final clauses 184
  noun clauses
    as subject 186, 187
    as object 188–193
    in apposition 194
Future tense 107
    in final clauses 199, 204
    in conditional clauses 242
    participle 265
    infinitive 112
    periphrastic form 114

General suppositions 244
Genitive case 23–31
    genitive absolute 35
    in comparisons 33
    of definition 31
    objective 28
    partitive 26
    of possession 24
    of price 30
    of source or material 25
    subjective 27
    of time 29
    after verbs 34
    after adjectives 32
Gnomic aorist 95

Historic present 88
Hortatory subjunctive 119

Imperative mood 124, 125
    force of tenses of 125
Imperfect tense 89–90
    distinction in meaning between aorist and imperfect 101, 102
    imperfect of attempted action 90
    periphrastic form of 114
Indicative mood 78
Infinitive mood 133–179
    imperative infinitive 137
    in consecutive clauses 139
    in final clauses 138
    in noun clauses
      as subject 142
      as object 144–168
      in apposition 169
    in temporal clauses 140
    with the article 172
    with τοῦ 174–179
    substitutes for 134
    negatives with 267
Instrumental case 36, 42

Local clauses 220
    definite 221, 222
    indefinite 221, 223, 224
Locative Case 36, 40

Middle voice 81, 82
Moods in general 78

Negatives 267
Nominative case 8
    used as vocative 13

Object clauses
    after verbs of exhorting 159
    after verbs of fear and danger 166
    after verbs of striving 165
    in dependent statements 145–157
Oblique cases 12
Optative mood 131
    in conditional clauses 243
    in dependent questions 161
    potential optative 132, 275
    in wishes 131
    Classical use in final clauses 184
    Classical use in dependent statements 154, 157
    Classical use after πρίν 217

Participles 255–266 a
  tenses of 259–266 a
  in dependent statements 150
  negative with 267
  adjectival use 256
  adverbial use 256
  conditional 245
  causal 227
  concessive 248
  final 203
  temporal 218
Passive voice 79
Perfect tense 96, 97
  difference between perfect and
    aorist 101, 103
  periphrastic form 114
Phrase, definition of 115
Pluperfect tense 98–100
Potential optative 275
Predicative nouns and adjectives 11
Prepositions
  governing genitive 4
  governing dative 5
  governing accusative 3
  governing genitive and accusative 6
  governing genitive, dative, and
    accusative 7
  in composition with Verbs, appen-
    dix to section 1, pp. 27, 32
Present tense 85–88
  of attempted action 86
  historic 88
  periphrastic form of 114
Prohibitions 126–130
Pronouns 49–67
  demonstrative 57
  indefinite 59
  interrogative 58
  personal 50–53
  reflexive 55
  relative 60–67
Protasis 235

Questions 268
Questions, dependent 160–162

Relative clauses
  definite 251
  indefinite 252

Relative expressing purpose 204
  pronoun 60–67
  case of 60
  assimilation of 63–66

Sentences 115
  simple 115
  complex 115, 117
  compound 115, 116
Subject and predicate 8
Subjunctive mood
  generally 78
  deliberative 121, 122
  hortatory 119, 120
  in prohibitions 126, 129, 130
  in consecutive clauses after ἵνα 185
  in final clauses 184, 198
  in noun clauses after ἵνα etc. 186–196
  in conditional clauses 241, 244
  in indefinite relative clauses 252
  in indefinite temporal clauses 208, 209
  in indefinite local clauses 224
  after ἕως 213, 214
  negative with 267
Subordinate clauses classified 118
  in dependent statements 156, 157

Temporal clauses 205–219
  definite 206, 207
  indefinite 206, 208, 209
  introduced by ἕως 211–215
  introduced by πρίν 216, 217
  expressed by a participle 218
  expressed by infinitive with article 219
Tenses in general 83, 84
  in indicative mood 83–107
  in dependent moods 108–113
  in reported speech 113, 151–157
  in the imperative 125
  in the participle 259–266 a

Vocative case 13
Voice 79–82

Wishes 131

GREEK INDEX

ἄν, general use of 272–277
αὐτός 51, ὁ αὐτός 53
ἄφες, ἄφετε followed by Hortatory
    Subjunctive 120
ἄχρι etc. 215
βούλεσθε followed by Deliberative
    Subjunctive 122
διά with articular Infinitive 228
ἐάν used for ἄν in Indefinite Relative
    clauses 252
ἐὰν καί concessive 246
εἰ in Conditional sentences 236
εἰ Interrogative 268
εἰ καί concessive 246
εἰς with articular Infinitive 202
ἐκεῖνος 52
ἐν with articular Infinitive 219
ἐπεί, ἐπειδή causal 225
ἐφ᾽ ᾧ causal 225
ἕως 211
ἤ in comparisons 249
θέλεις, θέλετε followed by Deliberative
    Subjunctive 122
ἵνα, special chapter on 180–196
ἵνα in commands 183
    in Consecutive clauses 185
    in Final clauses 184, 198
    in Noun clauses
        as subject 186
        as object 188–193
        in apposition 194
    in explanatory clauses 195, 196
καὶ εἰ, καὶ ἐάν concessive 247

καίπερ concessive 246
μέλλω 114
μετά with articular Infinitive 219
μέχρι 215
μή negative 267
    in questions 270
    in Final clauses 198
    in Object clauses
        after verbs of fear and danger
            192
        after verbs meaning to take
            heed 191
ὅπως in Final clauses 198
    in Object clauses after verbs of
        exhorting 188
    in Object clauses after verbs of
        striving 165
ὅτι meaning "because" 225
    introducing a dependent state-
        ment 146, 153
    redundant before a direct quota-
        tion or question 158
οὐ negative 267
    in questions 269
οὐ μή 123
οὗτος 52
πρίν 216
πρό with articular Infinitive 219
τοῦ with Infinitive 174–178
ὡς with a causal participle 229
ὡς, ὥσπερ in comparisons 249
ὥστε with Indicative 232
    with Infinitive 231
    introducing a principal clause 233

INDEX OF TEXTS

ST MATTHEW

1. 21	....	107
2. 9	....	212
2. 10	....	17
2. 13	....	114, 175
2. 20	....	261
3. 4	....	51
3. 11	....	170, 195
3. 12	....	42
3. 14	....	90
3. 17	....	106
4. 2	....	263
4. 3	....	189
5. 3	....	41, 47, 71
5. 4	....	71
5. 6	....	260
5. 17	....	110
5. 22	....	32
5. 23	....	109
5. 29	....	187
5. 41	....	253
5. 42	....	124
6. 1	....	42, 173, 202
6. 8	....	62, 219
6. 11	....	110, 125
6. 19	....	222
6. 25	....	38
6. 27	....	258
6. 50	....	127
7. 1	....	184, 198
7. 4	....	120
7. 19	....	85
7. 23	....	69
7. 25	....	99
8. 3	....	92
8. 8	....	195
8. 25	....	85
9. 33	....	35
10. 2	....	10
10. 9	....	129
10. 21	....	10
10. 25	....	187
10. 29	....	30
10. 32	....	253
11. 25	....	105
12. 3	....	105
12. 28	....	106
13. 4	....	1
13. 25	....	219
13. 32	....	231
13. 55	....	269
14. 3	....	100
14. 14	....	218
14. 32	....	218
15. 20	....	172
16. 18	.. ..	68
16. 21	....	40
17. 20	....	241
18. 4	....	253
18. 6	....	187
18. 12	....	39
18. 14	....	186
18. 25	....	35, 159, 226
18. 30	....	214
18. 32	....	225
18. 33	....	249
19. 1	....	207
19. 6	....	233
19. 14	....	94
19. 18	....	73
19. 21	....	149
19. 24	....	249
20. 10	....	153
20. 19	....	202
21. 24	....	19
21. 32	....	176
21. 35	....	54
21. 41	....	204
22. 3	....	201
22. 21	....	70
22. 23	....	267
24. 4	....	191
24. 12	....	228
24. 24	....	201 a
24. 27	....	249
24. 38	....	66
24. 43	....	162
25. 5	....	35
25. 8	....	85
25. 9	....	123
26. 13	....	224
26. 17	....	122
26. 18	....	88
26. 32	....	219
26. 34	....	140, 216
26. 35	....	247
26. 43	....	114
26. 44	....	53

ST MATTHEW (*cont.*)

26. 46	....	81
26. 55	....	102
26. 66	....	32
27. 1	....	201 *a*
27. 4	....	264
27. 5	....	81
27. 8	....	105
27. 20	....	94
27. 24	....	69
27. 36	....	170
27. 43	....	97
27. 49	....	265
27. 52	....	266
28. 13	....	266

ST MARK

1. 6	....	20
1. 7	....	135
1. 11	....	106
1. 22	....	258
1. 31	....	110
1. 32	....	254
1. 45	....	54
2. 5	....	87
2. 13	....	116
2. 15	....	142
2. 15, 16	......	68
2. 20	....	210
3. 8	....	163
3. 11	....	208
3. 29	....	32
4. 6	....	173
4. 21	....	158
4. 26	....	249
4. 37	....	139
4. 38	....	143
4. 39	....	111
5. 19	....	103
5. 23	....	183
5. 35	....	127
5. 39	....	106
6. 10	....	213
6. 21	....	158
6. 34	....	19
6. 50	....	127
6. 56	....	223
7. 4	....	81
8. 14	....	100
8. 29	....	264
9. 12	....	186
9. 22	....	124
9. 23	....	73
9. 35	....	149

9. 38	....	90
10. 18	....	21
10. 32	....	114
10. 36	....	122
10. 38	....	81
10. 43	....	252
11. 25	....	253
11. 27	....	88
11. 28	....	195
12. 41	....	89, 102
13. 2	....	123
13. 11	....	209
13. 21	....	128
14. 11	....	37
14. 31	....	123
14. 61	....	93, 102
15. 4	....	163
15. 6	....	89
15. 20	....	19
15. 23	....	90
15. 44	....	160, **167**
16. 6	....	106
16. 20	....	259

ST LUKE

1. 4	....	66
1. 9	....	179
1. 20	....	64, 66
1. 21	....	114, 219
1. 38	....	131
1. 43	....	194
1. 59	....	90
1. 62	....	73, 277
1. 76	....	175
1. 77	....	175, 202
1. 79	....	175
2. 5	....	81
2. 21	....	219
2. 22	....	175
2. 24	....	175
2. 26	....	114, 217
3. 10	....	121
3. 19	....	66
3. 22	....	106
4. 2	....	267
4. 3	....	238
4. 15	....	258
4. 16	....	254
4. 35	....	22
5. 7	....	175, 258
5. 9	....	63
5. 10	....	114
5. 26	....	105
5. 35	....	210

ST LUKE (*cont.*)

6. 11	....	277
7. 6	....	195
7. 16	....	106
7. 39	....	239
8. 5	....	173
8. 8	....	170
8. 27	....	100
8. 29	....	40
8. 46	....	150
8. 49	....	127
9. 25	....	245, 264
9. 36	....	65
9. 38	....	159
9. 46	....	277
9. 47	....	1
9. 52	....	201 a
10. 2	....	189
10. 4	....	130
10. 7	....	69, 128
10. 21	....	13
10. 39	....	57
10. 40	....	143
11. 3	....	109, 125
11. 18	....	148
11. 46	....	17, 69
12. 5	....	161
12. 48	....	67
13. 24	....	165
13. 28	....	210
14. 8	....	130
14. 20	....	106
15. 4	....	213
15. 18	....	266 a
15. 19	....	195
15. 20	....	266 a
15. 32	....	93, 106
16. 1	....	59
16. 4	....	95
16. 8	....	31
16. 12	....	130
17. 1	....	177
17. 2	....	187
17. 4	....	110
17. 6	....	245 a
17. 13	....	13
17. 27	....	89
18. 14	....	57
18. 25	....	142
18. 36	....	161
19. 8	....	88
19. 23	....	275
19. 37	....	66
20. 6	....	114
20. 10	....	199
20. 22	....	142
20. 26	....	93
20. 41	....	148
21. 6	....	178
21. 24	....	114
22. 2	....	73
22. 6	....	187
22. 23	....	73, 161
22. 37	....	73
22. 41	....	18
22. 49	....	1
23. 15	....	42
23. 28	....	127
23. 33	....	54
24. 23	....	156
24. 25	....	178
24. 34	....	106

ST JOHN

1. 2	....	52
1. 6	....	39
1. 7	....	184, 198
1. 14	....	15
1. 27	....	135, 195
1. 30	....	251
1. 39	....	162
1. 50	....	33
2. 12	....	18
2. 16	....	127
2. 20	....	40
2. 21	....	52
3. 2	....	29
3. 10	....	76
3. 16	....	232
4. 10	....	239
4. 14	....	63
4. 29	....	270
4. 34	....	186
4. 47	....	68, 189
4. 52	....	93
5. 7	....	195
5. 11	....	54
5. 13	....	263
5. 14	....	127
5. 46	....	239
6. 29	....	194
6. 37	....	123
6. 39	....	194
6. 40	....	194
6. 63	....	251
6. 69	....	97
7. 17	....	117
7. 31	....	65
7. 32	....	150

ST JOHN (*cont.*)

7. 47	149
7. 51	270
8. 16	247
8. 39	245 *a*
8. 56	196
9. 2	181, 185
9. 4	211
9. 9	158
9. 22	99, 196
10. 8	10
10. 32	86
10. 37	128
11. 9	244
11. 31	153
11. 36	89
11. 50	187
12. 10	190
12. 17	261
12. 19	106
12. 23	195
12. 29	16, 148
12. 34	50
13. 1	106
13. 12	100
15. 6	106
15. 8	194
15. 13	194
16. 24	81
17. 3	194
17. 8	1
17. 19	81
17. 25	106
18. 11	123
18. 30	267
18. 39	186
19. 2	40
19. 25	70
19. 30	100
21. 2	70
21. 3	138
21. 19	259
21. 23	88
21. 25	148

ACTS

1. 3	42, 219
1. 4	159
1. 22	64
2. 13	258
2. 42	68
2. 47	266 *a*
3. 2	89
3. 12	177

3. 26	203
4. 34	261
5. 3	139, 234
5. 24	277
5. 28	97
6. 3	204
7. 19	178
7. 26	90
7. 52	105
7. 60	93
8. 6	219
8. 11	40
8. 19	194
8. 23	150
8. 31	132, 245 *a*, 275
8. 33	275
9. 34	87
9. 39	100
10. 17	266, 277
10. 18	160
10. 25	177
12. 3	227
13. 20	40
13. 28	248
13. 33	264
14. 8	40
14. 9	178
14. 16	40
14. 19	111
15. 10	171, 196
15. 13	93
15. 20	177
15. 28	169
16. 27	111
17. 11	161
17. 18	132, 275
17. 28	68
17. 32	54
18. 9	129
18. 10	176
18. 24	41
18. 25	20
19. 13	69
19. 32	99
20. 3	177
21. 11	57
21. 12	177
21. 16	67
21. 28	103
21. 33	161
21. 38	76
22. 5	203
23. 10	192
23. 15	178

ACTS (*cont.*)

23. 20	....	177, 229
23. 26	....	137
23. 30	....	95, 112
24. 11	....	265
24. 15	....	47
24. 19	....	245 *a*
25. 11	....	172
25. 16	....	217
25. 18	....	66
25. 26	....	161
26. 11	....	90
26. 29	....	275
27. 1	....	177
27. 13	....	111
27. 30	....	229
27. 34	....	7
27. 42	....	186
27. 43	....	94
28. 27	....	184, 193
28. 30	....	92

ROMANS

1. 22	....	149
2. 1	....	53
2. 4	....	86
4. 2	....	238
4. 11	....	31
4. 12	....	40
6. 6	....	176
6. 12	....	128
6. 17	....	67
7. 3	....	176
8. 9	....	267
8. 12	....	178
8. 26	....	73
8. 35	....	27
9. 3	....	149
11. 20	....	42
12. 15	....	137
13. 9	....	73
13. 10	....	71
13. 11	....	170, 195
14. 2	....	54
14. 4	....	38
14. 5	....	54
14. 9	....	93
15. 14	....	111, 266
15. 22	....	179
16. 25	....	40

I CORINTHIANS

1. 4	....	263
1. 17	....	138
1. 18	....	28, 266 *a*
1. 23	....	266
1. 25	....	48
2. 8	....	239
3. 2	....	17
4. 2	....	186
4. 3	....	187
4. 17	....	19
5. 11	....	95
7. 28	....	86, 245 *a*
7. 29	....	183
7. 36	....	124
9. 10	....	179
9. 18	....	194
9. 25	....	22
10. 2	....	81
10. 16	....	67
10. 30	....	42
11. 27	....	32
11. 29	....	245
12. 15	....	267
14. 5	....	135
14. 39	....	128
15. 4	....	103
15. 31	....	85
15. 32	....	88
15. 37	....	112, 265
16. 4	....	179

II CORINTHIANS

1. 8	....	179
2. 1	....	172
2. 13	....	228
2. 17	....	114
5. 20	....	109
8. 7	....	183
8. 9	....	93
8. 11	....	179
10. 2	....	149
11. 25	....	92
12. 20	....	192

GALATIANS

1. 23	....	261
2. 10	....	165, 183
2. 12	....	219
2. 13	....	232
2. 27	....	193
3. 23	....	219
4. 11	....	193
5. 1	....	128
5. 4	....	86
5. 14	....	73
6. 9	....	245
6. 11	....	163

EPHESIANS

4. 9	....	73
4. 26	....	128
5. 33	....	183
6. 22	....	95

PHILIPPIANS

1. 18	....	107
2. 2	....	196
2. 25	....	95
2. 28	....	95
3. 1	....	109
3. 10	....	175
3. 16	....	137
3. 21	....	179

COLOSSIANS

2. 5	....	246
4. 6	....	139
4. 8	....	95
4. 16	....	190

I THESSALONIANS

2. 4	....	20
2. 7	....	249
2. 16	....	106
3. 5	....	195
4. 3	....	169
5. 4	....	185

I TIMOTHY

3. 11	....	68
4. 4	....	245
4. 14	....	128
5. 22	....	128
6. 5	....	68

II TIMOTHY

1. 8	....	129
1. 9	....	266 a
2. 12	....	242
2. 19	....	106
4. 7	....	97
4. 8	....	111
4. 9	....	165
4. 11	....	258

TITUS

| 2. 2 | .... | 137 |

PHILEMON

| 12. | .... | 95 |

HEBREWS

2. 3	....	245
2. 15	....	32
5. 5	....	139, 234
5. 8	....	246
6. 10	....	139, 185, 234
10. 31	....	68
10. 36	....	185
11. 15	....	170
13. 24	....	71

JAMES

1. 11	....	95
1. 24	....	95
1. 27	....	169
2. 14	....	69
2. 19	....	10
2. 25	....	40
4. 13	....	57
5. 17	....	177

I PETER

1. 24	....	95
3. 14	....	243
3. 17	....	68
4. 17	....	178

II PETER

| 1. 10 | .... | 81 |

I JOHN

1. 9	....	185
2. 6	....	52
3. 1	....	194
3. 4	....	76
3. 11	....	194
3. 13	....	167
3. 23	....	194
4. 1	....	128
4. 7	....	119
4. 18	....	69
4. 21	....	194
5. 3	....	194

II JOHN

| 6. | .... | 194 |

III JOHN

| 4. | .... | 194 |
| 6. | .... | 264 |

REVELATION

2. 1	....	57
8. 1	....	210
9. 4, 5	....	186
9. 20	....	185
14. 13	....	183